ghetto bastard

A Memoir

*Life is only as fair
as* you *make it.*

T. H. Moore

Copyright © 2024 by Tarik H. Moore

Published by:
In Third Person Publishing
P.O. Box 3622
Baltimore, MD 21214

www.thmoorenovels.com

All rights reserved. Printed in the United States of America. No part of this book may be used or reproduced in any manner without written permission except in the case of brief quotations embodied in critical articles and reviews.

This is a work of nonfiction, a memoir that reflects the author's present recollections of experiences over time in the near and distant past. Some names and identifying details have been changed to protect the privacy of people represented. Some events have been compressed and some dialog has been recreated.

Cover artwork by Adam Hay
Interior book design by David Provolo

First Edition July 2024

Library of Congress Cataloging-in-Publication Data is available upon request.

Hardcover ISBN: 978-0-9779519-4-9
Paperback ISBN: 978-0-9779519-5-6

Mom, thank you for everything…

Acknowledgments

Ms. Sheila "Sheeky" Jackson, or the person known more affectionately as Mom, I would be remiss to neglect thanking you for the countless sacrifices you made on my behalf. You provided an environment of safety, consistency, and support that I needed to thrive. The education you financed during my early and formative years directly correlates to my successful navigation of this experience called life.

For some, reading this story may be difficult, jarring, and met with instinctual defensiveness. To those who do fall victim to that defensiveness, please know this book comes from a place of love. I accept the probability of sharp criticism that may be on my horizon as this very public display of vulnerability may trigger some readers. It's my hope that my readers understand my release of these memories—I use the word "release" intentionally—was necessary…for me.

I hope you, the reader of the following pages, will do so with an open heart and mind. I hope my point of view in the following chronicle of my life experiences in some way helps others who may have experiences and struggles that parallel mine. I hope this book is a tool you can leverage to exorcise your own demons, as it has been for me.

Most of all, I hope these words ultimately bring you the relief and healing that writing it has brought me.

Preface

*One cannot heal unless they first confront, share,
and process their trauma(s).*

I was once asked by a friend, "Tarik, have you noticed you gravitate toward life's struggles instead of repelling them?" Initially, I took her comment as a joke until I saw the sincerity in her face. In addition, I didn't comprehend the significance and depth of her question. I returned a blank stare, coupled with my head tilted at a forty-five-degree angle. Much like a family dog communicating to its owner, I didn't understand.

"I'm not following you. Ask the question another way," I replied.

For a moment, she broke eye contact with me and her eyes shot to a corner of her mind, searching for the proper response.

"You've made it out of Camden, Tarik. But your routine and habits, some of your life choices—they're the choices and habits of someone still in survival mode. If this was a race, you've lapped those still surviving. You're thriving now."

Finally, I understood what she meant. But I didn't receive her constructive criticism well. My emotional intelligence hadn't matured to the level I needed, despite my forty-plus years of age and life experience. The habits and routines she was questioning processed incorrectly in my mind. I heard them as an insult. I instinctively became defensive of what I perceived as a "dis" or *dis*respect. *Dis*respect, in my world, meant you were deserving of one of my many stockpiled, verbally abusive retorts.

Who duh fuck she think she talking to?

My tongue reeled back like a cobra, sliding across the roof of my mouth, ready to strike with the ferocity of a wet bull whip and the precision of a surgeon's scalpel.

Tarik, no! Take a breath!

I performed a mental exercise a therapist introduced me to years ago. My anger subsided just enough before I said something I couldn't take back.

Remove the emotion of the words that triggered you, Tarik. Instead, focus on the literal meaning of the question being asked. Respond as if you are Mr. Spock, the Vulcan from Star Trek. *Let reason and logic dictate how you're listening and how you respond.*

So that's what I did. I ignored the emotional response swelling inside me and objectively audited her question. A calming sensation washed over me like a warm wave. A chill traversed my body that instigated goose bumps on my forearms. I replayed her question in my mind. My eyes bounced side to side, searching the imaginary heavens above for inspiration and clarity.

She's not insulting you, Tarik. She's trying to understand you.

Suddenly, an honest self-critique of my own life behaviors and habits overwhelmed me. I could only equate the moment to the experience of devout churchgoers experiencing the "Holy Ghost"—well, minus the part where people speak in tongues, cry, and fall out as if possessed. The spiritual manifestation was immediately followed by a symphony of corresponding traumas associated with each flashing memory. The memories flooding my mind could only be described as similar to those of someone facing certain death. Despite my experience not being death-induced, there still remained a lifetime chronicling of behavior that I could directly attribute to traditions and behaviors I learned directly or indirectly from my environment or the inhabitants of the village that raised me.

Each habit and learned behavior I'd absorbed up until this point could be traced and correlated to an accompanying trauma. And much like those who experienced these flashes before their demise, the phenomenon equally prefaced the death of my previous way of thinking and living.

"Tarik? You still there?" she questioned, snapping me out of my self-induced trance.

"Huh? Uh…yeah. Of course," I lied. The truth was I was still processing, not wanting to ignore her but equally not setting loose my epiphany. I had to concede, the critique was honest and accurate. I'd become ignorant of the rut I was stuck in—a repetitive cycle of questionable and sometimes blatantly bad decisions. Decisions based on my experienced social norms, destructive traditions, and subliminal conditioning I needed to purge to experience and enjoy a life I wanted to have. A life I'd earned and deserved to relish, on my terms, free of outside influences.

My objective in writing *Ghetto Bastard: A Memoir* is to take an honest audit of my life choices. I attempt to take responsibility for the bad choices I've made while also paying homage to those who've contributed to my evolution toward a more righteous and purposeful existence. The following body of work is a chronological account of my life traumas in three parts:

Part I: Sex & Relationships
Part II: Parents & Family
Part III: Violence & Racism

For some readers, my story will be jarring. You all should know the development of this book is rooted in love—tough love—and should never be misconstrued with any intention to instigate conflict. The memories I've experienced, processed, and now present in this book are derived from my honest perspective in as fair an account as my recollection could manage.

Some names and details have been omitted to preserve anonymity. I've purposely omitted details and dialogue I determined would not be constructive or in line with delivering the message I intend. My message isn't meant to hurt or cast blame of my life experiences upon anyone. I did not write this as some twisted form of self-pity.

It is my sincerest intention that sharing my story may help readers identify and process their own traumatic or questionable experiences. Yet I know, despite my best efforts, I will not be able to satisfy everyone. My goal is to create a space within the confines of these pages for others to nurture their own process of healing that is much overdue for far too many of us. Especially men.

Look where you came from. You made it out, Tarik. Why are you still living like you haven't? Your routine and habits, your life choices. You're still living like you never left.

I wonder how many times I've missed others asking me the same question when I wasn't ready to hear it or was too immature to properly process it. The honest short answer to her question is the routine and habits I displayed before writing this book were what was familiar to me. That state of being and surviving was all I and the people I'd known up to that point had ever experienced. It was my life's version of what "normal" was. The only glimpse of an affluent African-American family I had exposure to was Heathcliff and Clair Huxtable from the hit television sitcom *The Cosby Show*. In short, an affluent Black family where the husband was a doctor and his beautiful wife was a bilingual attorney only existed on television, in my world.

To give you some additional clarity, I didn't realize until I was eighteen years old and matriculated as a college student that every African-American and Spanish-speaking person did *not* grow up in a ghetto or hood. I did not realize that it wasn't a badge of honor having so many street fights that you couldn't pinpoint which fight caused your permanent scar—for me, on my right temple. It simply meant you were raised surrounded by and eventually became accustomed to violence. I didn't realize that the students I shared classes with at Jersey City State College did not share my experience of being raised in a home originally built in 1859 where the bathroom did not have a showerhead. Many friends I've known my whole life won't know until reading this paragraph that I could only take baths because my mother didn't have extra money to commission a contractor to install a showerhead. I was born in December of 1975, and it wasn't until September of 1993 that I had daily access to a shower, thanks to my college dormitory.

My version of normal was my grandmother, Edith Jackson, possessing only an eighth-grade level of education. You see, she and her thirteen other siblings were raised on a seventy-nine-acre family farm in a deep rural South Carolina town called Little Mountain. At that time, Little Mountain's total population was below four hundred. Today's population is approximately three hundred. In her day and time, continuing her education past the eighth grade wasn't mandatory because the family farm was what literally put food on the table and what little money they earned in the savings account.

My grandmother would eventually marry and move her family north from South Carolina to New York for a short stint before finally settling in southern New Jersey, where she could afford a home. My mother, her youngest of five daughters, eventually attained a higher level of education than her mother by earning her high school diploma from Camden High School and her associate degree from Camden County Community College. The jobs my mother maintained most of her life compensated her a meager $30,000 to $35,000 a year before I left for undergrad.

My other normal was my father being incarcerated in county jail for a little over a year for selling marijuana his first year in college. After jail, he had difficulty finding steady work, so he was a nonfactor when it came to financially supporting me. As a result, my mother and I soon learned life would be only as fair as we made it. So we survived by living financially thin. To this day, my friends joke about how "frugal" I am, but I know they're just being nice and don't want to call me cheap. The truth is, I can't help it. For the first eighteen years of my life, I was taught and cultivated my own methods of making food, drink, clothing, and shelter stretch. We had everything we needed and none of the things we wanted.

In layman's terms, we were poor and barely living above the poverty line. For example, at one point, my mother applied for public assistance in the form of food stamps and the government determined her $30,000 annual salary was above the qualifying threshold. What that meant for my household was a refrigerator and cabinets full of off-brand cereal and food in a city already considered a food desert. My mother shopped for her clothes at thrift stores, and bobo sneakers were standard for me. Anything outside our basic needs of food, water, shelter, love, and my private school tuition were a luxury…literally.

I'm sure some of you may be thinking that a private school education is a luxury when public school education is available. You're right; my Catholic schools were not cheap but the public schools in my city left much to be desired. Luckily, my mother always maintained great credit so whenever my tuition was due, the banks and predatory lenders always approved her lines of credit, leveraged against our house, of course. That's how she afforded my tuition, uniforms, and any other expenses associated with my education and extracurricular activities.

I rarely had nice clothes outside of my Catholic school uniform. I had one pair of sneakers at a time. I had one pair of brown, hard-bottom, penny loafer shoes for school and church, and both usually were on sale for under $30. My clothes would be replaced only after I outgrew them. Neighborhood kids would tease me consistently about expecting a flood because the hem on my pants or jeans rose high enough to reveal my off-white socks that were losing their elastic and falling to my ankles. I'd earn a new pair of sneakers or shoes only after I showed my mother the rain I'd walked to school in that day had finally penetrated my thinning soles and had soaked my socks.

Eventually, I would realize I was one of the poorer kids of my poor friends. The usual teasing or clowning always revolved around the whack clothes I wore since I couldn't afford the latest trends and styles. I was eleven years old when I finally realized for the first time our economic status. So, like most of the men and some women in my family, I became an entrepreneur. I started my first business selling homemade Italian water ice based on a recipe my grandmother taught me. Her first lesson to me about self-sufficiency and how to hustle came after a summer of her watching me spend what little pocket change I had devouring corner-store-bought water ice.

My mother only allowed me to work during the summer because for her, my education came before everything. The personal loans and equity lines of credit she would be approved for were backed by our meager $40,000 single-family row house she'd inherited from my grandmother as collateral. Yup, my mother literally mortgaged my future by betting on my education. She even started my education in kindergarten a year earlier than I was supposed to. I would remain in Catholic school until the conclusion of my freshman year of high school, when we finally had to accept a premiere parochial high school education was just too expensive and a burden on our household.

So, starting at eleven years old, until I was old enough to work a real job, I hustled homemade water ice. I cut people's lawns in the summer and shoveled snow in the winter. I bagged groceries for tips during the first week of the month, when markets were overrun with customers who had received the food stamps we didn't qualify for. Before I could legally get a job, I did whatever work I could to stack money to finance my own wants and contribute to the overall needs of me and my mother's household.

The money I earned didn't amount to enough to cover a utility bill, but it did fund my mother's bus and train fare to and from work every day during those summer months. Where I'm from, it's not uncommon for the children in my peer group to contribute to their household's overall income. It was merely a Northern adaptation of my family's Southern tradition of contributing to the upkeep of the family farm. Southern farmers purposely had multiple children because each child would eventually grow strong and competent enough to help work the farm. The more children they had, the fewer farmhands farmers like my great-grandfather had to hire.

With so many of my community migrating North from the terrors of Southern living, it's no wonder my generation's eventual indoctrination into "hustle" mentality. For many of us reared in America's ghettos, we either hustled or starved. Those worse off than I had to trap or die. Some of us were literally fighting or hustling for our survival.

This constant state of hustling was my mother's and my "normal." A never-ending state of making ends meet, robbing Peter to pay Paul, and squeezing every cent out of every dollar. After eighteen years of conditioned hustling during my formative years, I could only instinctively deduce this was what normal life was like. But now that I'm an adult with a larger worldview and breadth of life experience, I know that how and where I was raised isn't the universal normal. I've had to reprogram my way of thinking and behavior to grow comfortable in the boring stillness I find myself in now without a crisis to solve.

My most recent therapist—I've had two in my lifetime—reminds me constantly when I get anxious or when, as I describe it in jest, I "wake up feeling manic," that it's okay to have no emergency to attend to. I can celebrate my new normal as not having to scramble to make ends meet every month. Boring is okay compared to a chaotic state of survival mode.

I applaud pop culture and the media in the last few years for highlighting the importance of addressing mental health. In the forefront of this movement, I've noticed many people who don't look like me expressing their increased levels of anxiety coupled by their outcry for medical remedies like Xanax, Lexapro, and Zoloft, to name a few. Sorry but not sorry, my community reserves no sympathy for you. The truth is, for people like me, from my community, experiencing anxiety in such constant doses doesn't allow it to register significantly on our mental health scale. Sadly, for a community with four centuries of experience with being human trafficked, tortured, raped, murdered, sold as cattle, and ultimately "freed," only to be oppressed as second-class citizens, imprisoned on minor or trumped-up offenses, anxiety is a mythical phenomenon we shrug off as status quo in America. So, in short, you all have some catching up to do.

Introduction

"Okay, y'all. I'm leaving to go to work," my aunt announced. She retrieved her coat from the small closet directly across from the half-bathroom in my grandmother Edith's house.

"Already?" my mother asked, a slight hint of disappointment in her voice.

"Yes, Sheeky," she responded, calling her baby sister by her childhood nickname. "I have to work the overnight shift, but I'll see you all next Sunday as usual." Sunday dinner at my grandmother's house had been a tradition in our family since she relocated from rural South Carolina. My aunt walked back into the dining room, where all the adults congregated, while I took up my customary place in the middle of the carpeted living room floor, a few feet in front of the television.

My aunt gave everyone a hug and kissed my grandmother on the cheek before heading back to the living room toward the door.

"Tarik, you're too close to the TV. You're going to ruin your eyes," she said, loud enough so my mother could hear her correct me. My family took turns warning me of the dangers of watching my grandmother's floor-model television so closely the images probably reflected off my face. But the TV was the perfect babysitter for me. I wouldn't move for hours, as if I were in a trance.

"Tarik…" my mother sounded off as I scooted back another two feet until my back rested against the red velvet sofa encased in thick, protective plastic. I locked eyes with my aunt and we smiled at each other before she left, closing the solid wood door behind her.

"Hey, you gotta light?" he asked. A woman in her early thirties sat patiently on a metal bench at the elevated train platform, waiting for one of the last trains on the schedule for the night. She looked up at the young man, accompanied by two others who appeared to be in the same age range as her own children.

"Yeah, sure," she said, taking a short drag from her Newport cigarette before looking into her purse in search of a lighter. Once she retrieved it, she glanced back up at the young man, only to meet the sight of his fist flying toward her pretty, delicate face.

She screamed from the impact of his large hand knocking her off the bench and onto the cold, concrete platform. "Help!" she cried out in vain on the empty platform as the three young men surrounded her, kicking and punching her as if she were a man who had wronged them. Tan-colored suede construction boots with steel toes crashed against the ribs of her slender frame. A barrage of fists descended upon her like archer's arrows, eventually finding their target, splattering the concrete with countless crimson spots of her blood.

With no one to intervene and this train station being notorious for juvenile delinquents destroying the few closed-circuit cameras, there was no motivation for the trio to hold back from their assault until they eventually exhausted themselves. Hunched over, two of them rested their palms on their thighs while the other took a nonchalant seat on the metal bench their victim had occupied. He snatched her purse from the ground and rummaged through the contents. Finally finding something to his liking, he pulled the few bills from his victim's worn wallet, shoved them into his pocket, and discarded what remained of the wallet onto the railroad tracks.

He nodded at his two accomplices before getting up and heading toward the glass doors leading to the descending steps and the station's exit. The two who remained grabbed their unconscious victim, each taking an arm, their victim's head bobbing limp as a stream of blood poured from her mouth. Her nurse's aide uniform was stained with the dirt imprints of their boots. They both looked at each other and, without a word, nodded and tossed her limp body onto the tracks four feet below.

Her delicate body crashed against unwelcoming wood, gravel, and metal.

The two smirked at each other when they saw the oncoming train's headlights in the distance as it unknowingly advanced toward their motionless victim. They darted to the glass doors only a few moments before the train was close enough to see them or their victim. A few seconds later, the train's horn sounded off, interrupted only by the sound of urgently squealing brakes that violently woke me from my nightmare.

I obviously wasn't there when my aunt was assaulted and murdered, but because I was raised as an only child with a vivid, active imagination, the above is how the recurring dream of her murder manifests itself. With dreams and nightmares being so nonsensical, there are deviations in the details of the assault and how it was initiated on that train platform, but the violent conclusion remains the same and the sound of those squealing brakes is what always wakes me.

My Aunt Janice was murdered when I was eleven, and it would unfortunately serve as my initiation to how heartless and cruel mankind can be. It would also serve as the first and only time in my life when I was sincerely in fear of my own life. That fear would eventually dissipate, as my emotional coat of armor cured. Additional coats of armor would follow, layering me repeatedly, growing thicker as additional experiences of overt violence spanning from childhood to adulthood hardened my heart. Unbeknownst to me, and to the detriment of those in my orbit who were unaware of my life's experiences, my hardening manifested itself as meanness.

I became fearless; my mother, a conservative woman, preferred to call me "reckless." For me, though, my closed heart became a hallmark that I foolishly prided myself on. To this day, despite being filled with sadness, I can't bring myself to cry at funerals. That emotional part of me has been broken. I've developed a talent for keeping my head and remaining abnormally calm in times of chaos.

When faced with extremely uncomfortable situations, I mentally recuse myself until the situation has concluded. I admit, it scares me sometimes to know I can mentally check out at my discretion.

Years ago, a coworker commented on my steady, calm demeanor while we were neck-deep in a system outage and everyone was scrambling to diagnose and figure out the remedy before we could potentially face a financial penalty, estimated in the tens of thousands for every hour of downtime.

"How can you be so calm?" she asked as I focused on the screen of my laptop, rapidly hitting the keys, troubleshooting the issue like everyone else.

I turned my head to respond to her while my fingers continued banging away. "I've had plenty of practice."

I'd been stuck in a rut of unhealthy behavior longer than I care to admit. If I'm being honest, my unhealthy habits at times polluted my foundational character for most of my adult life. Some of you reading this whom I call friends, family, significant others, and even associates may be familiar with the unhealthy rut I'm referring to. The rotation of binge drinking, secluded consumption of cannabis, and hypersexualized dating. The last of the three—I have been the saboteur of countless potentially monogamous relationships—includes more than I care to admit.

Whether I chose these vices consciously or was genetically predisposed to them, they never failed to provide the on-demand comfort and pleasure I needed in that moment. Being reared in an existence of perpetual survival and constant wanting, it's easy to conclude how I became obsessed with repetitively experimenting with the short-lived, artificial pleasures sex, alcohol, and weed provided. Occasionally, I'd have to pay a hangover tax for nights I overindulged in drink. Not to mention that I once developed pneumonia after a month-long binge of daily cannabis use that unceremoniously collided with my contracting COVID. If any law enforcement officers are reading this, you can relax; my recreational use of cannabis was legalized in the state I was a resident of. So *please,* for both our sakes, keep your no-knock-warrant-abusing asses away from my door unless you want to get shot.

The first time I questioned whether I had developed an addiction to alcohol was after a date with a young lady I wasn't necessarily fond of, but she was gorgeous, so I endured with hopes I'd be funny and charming enough to ultimately bed her in the near future. To lubricate the grinding gears of the subpar evening, I indulged in one, probably two more drinks than I should have. By the time I realized I was intoxicated, it was too late. Too late to chase the alcohol with water to dilute my inebriation. Too late to reel back in a response the filter between my brain and mouth should have caught like a fishing net.

"You're such a good listener and very easy to talk to," my date said, paying a sincere compliment.

"I paid a price to be this way," I responded mindlessly. The heavy fog of my inebriation clouded my reason. Instantly, from across the small table of a trendy, overpriced Philadelphia restaurant, the smile that once adorned her face vanished. Replacing it was an expression of perplexity.

Shit! Tarik, you and your mouth!

"What do you mean?" she questioned, carefully lowering the base of her wineglass onto the white tablecloth. She carefully swirled the Caymus Cabernet along the side of the large glass for a second before allowing it to come to a rest. She leaned forward, resting her elbows on the table, fully engaged.

Change the subject, Tarik.

"I didn't mean anything by it. Obviously, my bad joke bombed," I said, accentuating a forced smile coupled by practiced charm. I hoped to derail her curiosity.

"Oh...okay," she responded, obviously disappointed, followed by a peculiar look that let me know she didn't believe me. Her body language and conversation changed from that point on. Quickly, I understood there would be no sex for me that night with her, or in the future, for that matter. This would probably be our first and last date. The good news was, I honestly didn't care. All that mattered was very soon, this cordial exchange of pleasantries would come to an end, leaving me the rest of my night to emotionally haze myself over a careless moment of emotional vulnerability.

For my fellow suffering kindred spirits who've managed to neatly wrap their lives in a cloak of presumed exterior happiness despite the turmoil that's spinning inside us, I wrote this book for you. Despite our maintaining the lie we tell our family and friends—*I'm okay, I'm good*—we know it's a farce. The emotional baggage we suppress remains harmful to us as we march forward, persevering and enduring like good soldiers. We conceal our pain behind the guise of strength because being in survival mode demands it of us.

Just like in the blockbuster movie, *A League of Their Own*, where the phrase, "There's no crying in baseball" was coined, life in the ghetto doesn't allow for crying or softness. To successfully navigate Southwest Philly and Camden, New Jersey, one can become mean, desensitized to violence and crime. It's not a coincidence that I don't smile naturally. My smile, absent a good joke, is artificial. It's a byproduct of my concerted adult decision to practice smiling in my bathroom mirror. In addition to my practice smiles, there are the masks I've created to distract family, friends, and even strangers from my subconscious scars and feelings of melancholy. This mask is my countermeasure so the people I interact with won't discover my suppressed frowns or tears and disappointment.

I paid a price to be this way.

My date that fateful night was one of the rare moments when I was compelled, directly or indirectly, to take a deliberate accounting of my life and behavior. That night forced me to tally my bad decisions and behavior as if they were leaves spawned from a tree where trauma lay at the roots. And every year, every fall season, those leaves of self-destruction accumulated like revolving debt. And much like a person drowning in financial debt and lacking the fiscal resources to eliminate that debt, I was at an emotional impasse that I could no longer manage without help and therapeutic guidance.

That guidance would correct my emotional unavailability. An unavailability that I'd forged in the communal fire of lacking emotional expression at home and among my closest friends. I was reared in the philosophy that "real men suffer in silence," the status quo in my community. Brainwashed by the same community that regards therapy in the same breath as witchcraft, despite it being a therapeutic witchcraft the men in my family and community so desperately need. But the trick is, the unexplainable magic of this witchcraft only reveals its benefits once you make a personal sacrifice of faith to a stranger—a well-educated stranger, but a stranger, nonetheless.

Some who read this story will cringe. Some family members may, if they haven't already, curse my name with each passing chapter. However, I can't please everyone, so my readers' potential displeasure will have to take a back seat to the story—my story—that I need to tell.

With that said, in some African, Middle Eastern, and ancient Greek societies, when a young man reaches a certain age, typically when puberty kicks in, he is taken away from his mother by the men of his community. This action initiates the cultural and ritualistic process the young man will experience as their rite of passage into manhood. That young man is then taught to wrestle and fight, build a home, hunt, and any other skills he needs to protect and provide for his future family.

My family has a similar rite of passage, crafted out of meanness and violence. Shying away from this tradition was unheard of. The most egregious of my bloodline, some of whom are my cousins, sprinted toward our traditions with balled fists and open arms. Street fights with our neighbors, strangers from other neighborhoods, or even amongst our own bloodline weren't uncommon. I was born into a kinship that too often displays the character traits typical of a pack of wolves protecting their den or foraging their territory for sustenance. And then there are those moments of peace where survival isn't at the forefront, where my family members are as equally loving and territorial of our pack's safety and wellbeing as we are ruthless and merciless to our foes.

My pack is aggressive, fearless, and, in times of desperation, exploitive. Being the youngest in my generation, I was afforded the protection my family commanded. Our numbers and reputation for viciousness toward outsiders were earned before my prepubescent days.

Human nature's rigid rules of self-preservation transcend blood. Self-preservation demands even the youngest to push and snarl their way through and past the bigger, more aggressive, and sinister to devour their portion of life's carcass to ensure their own survival. It's saddening to acknowledge my kin being capable of only flashes of civility and love toward one another. There are family moments I will always relish like gold, but life has also shown me those moments are fleeting. Because in an instant, without warning, those beautiful moments can dissipate like steam ascending into the air until we gradually lose sight of them.

Whether my life experiences were the result of an unseen order of natural selection or the fallout of the family I was helpless in choosing, I acknowledge that I am damaged. I don't make that statement lightheartedly or to seek some dysfunctional form of pity. My family, like many in this country, have life experiences rooted solely in survival. Unfortunately, this sustained state of survival over a significant period of time normalizes greed, jealousy, and ultimately, violence.

Consequently, the fallout from these self-destructive practices is impossible to confine, and its dysfunction spills unknowingly over generational brims. Its aftereffects spatter like blood on not only the intended victims of said violence, but also soils the spirit of unintended victims, those innocent bystanders, as we call them. Our children.

part I
SEX & RELATIONSHIPS

chapter 1

My mother left my father not long after I was born, after one too many nights of him coming home late. "Where the hell have you been? It's almost three in the morning!" my mother questioned.

"Last I checked, we ain't married. I can come and go as I please," my father shot back, inebriated.

"You know what…?" my mother responded with a calm change from her initial tone. "You're right. We aren't married." That would be the last night we spent in my father's one-bedroom apartment in Philly.

Before my seventh birthday, amid the backdrop of a dirty and dilapidated toolshed that sat alongside the apartment building my mother settled us into after leaving my father, the preconceived societal notion and the sacred sanctity of what sex should be for me was ruined.

I met a girl who also lived in our building. She was older by only two or three years but her exposure to sex obviously preceded mine. Who exposed her and under what circumstances I never knew or had the chance to ask her about before her family abruptly moved out of the building.

What was obvious though was that she was about to share with me the same sexual exploitation someone had exposed her to. As children typically do, they mimic the behavior taught to them by the adults they trust. We were not strangers to each other, or to the empty tool shed we occupied. Our parents thought nothing of us treating it as a clubhouse. In fact, they were at ease if their children used it, because of its proximity to the building. Especially those parents whose apartment windows hovered above the shed, giving them easy access to our whereabouts while they prepared dinner or any of the other after-work rituals they busied themselves with to distract them from the stress of that day's labor. After our parents had decompressed from the day, they could conveniently shout down and call us in for dinner or reprimand us if our roughhousing or language became too intense.

For us kids, the toolshed mimicked the treehouse or clubhouses the characters on our favorite television shows always treated as their own childlike homes.

We treated our clubhouse as if it were our own apartment, minus the rent payments—a single-room, unfurnished studio for kids only. Such accommodations, driven by our imaginations, spawned the family kids' game, "house." On this particular day, the neighbor girl and I played that exact game, where I, being the only boy, by default acted as the husband and she, the only girl, by default was my wife. Not having my father living with us, I only had the examples of White husbands to mimic from the television shows my mother and I watched after dinner.

Our clubhouse had an old, rickety wood door with a missing doorknob but a small deadbolt lock that we could use to lock ourselves in once inside. With no space for us to designate as a kitchen, bathroom, or bedroom, our imaginations provided the interior design.

"Okay, Tarik, you're the dad and I'm the mom. It's almost dark so I have to cook dinner, and after you eat you have to give me a kiss. Okay?"

"Okay." I eagerly agreed because I'd never kissed a girl before. Now that we'd made our pact, she turned around, looking over the dusty, empty wooden shelf along the wall of the shed, stirring imaginary contents with invisible spoons, pots, and pans. I simply stood behind her with my hands in my pockets, doing my part concocting the wavy imagery of the feast she was preparing just for us. Occasionally, she would look over her shoulder at me and smile. I imagined that's how her mother smiled at her live-in boyfriend when she cooked for him. She was the only kid in my building whose mother had a man living with them.

"Okay, it's ready," she said, grabbing and setting imaginary plates from nonexistent shelves and placing them on an invisible dinner table. With her petite hands and skinny arms, she placed transparent scoops of food neatly on the plates.

"That's your mashed potatoes, here's your vegetables, and here's your steak, honey," she said with pride.

"Thank you, honey," I replied, using my imaginary utensils to graciously shovel air into my open mouth.

"Where's my kiss?" she reminded me, taking two steps closer. I hadn't forgotten, I was just shy, and I had planned to make my move after I'd finished eating. She had other plans. I placed my make-believe plate down on the table between us and moved closer to her. The rubber tips of our sneakers kissed before we could. She was taller so she bent over with the cutest of smiles to give me a loud peck on the lips before snapping her neck back. That was my first kiss. I liked it, returned a nervous smile back, and leaned in for another, this time craning my neck up and poking my lips out to meet her lips again, copying the same neck snap. Our kiss echoed in the empty shed. A simultaneous smile shared between us lit the darkening shed now that the sun was retiring for the day and surrendering the sky to the moon.

"You want to keep going?" she asked.

"Uh, yeah," I responded, thinking more kissing lay in store for me. Then she reached down and felt in between my thighs until settling her soft touch on my groin. She grabbed at the space where my He-Man underwear had compacted my penis and testicles. A shiver-like sensation shot through my body.

"Oh, shit!" I said. That instigated another smile from her. She removed her hand from my groin and repositioned it to slide down the front of my shorts to take a handful of what she was previously holding, except this time skin to skin. I was so nervous my body didn't respond to her touch, but her soft contact was pleasant.

"Here, do the same thing to me," she said, untying the drawstring of her shorts and pulling the elastic forward to make room for my hand to explore her body as she'd done with mine. It was the first time I'd touched a girl like that and, honestly, I didn't know what I was even reaching for or what to expect to find down there. I fumbled around, more surprised and confused than anything. Sensing my confusion, she removed her hand from my shorts.

"Go 'head, look," she instructed, using both her hands to pull her shorts forward until I could clearly see the slit that indicated the beginning of her prepubescent labia.

"See, right there," she said, pushing down her pants and positioning my fingers. I gasped, feeling the startling difference between a boy's and a girl's legs.

"What's that?" I exclaimed in both confusion and excitement. She smiled again.

"Lisa?" her mother's boyfriend shouted from the second-floor window above the shed. Her smile dropped. She ripped my hand from in between her thighs and rushed to fix her shorts.

"Lisa! Time to come in!" he shouted again.

"Here I come!" she yelled back before darting out of the shed, leaving me there alone to revel in my exciting experience. A few seconds later, my mother bellowed.

"Taaare! Dinner!" she sang, using only the first syllable of my name. I slyly poked my head out the open doorway just in time to watch Lisa dash around toward the front of the building. The sun was disappearing, and the streetlights were stuttering on. I dashed off in the same direction as Lisa had only moments ago.

"Here I come!" I responded. Strangely, that was the last time I'd see Lisa again. That would be our first and only intimate rendezvous in the shed. Years later, at the ages of nine and thirteen, I would have two similar experiences to what I'd had with Lisa. These later encounters would introduce me to more advanced intricacies of sex. Both instances were initiated by older women. What I'm about to say next may be unsettling to those who have suffered sexual molestation or assault, but I'd be lying if I said I was not a willing participant in their taking advantage of my naivete. In fact, I looked forward to seeing the adult woman I had experiences with when I was thirteen years old. Why, you may ask? Because it was exciting having this secret "relationship" with an older woman, and frankly, to a pubescent boy with raging hormones, getting to experiment with sex and a woman's body was very pleasurable to me.

We'll call this mystery lady Shelly. She lived across the street from a friend I visited frequently after I figured out the route to his house using NJ Transit and transferring over to Philly's SEPTA bus system. It took me an hour to get there, but my friend's house was a free-for-all because his parents worked all the time. I could count on one hand how many times I'd seen them at the house while we were there playing video games or running the streets chasing girls.

That's how I met Shelly. She was sitting on her porch, which overlooked the streets where we chased after girls. She graduated from high school but didn't go to college afterwards. She was living at home with her mother and working. She was either in her late teens, maybe early twenties at the most, and was very attractive. The teenage boys in the neighborhood all had a crush on her because of her natural brown beauty and shapely figure, despite being naturally thin. She was slim-thick, with her butt being her best physical asset and she knew it. How do I know? Because she mooned me one day while I was visiting my friend. We'll call my friend Kenya.

"A'ight, man, I gotta go so I don't miss this bus," I said to Kenya after beating him in a video game we'd been playing obsessively since my arrival earlier in the day.

"Come on, man, one more game. You can catch the next bus."

"Nah, man. The next bus won't get me home in time for dinner and I'm not trying to hear my mom's mouth," I said, dapping him up and tapping my pockets with my palms to make sure I had my wallet and keys. "I'll holla." I shot out the door, leaving Kenya to continue the game without me in his empty house. I traversed down the steep, twenty-plus steps until I reached the sidewalk, making a left, then power-walked up the block in the direction of my SEPTA bus stop.

From the corner of my eye, I could see Shelly sitting on her porch in furry slippers, a denim miniskirt, and a small, gray, short-sleeve T-shirt that barely covered her navel. Seeing her, I instinctively smiled. Still too shy to initiate conversation with a girl, I waved my hand and she returned the gesture with a smile of her own. I always liked her smile. Then her wave changed from "hello" to "come here," and my heart leapt. I could feel my smile intensify to the point my cheeks were tight. The block was dark and empty except for her. As I climbed the steps from the sidewalk to her porch, I took a few more steps and passed her door, arriving just a few feet in front of her and the small section of porch where she'd positioned the chair she used for people watching.

"Hiii, Tarik. You little cutey," she sang, instigating the largest smile. My leg shook from nervousness. She uncrossed her legs and leaned forward in the cushioned metal porch chair, closing the distance between us. Then it happened. She kissed me on the cheek. But it wasn't how my aunts or my grandmother kissed me on the cheek. Shelly's kiss was full, with moist lips, and ended with the subtlest smacking noise that gently echoed in my ear. The raging pubescent hormones in my body instantly responded to her flirtation.

She noticed and smiled.

"Don't you have a bus to catch?" she reminded me.

"Oh shit!" I said looking at my cheap, plastic, digital watch.

"Get home safe," she said, before twiddling her fingers at me to let me know that there would be only one surprise kiss. I hesitated for a slight second, disappointed it was over so quickly but excited it happened. I turned and left without a word. Just scurried off like a scared mouse with the smile of a Super Bowl champion.

"See you next time you visit," she said before I reached the last step. I turned around to wave bye, and at the top of the dark steps, there she was, her backside to me, looking over her shoulder with both her palms carefully placed on the faux back pockets of her miniskirt. We made eye contact again before she smiled, whipping her head to either side, quickly checking if the coast was clear before pulling her skirt up and resting it on her hips, revealing her perfectly symmetrical ass and toned thighs. My jaw dropped and a throbbing exploded in my pants. She laughed before pulling her skirt back down, ending my personal peep show. Then she slyly pointed to the top of the block where people were already gathered, where I should already be. I took off, sprinting up the block, knowing my bus would soon arrive.

"See you next time!" I shouted back at Shelly, and I meant it. My next visit, I stopped by Shelly's house first before heading over to Kenya's.

Looking back on those instances now as an adult, I fully understand I was molested despite not feeling that in the moment. With my first two experiences, because they happened with girls close to my age, I can easily categorize them as merely young sexual curiosity, playing out of the supervision of adults. Yet, in comparison, when I purposely force myself to reflect on the moments I shared with Shelly, I'm conflicted by why I don't feel guilt or remorse for enjoying those experiences with a significantly older woman. Because if the gender dynamics were reversed and I was a 13-year-old girl and Shelly was a 19- to 20-year-old man, I would be instantly disgusted and enraged at such perversion.

But I would be naïve to not acknowledge that my exposure to sexual touching and certain sexual acts so early and at such an immature stage of my life had a hypersexualizing effect on me. It warped my perception of what sex should be. With every premature act, the sensual intimacy and emotional connection of two people finding and sharing love through touch had been omitted. I just knew what sexual touching was, how the act of sex was performed, and how I could achieve orgasm and make a woman climax by touch of hands and mouth. Yes, in those later meet-ups with Shelly, she introduced and taught me about oral sex. I wouldn't officially lose my virginity by intercourse until I was a senior in high school.

The emotions that should correlate with the act of sex and lovemaking were never part of my sexual education. Consequently, my ability to make meaningful emotional connections was stunted once I began having real relationships with women. I unfortunately associated attaining sexual climax with achieving and sustaining love between a man and woman.

chapter 2

The first New Year's I remember celebrating would happen after my eighth birthday while also coinciding with my second sexual experience. This time, instead of it being shared with a girl from my apartment building or an older woman like Shelly, this experience would happen with a family friend. She was also older by two or three years and was the niece of one of my aunt's husbands. This New Year's fell upon a weekend, so my mother arranged for me to spend it with my aunt and her son since he and I were so close.

My aunt and her husband had just bought a new home. Up to that point in my life, my aunt's new home was the largest I'd seen and visited. It was a sprawling mini-mansion in Philadelphia. She'd married a large, authoritarian man with a Jheri curl. I'd always been grateful my mother didn't buy into the whole Jheri curl fad when it was popular. Many pillowcases and clear complexions have been ruined by that insane hair style, but I digress.

My aunt's husband had a niece—we'll also call her Shelly—and a nephew in the same age range as my cousin and me, so they spent the night at the large house as well. Despite my being so young and inexperienced with girls, it was apparent, not long after their arrival, and this being the first time I'd met them, that the niece had a crush on me. Shelly wore a smile whenever we talked, and it would disappear when she interacted with my cousin. It was also apparent my cousin didn't like losing her attention to me. I had plenty of practice recognizing and countering his jealous microaggressions, such as his trying to steal my friends or snitching to my mother when I used profanity. I never understood his jealous competition with me, but I noticed the idea of me getting in trouble or being punished by my mother gave him satisfaction.

This holiday weekend would be no different. Whenever the opportunity presented itself, he'd try winning Shelly's attention. His overzealousness, compared with my nonchalant and shy demeanor, only enhanced her curiosity in me. In fact, I was always naturally a shy child. By the time I was brave enough to initiate talking to a girl, it was only under the circumstances that it was blatantly obvious she liked me so I had nothing to lose.

I'm embarrassed now to admit that on one too many occasions, when a girl I wasn't attracted to expressed her feelings for me, I'd just go along with it because I didn't have the courage to tell her the truth. Back then, it was easier to be the nice guy my mother and Catholic school taught me to be, hoping the girl would eventually lose interest, or to avoid her the best I could. In short, I was a runner and I'd developed the habit of disappearing from situations or people that made me uncomfortable. I was a coward. Ultimately, the girl my cousin wanted to steal from me would gravitate toward and engage with me without any effort on my part.

Now, back to New Year's Eve at my aunt's house.

My aunt always had great taste in real estate. And out of the houses or high-rise condos she'd lived in over the years, this house was my favorite. They had a dog and a large backyard the size of half a football field. The previous owners must have been horse lovers because the property had two empty stables in a miniature barn. It was the perfect playground, where we four kids could play safely unattended until we were exhausted. Helicopter parents didn't exist in my generation. A kid running the streets until the streetlights came on was the norm for city kids like us. Avoiding calamitous injury, climbing both trees and random structures, even surviving near-death experiences taught us necessary survival skills absent in today's generation, for better or worse.

After every meal that weekend, we four kids would shoot out the back door to burn off the energy of my aunt's latest meal. I liked staying over at her house, despite her son's routine callous behavior, because my aunt is a great cook. Plus, as long as we weren't causing any major ruckus, I could stay up later than usual on Saturday nights, though that meant being tired for church in the morning. That year would be the first and only time I'd see the annual Philadelphia Mummers Parade in person instead of on my local television station.

"Sean! Wake your guests up, and you all take turns getting in the shower!" my aunt yelled from down the long, sprawling hallway where the primary bedroom was located. I instantly opened my eyes, as my aunt's morning wake-up call had a tone and cadence eerily like my mother's.

"Wake y'all asses up!" Sean said. "It's my house so I get the shower first." His small body shot out of bed, through the door, and down the hall toward the bathroom in a blur of Batman pajamas. The rest of us slowly sat up at our own pace, then the younger nephew shot out of bed behind Sean.

"I'm getting some cereal. Auntie got Cinnamon Toast Crunch yesterday," he said, excited. Now, only Shelly and I remained in bed. She looked over at me and smiled.

"Good morning," she said, wiping the sleep from her eyes from the far side of the bed.

"Morning," I returned. Then she jumped from under the covers, walked the length of the king-sized bed the four of us shared until she reached my side, and slid back under the sheets with only two feet between us. I lay on my left side, propping my head up with the palm of my hand. It being winter and the house large and hard to heat evenly, I enjoyed the warm comfort being beneath the sheets provided.

"You kiss a girl yet?" she asked.

"Yes, but just one," I replied, nervousness adding a slight tremble to my voice.

"So, you have a girlfriend?"

"I'm eight. I'm too young for a girlfriend," I explained. She smiled and slid closer to me, shortening the distance between us to an arm's reach. Neither of us had brushed our teeth before bed and so her morning breath greeted my nostrils with every word she spoke. I wondered if she could smell mine as well.

"Well, what about this? Ever done this before?" she asked, fumbling her left hand beneath the sheets until they found the space between my legs where my penis was already erect from needing to use the bathroom. Feeling me hard and seeing me smiling in enjoyment of her touch, she repositioned her hand inside of my loose pajamas. There was no hesitation to her methodical stroking of my penis.

This feels so good!

"You like that?" she asked as my body periodically felt a jolt of exhilaration from her caress. My breathing intensified and I wondered if she could hear my heartbeat, as it seemed amplified by ten from my perception.

"I-it f-feels g-good," I stuttered in prepubescent pleasure. It was my introduction to the joys of masturbation before I even knew such a word and concept existed. Admittedly, I knew something about it was wrong because it was something we would not be doing if we weren't alone. But I also didn't want her to stop. She was enjoying how she was making me feel, gauging from how her smile grew larger with every passing moment, in addition to the increased velocity of her hand motion.

"Here, touch me too," she directed before I could muster the courage to initiate reciprocation. I reached over and touched her chest through her long, white nightgown, and we both giggled as our innocence faded away bit by bit.

"You have a boyfriend?" I asked.

"No."

"How you know about this, then?" I asked, now more relaxed than ever.

"I can't tell you. It's a secret—"

"What y'all doin'!" Sean said, standing in shock in the doorway. We had both been so distracted we didn't notice he'd returned from his brief shower. We simultaneously jerked our hands back from one another.

"*Nothing!*" we lied in unison. She jumped out from under the covers and out of the bed, with her bare feet against the cold, hardwood floors. I sat up, my mouth propped open, unsure what to do next.

"Ooooh! Y'all was doin' iiit!" Sean sang in a low, sinister tone.

"Shut up! No, we weren't," she said. "That's not doin' it."

"Shhhh!" I shot at Sean, scared my aunt and her husband would hear him. Sean frowned and ran toward her with his bath towel wrapped around his waist.

"Yes, y'all were. Y'all was doin' this," he accused again, but this time wrapping his arms around her torso before he started dry humping her like a dog in heat. He thrusted so ferociously the friction caused his towel to fall to the floor. Every inch of his body was exposed, with his groin grinding against her. "Y'all was doin' this. I saw you!"

"*No, we wasn't!*" she yelled as tears welled up in her eyes, looking at me catatonic beneath the covers. Whenever I relive that day, I'm unsure if her objection to his accusation was because she was embarrassed he was humping her in front of me or because he was performing this terrible act without the consent she'd granted me.

"Get off of me!" she yelled, startling Sean enough to pull herself away from him. She ran out the door in a sprint down the hallway until the sound of her banging on my aunt's bedroom door sent chills down my spine.

"She's going to tell on us," Sean said.

"Us? I didn't do anything," I shot back, terrified. We heard the door suddenly open and shut soundly behind her, then the sound of her muffled, frantic voice mixed with both my aunt's and her husband's. My heart pounded. Sean grabbed his towel from the wood floor.

"Sean! Tarik! Get in here now!" my aunt's husband shouted. We looked at each other, both of us jockeying to be the last person to traverse that hallway and pass through their bedroom door. Sean fashioned his towel around his waist and tied it tightly as he could with shaking hands. We stopped the moment our feet passed the doorway. My hand grabbed the wrist of my other arm.

We're going to get a beating. Then they're going to tell my mom and I'm going to get another beating.

From across the room, I saw my aunt and her husband sitting side by side on the edge of the bed. Shelly stood behind her uncle, head down, refusing to look at Sean or me. I'd never seen such disappointment in my aunt's face.

"How would you like it if someone did that to your mothers?" my aunt's husband scolded. Before I could respond, Sean spoke out for both of us, as if we'd discussed it before arrival.

"Everything she said is true and we're sorry."

What? We don't even know what she said. And what are you talking about, we're sorry? There is no we in what you did!

"Tarik, I'm calling your mother and you're going home. Now the both of you go back in the room and sit there until we decide your punishment," my aunt's husband ordered. As soon as he completed his sentence, we crashed into each other trying to both run out the door, down the hallway, and back to the scene of my cousin's crime. When we got back to the room, Sean immediately threw his towel to the floor and hurried to dress himself in the clothes his mother had ironed for him the night before. I sat on the bed, hands folded, with a million thoughts shooting through my young mind. When Sean finished dressing, he nonchalantly sat on the bed, looking at me.

"You think he gonna beat us?" he asked me.

"Us? You grinded on her, not me!" I whispered through tight lips and gritted teeth.

"Don't matter now," he replied, before running over to the dresser where an old newspaper was lying. He started taking the pages out and stuffing them down his pants legs and even more around his butt. His pants looked like they had cellulite.

"What are you doing?" I demanded.

"If he beat us, this will make it not hurt as much. You seen him—that motherfucker big."

chapter 3

During the forty-eight years I've navigated this experience called life, I've only cohabitated with one woman, and it also just so happens to be the worst relationship I ever had. From the first date, all the red flags were there, and I ignored them…because she was gorgeous. I'd always been a fool for a pretty face.

Our first time out we had an argument. She was rude, uncouth, and as the grand finale, she drank too much at the bar we went to after dinner. The evening was so embarrassing for me because she had become belligerent. So belligerent I paid our bar tab and calmly walked away from her, leaving her at the bar after she made a scene. I had every intention of getting into my car and leaving her in downtown Baltimore just to get away from the public spectacle she was causing. Instead, like a dummy, I drove her home and she spent the ride crying and apologizing.

Five months later, I agreed to let her move into my apartment after her lease had expired. A month into it, I knew I'd made a huge mistake. We argued constantly and she had these unexplained mood swings. Once, we got into an argument about her either smoking or drinking every night. She grabbed her keys, stormed out of the apartment, and didn't come back for an hour. Honestly, I welcomed the silence, thinking she needed time to calm down, but I was wrong. What I didn't find out until two months later was, she had grabbed my keys as well, went into my car, stole the registration from my glove compartment, and threw it into one of the large dumpsters outside our apartment complex. I didn't realize it was gone until I was pulled over during a traffic stop and I had nothing to produce to the officer as proof the car was mine. I know, I know. You have my permission to judge me and call me names for choosing a terrible mate and enduring a terrible relationship. I deserve it.

Finally, nine months into us being together, I made plans to go out with my friends and she cut the pockets out of my jeans so I wouldn't go; then she threw her phone at me, tried to start a physical fight, and topped it all off with threatening to shoot me with the gun she owned. I called the police to have her removed from my apartment, filed a restraining order, and that was the last time we saw each other.

Before that awful experience, I'd always prided myself on the fact that I never had a relationship where I could describe my ex as "crazy." To this day, I've never invoked her name again. I even forbade my closest friends from mentioning her name for a few months until I was sure she was gone and out of my life for good. I'm not superstitious, but erring on the side of caution, I muted her amongst my circle just in case the mere mention of her name could conjure her evil ass back into existence to wreak more havoc in my life.

I would later find out she had mental health issues, as did others in her family. And instead of taking her medication, she self-medicated with cannabis, alcohol, and prescription pills. You see, she was the type of woman who had grown up in a house built in chaos. Love, for her, was demonstrated by conflict, yelling, and fights. To her, those were the displays of the passion you had for your significant other. Her thought processes and reasoning translated my lack of jealousy or insecurity about other men who desired her as my not loving or valuing her. Like the infamous scene from the movie *The Five Heartbeats*, she needed a man who "needed to fight every night to prove my love!"

I'm not a big fan of clichés, but there is one I do find comforting.

The saying goes that some people aren't meant to be in your life forever. Sometimes they're introduced into your life as a lesson. A teachable moment. This young lady from a city I won't name at the advice of my lawyer and editors was only meant to be in my life for a couple of seasons and to deliver a message, however painful and toxic the methodology. What good did I pull from this nine-month whirlwind of aggression and emotional violence? At the tail end of an alcohol and cannabis binge, she said to me, "Tarik, you know how to fuck but you don't know how to make love." It was without a doubt the meanest yet the most sobering evaluation I'd ever received outside of my many therapy sessions. And the sad part is, she was right.

Despite the three instances when I was prematurely introduced to sexual activity, I was the last to lose my virginity in my circle of high school friends. Even worse, I didn't learn about sex, its emotional significance, and consequences from a responsible adult like my mother or father. Like most, I uncomfortably sat through the sexual education portion of my health class in high school and watched the all-too-familiar birth-of-a-child video. However, my in-depth lessons about how to have sex, how to choose the right partner, and most importantly, the emotional significance and connection initiated through the act of sex were mysteries I'd have to learn on my own.

Ultimately, I learned the intricacies of sex from the worst places possible. There were vague pieces here and there, courtesy of rumor and innuendo during locker room stories shared between neighborhood friends and my teammates from the plethora of sports I played. But the most significant *miseducation* I received about sex came from pornography. My introduction to dysfunctional sex came by way of a VCR tape I stole from my dad's secret porn stash. I was at his apartment, left to my own devices, while he and a friend went outside to smoke weed on a large wall where they'd perch themselves to flirt with passing women.

This was the age of Erol's and eventually, Blockbuster Video.

My father owned two VCRs so he could duplicate movies he'd rented. He, like many fathers in America, had a modest porn stash. My father kept his stash locked in a bedroom closet using a simple three-number combination lock. I'm guessing he never suspected that I'd be curious enough to wonder what was so valuable he had to lock it despite him living alone. Honestly, he probably would have been better off leaving the door unlocked because once I saw that combination lock, it only piqued my curiosity.

Being an inquisitive teenager, I needed to know what was behind that door. I remember initially treating it like a contest, wondering what lay behind the curtains of one of the popular daytime game shows I watched at home during the summer. I guessed maybe it was a gun or perhaps a safe. So, one sunny weekend while he and his friend sat on the wall, I went snooping. I made sure the door was locked and the safety chain was applied, just in case they came back unexpectedly.

Ignoring my increasing heart rate, sweaty palms, and trembling hands, I turned the three number dials to 000 before systematically increasing the dial one number at a time until I eventually reached 181. When I pulled the lock and it opened, I immediately locked it again.

"181, 181, 181," I repeated while running back to the front window where I could see my dad and his friend still on the wall. I watched them for another minute or two until I saw my dad's friend retrieving a cigarette lighter from his pocket and passing it to my father, who was preparing to light another joint. I dashed back to the closet door, knowing I still had time before they'd be coming back. At least another fifteen to twenty minutes to finish the joint and enjoy the oncoming high. Even longer with the weather being nice and the foot traffic of women who would more than likely pass by, since it was a Saturday afternoon.

181, 181, 181.

I was so excited I ran to the bathroom to relieve myself. I didn't even wash my hands before rushing back to the closet door. "181."

I dialed to unlock the closet again and opened the door to find two standard-size moving boxes sitting at the bottom of the closet with a busty blonde woman staring up at me from a *Hustler* magazine. My eyes lit up and my jaw dropped before I reached down to grab the magazine on top. I eagerly flipped through the pages to find glossy sheet after sheet of beautiful women with perfectly round breasts, legs spread wide, leaving nothing to the imagination. They were a little bit on the skinny side for my taste, but I greeted them with a raging erection, nonetheless.

I made my way through two magazines, flipping through the pages, getting more and more excited with every turn of a new page. When done, I made sure to place them back how I found them so my amateur breaking and entering wouldn't be discovered. I ran back to the front window in the living room to spy on my dad. They were still taking pulls on the joint. I dashed back to the closet. A slight layer of perspiration was developing while my erection led the way.

After sifting through more magazines, I noticed, tucked to the side of the 8.5x11-inch magazines, three black VHS tapes. My eyes lit up, slightly disappointed I didn't see them at first. My hands began to tremble again as I picked up the tapes with no labels. I could feel my heart pound in my throat. A sensation of heat emanated from my ear cartilage. I instantly placed all the magazines and VHS tapes back how I found them, minus the one I had in my hand. I closed the closet, pushed the combination lock back, and spun the dials before heading back into the living room where my dad's VCR waited for me.

I stole one more look out the window.

Yes! Still there. I'll just watch a few minutes to see what's on the tape and put it back.

I pushed the VHS tape into the VCR. The gears inside it churned for two seconds before they came to a rest. I pressed play. I was greeted by what I thought then was the most beautiful woman, with caramel-brown skin, full lips, curly shoulder-length hair, and the curvaceous body the centerfolds in the magazines were sorely missing. A couple of minutes later, the brown beauty wrapped her lips and tongue around a White guy's penis. I was in shock.

Pee comes out of there!

The expression on the man's face whose penis she was devouring was lit with ecstasy. Then it happened: he ejaculated on her chest. She spread what remained on her lips and slurped the rest with her tongue. I was in awe. I had just been introduced to Vanessa del Rio and I was in lust with her!

The conclusion of the weekend couldn't have come faster for me. I never returned the tape to the closet. I shoved it to the very bottom of my backpack beneath my clothes and wrapped it in my underwear. With only a few minutes of sampling the video, I'd decided Vanessa was coming home with me—damn the consequences. If my dad asked me about the missing tape, I would just deny, deny, deny! She was mine and would be worth the ass whooping.

Four years later, during the summer of 1992, I would apply everything the four-hour Vanessa del Rio compilation porn tape had taught me. For weeks, I'd been convincing my girlfriend at the time to come over to my house while my mother was at work so we could have sex. We planned for her to meet me at my house at ten o'clock one Tuesday morning when she didn't have to babysit her younger brother. That week, her younger brother's dad had picked him up, leaving my girlfriend free of babysitting duty.

At 10:14 that morning, she knocked on my door and I shot up from the couch to hurry her inside before any of my neighbors could see and notify my mother I had a girl over. She and I exchanged the most mischievous of smiles and hugged as I closed both the porch screen and vestibule door behind us. I let my hands slide down to her round backside, instigating a giggle from her. I pulled her body into mine, initiating a slow, swaying grind based on our own rhythm.

"Come on, let's go upstairs," I suggested, wasting no time. She nodded in agreement. We ascended the stairs, and once at the top, I led her directly into my bedroom.

"Lemme help you with this," I joked, removing her purse and placing it on top of my bedroom dresser. I hastily pulled off my T-shirt and discarded it next to her purse.

"You ready, huh?" she joked.

"Hell, yeah!" I responded. "I've been trying to get you over here for weeks." I closed the space in between us again so I could lead her over to my bed. I grabbed at the loose material of her blouse so I could free it from her fitted jeans. My slender, six-two frame stood in front of where she was seated on my bed. She was eye to eye with my protruding penis. I slyly smirked at her. She noticed my pulse, flexing my penis slightly up and down to the rhythm of my heartbeat.

"Uh-uh!" she said, craning her neck back. "We can fuck but I ain't sucking yo dick." I returned a smile, just happy to hear her confirm that sex was going to happen.

"That's cool," I agreed, not wanting to ruin the moment. Just the sound of her mentioning my penis and her mouth in the same sentence sent a sensation of heat racing up my body and ending at my ears. I leaned down to kiss her deeply. My tongue rolled around hers, and I sat next to her. Grabbing at her overdeveloped breast, I fumbled my way through unbuttoning her blouse. Moments later, we were both naked and under my bed sheets. I positioned myself in between her thick thighs, with my penis throbbing on the outside of her glistening labia.

Between the next few kisses, I reached down to grab a handful of myself and blindly rubbed my penis between her lips like I'd seen done to Vanessa del Rio just before the multitude of men I watched inserted themselves into the starlet. A jolt of pleasure ran through my pelvis the moment I felt how wet she was. I'd never felt a woman like this, and it was exhilarating. I repositioned myself closer on top of her and slowly thrusted my hips. The undershaft of my penis slid back and forth against her. A slight moan emerged from her mouth.

More moans erupted from us both as the enthusiasm of my thrust increased. I could feel her body increasingly respond to mine. A shock wave ran through me. I laid my full weight on her, reaching beneath her to grab two handfuls of as much of her ass as I could.

I was thrusting ferociously now. The same building sensation of exhilaration I experienced masturbating during countless bathroom sessions ran through my pelvis.

"You feel so fucking good!" I exclaimed, thrusting faster and harder. Using the handfuls of her ass, I pulled her into me at the same cadence as my thrusts.

"What are you doing?" she questioned suddenly.

"Huh? W-we're having sex!" I exclaimed, still amateurishly thrusting her. Only two seconds would pass before I realized her moaning had dissipated and she was staring at me emotionless and a little confused.

"What's wrong?" I asked, this time thrusting as hard as I could, hoping to evoke a reaction out of her. Any reaction. Then she said it.

"You know you're *not* inside of me, right?"

"Yes I am! I can feel it," I replied. She rolled her eyes.

"You're such a virgin. You're stroking in between my lips, Tarik," she said as kindly as a teenage girl could, considering the situation. "Here, let me show you." She reached down and grabbed a handful of my engorged penis to reposition me.

"Uuuhhh," she moaned, eyes lightly closed, and biting her lip. "Now, push slowly," she whispered. I did exactly as she instructed and that's when I felt myself slide into the most perfect place I'd ever been. Inside of her was a culmination of every wet dream I'd had. Better than any fantasy I'd developed in my head while lying in a warm bath with my soap-lathered hands wrapped around my penis.

Inside her was excitement and joy. Inside her was a feeling I'd never want to abandon. Inside her, at that moment, was heaven.

"Ooooh shiiit!" I sang as my body melted onto hers. My feverish thrust returned, this time relentlessly, as we both moaned at our own pleasure. My bed's wooden headboard banged against the wall. The pounding cadence excited me even more, as it brought back memories of the suggestive sex scenes of R-rated movies I'd watched on cable TV while my mother was at work or during weekends at my cousin's house in Philly.

I paced my thrusts to mimic what I'd seen in those R-rated movies. My breathing intensified; my right leg began to shake uncontrollably like a dog having his belly scratched. I continued to pound her mercilessly, knowing each stroke equaled pleasure. However, my pace was too much for my modest, twin-size bed and old metal clamps to hold both our weight. A millisecond of freefall followed by a large thud landed all my body weight and my penis into her.

"Tarik!" she cried out.

"Uuuuuuuhhhhhh!" I roared as my entire body tensed with an exhilaration of full-body pleasure that ran from my head down to my curling toes. I recklessly reached down between my legs at the last minute, pulling myself out of her vagina and ejaculating widely on her right thigh. I missed my mark of leaving a money shot of semen on her stomach, just how the men had done to Vanessa del Rio.

Next time I'll get it right!

I completely collapsed onto her, heaving my chest up and down in exhaustion and basking in the euphoria of my first sexual orgasm, conquest, and loss of my virginity.

YES!

I lay there a little while longer, panting on her selfishly, completely oblivious of my partner, before rolling off and heading to the bathroom to wash up in the sink. I grabbed my washcloth and the bar of Dial soap. I set the hot and cold faucets to create the perfect temperature of warming water. I worked up a good lather while looking at the glistening that both our bodily fluids coated my limp penis with. I was so proud of myself.

That's how you do it, nigga!

The bathroom door swung open, and that same expression of

disappointment had returned to her face from when she had to guide my penis inside herself.

"Uhh, what are you doing?" she asked, befuddled.

"Washing up. You want a rag too?" I asked, thinking how impressed she would be at my chivalry. She wasn't impressed. Instead, she took one step into the bathroom and reached past me to turn off the water. The four and a half minutes of pleasure I'd selfishly experienced would not cut it for her. I was a virgin up until today, but she was not. When we first began talking about sex, she'd confessed that she'd had sex with two other guys before me.

"Nigga! We not done! I still want to fuck, so we doin' it again!"

"You can do it more than once!?" I exclaimed in naivety and excitement.

She sucked her teeth and shook her head before leading me from the bathroom by my wet hand. She made a line down the hallway, landing us in my mother's bedroom. She climbed on top of the bed, placed a pillow under her head, and pulled me back in between her thighs.

"This time, don't pull out when you come."

Between the crossroads of my inexperienced naivety and witnessing porn scenes lasting a few minutes before the scene ending with the "money shot," my understanding of sex was deformed. In the pornography I was exposed to, there was no room for passion, patience, or even sensual foreplay. There may have been some oral sex exchange before the sex, but after the man reached orgasm in the infamous "money shot," the scene faded to black. From the ages of thirteen to sixteen, I learned from porn what making love or fucking was. They were not mutually exclusive. My perception of sex and intimacy wouldn't change until much later, when I updated my idea of making love to a slower version of fucking, with periodic kisses thrown in here and there, and whispering "I love you" like they do in movies. It wouldn't be until my thirties, courtesy of my nameless toxic terror, that I learned the act of making love was completely foreign to me.

chapter 4

One of the many consequences of young men being raised with limited exposure to proper male role models is the equally limited exposure to healthy relationships and what they look like. Young and impressionable, children live vicariously through the examples and emotions of their parents, aunts, uncles, and grandparents for the proper demonstration of love toward their significant others.

Speaking from my perspective, I was one of too many young men with absent fathers, raised by single mothers, some of whom raised us out of genuine love, others duty, and a rare few subconsciously resenting us for being constant reminders of the men who didn't love them back properly. Then there were the unintended consequences of some of these mothers who never received the love they gave away to the men they bore children for. They coddled their sons in an attempt to mold them into a version of man they'd wished our fathers would have been.

This is evident in some mother-son dynamics where mothers treat their sons more like de facto husbands once they come of age, expecting budding young men to shoulder the burden of premature adulthood. Before you misunderstand me, I'm not speaking of inappropriate sexual relationships, but rather, the act of placing adult responsibilities on their sons as protectors and providers. Labeling them "the man of the house," despite their having limited or no example of manhood to mimic.

Then there are the mothers who expect that their children will contribute to the financial stability of the home, rather than simply being children who are free to make mistakes while sorting out their purpose and place in this world. Finally, some mothers overstep when their sons choose a mate, subconsciously imposing their will on their child's choice of a life partner, as if their son's decision to love another woman besides them would take away the attention they were lacking from their missing significant other.

Loneliness is a terrible emotion to endure. I remember having a crush on a teenage neighbor who lived across the street. She'd developed earlier than the girls her age, resulting in her being curvaceous, like some grown women, rather than a 14-year-old girl. My mother noticed us spending more time together, and one summer evening after I came into the house for dinner, she inquired about our friendship.

"I notice you and Toi have been spending a lot of time together."

"Yeah, she's my girlfriend," I responded innocently, trying to subdue a budding smile. I didn't notice my mother's mood change until it was too late. Instead of the typical follow-up questions parents ask to gain additional information, my mother's initial response was shocking. Shocking because my mother never spoke a negative word about anyone unless provoked.

"You know she going to be fat when she gets older, right? She doesn't take care of herself like she should," my mother said callously, even mean-spiritedly. Our very first argument would immediately follow.

"Don't talk about my girl like that!" I instinctively responded, defending Toi's "honor," so to speak. It surprised me as much as my mother.

"Who do you think you're talking to?" she responded, standing over me to remind me she was an adult and still bigger than me. I wasn't intimidated. I hadn't done anything wrong. I didn't start this confrontation, she did. She was a grown woman in her thirties going out of her way to talk badly about a 14-year-old girl who hadn't done anything to her except express interest in her son.

Even as a teenager, I recognized my mother's response was fueled by some displaced emotion. It was an unjustified, immature comment. It was the first time it made me question her judgment and ultimately her intentions for giving me advice about women. It sent the message that this would be an aspect of life I would have to figure out on my own. I didn't want to be molded into some incompetent momma's boy who couldn't navigate the world without her approval.

Even a decade later, when we should have both been wiser from our collective life experiences, my mother's misguided opinion about the women I should pursue was only reinforced. At twenty-four years old, I'd begun dating a young lady who was attending an Ivy League medical school in Philadelphia. We were still in the early stages of courtship, and when I expressed to my mother that I might stop seeing her because I didn't believe us to be compatible, her response was equally as shocking as her comment about my childhood girlfriend.

"Don't break up with her, Tarik. Doctors make a lot of money and there's no guarantee you'll meet another one," she said plainly. I didn't respond in the same manner as to her insulting Toi so many years ago. Instead, I was disappointed—disappointed in her guidance because it sounded far too similar to the mindset of hood gold diggers I'd purposely avoided after graduating from college.

It also seemed eerily similar to the old-school advice of her generation to young women who solely attended college to hunt and latch onto men with high earning potential. And it rang too true to women of my generation who give advice equal to that of groupies who prey on men who are athletes and entertainers, hoping to latch on, maybe even get pregnant, so they can secure a meal ticket for the next eighteen years. Except in this instance, it was suggested that I become the hood gold digger and the young lady I was dating was the millionaire athlete or celebrity. Even worse was the insinuation that she may be the only doctor, or successful woman for that matter, I might meet despite my own personal accomplishments.

It was at this moment I realized my mother was projecting her approach to choosing a mate onto me. I knew unequivocally that I could not rely on her for guidance for some of my important life decisions. I don't say this to be callous. I say this to emphasize that at the mere age of twenty-four, I'd surpassed my mother philosophically and socioeconomically. The constraints she placed on her life would never apply to me, and unfortunately, she didn't see that despite being the person who knew me best of all. And if my own mother, the person who brought me into this world, didn't know who and what I was in that moment, then who did? How could I?

My point is, too many of us as young men are left to our own devices. Left to pit our will and wits against life in a battle of trial and error as we stumble our way through. And unfortunately, too many of these errors come at the expense of the women we enter relationships with and even love.

I've admittedly ruined my fair share of healthy relationships simply because I didn't know how to properly initiate, nurture, and maintain a relationship. At twenty-four, I could not account for one household where I witnessed a father who demonstrated genuine love for his wife in a home meticulously curated for a family. The concept was as foreign and majestic to me as the existence of Bigfoot and unicorns. And much like those two mystical creatures, I would only ever see them on television.

Heathcliff and Clair Huxtable of *The Cosby Show* were a fictional New York power couple. One where the father was a successful doctor who was happy with his intelligent, bilingual wife, an accomplished lawyer. They were my unicorns. A fictitious representation of a beautiful and majestic creation with wings that could take them anywhere they desired.

But the Huxtables weren't grounded in my reality. They were merely a concept for me to be in awe of for thirty minutes a week. A healthy distraction from the repeated romantic and financial failures of the adults surrounding me as a child. My exposure to nature versus nurture is real where I was raised, and the skills developed to survive nature rarely fit with romance. In fact, it clashed. Despite my best intentions and efforts, I've yet to negotiate a sustained healthy relationship for longer than two years. Being the youngest in my pack, I did not learn to value logic and compromise. I learned aggression as a way of life, survival at all costs as my primary objective, and that embracing love would weaken me.

"Bruh, what's up with you and Dee?" one of my best friends from college asked me one homecoming weekend.

"We not seeing each other anymore," I responded, hoping my lack of detail would satisfy his curiosity.

"What you do now?" he questioned, destroying all hope.

"Why it gotta be me?" I said with a smirk, knowing damn well it was, in fact, my fault. Again.

"Come on, bruh, you know I don't mean it that way, but you know how you can be sometimes, too."

"Yeah, I fucked this one up really good. Straight FUBAR. She's not coming back, and I can't blame her," I admitted.

"So, let me hear it. What happened?" he asked sincerely. "And I'm not asking to make you feel bad, but we need to get you right." This time, he had encouragement in his voice.

"Honestly, I don't know what it is. But I just do uncharacteristically dumb shit whenever I'm around her. One minute we're good and the next I'll say or do something that causes her to look at me like I've lost my damn mind. I'm not talking about regular mistakes. I'm talking about embarrassing, you'd think I haven't had any home training-level type of dumb shit. Bruh, I'm embarrassed for me," I said with a slight chuckle and a sincere shake of the head.

He joined in the laughter. "Give me an example," he requested.

"Okay, well, it was this one time where she invited me to her parents' house to meet her mother and father. She offered me a drink. Dee grabbed me a beer and we were all drinking, having a good time just conversing. I'd finished my beer, and when I leaned forward to get up from the couch, all the carbonation from the beer shot out of me and I belched. I'm talking loudly, too! Like Barney, the drunk barfly from *The Simpsons, loud!*" I said, shaking my head again, reliving the experience.

"Are you fucking serious?"

"Yeah, man, and I swear to God I didn't even realize I had to belch, or you know I would have curbed it or held it in or *anything* but that! The moment I leaned forward to get off the couch, it just shot out of me before I could even stop it. It was embarrassing as hell. I apologized to Dee and her mother so many times, hoping they'd realize it was an accident."

"That was your first mistake," he responded.

"Huh? What?" I questioned. "Burping? Duh!"

"No, dummy, you got too comfortable too soon. It's still early in y'all dating and you got so comfortable you were slouching on their couch. Our body language speaks to people too, sometime more than our words. You're at her house meeting her parents and you're slouching on their couch like you are right now, sitting across from me. Is that the impression you want to make? Is that the impression you'd make if you were at a job interview?"

"Of course not!" I responded.

"Exactly. Meeting a woman's parents is a job interview. They want to see how you present and respond under certain circumstances to make sure you deserve their daughter. You should've been sitting up straight, with laser focus on making the best of impressions. Instead, you got lax and belched! And you paid a price for it.

"So, what else happened? I know that can't be it. No one stops seeing someone because they belched once. What made her call it quits?" he questioned.

"I'm going to need a drink for this one," I admitted. "You're going to clown me when I tell you and I wouldn't blame you."

He didn't even wait for me to finish and had already risen from the couch opposite me. He disappeared into the kitchen, and I heard his cabinet doors open, followed by the sound of two glasses clinking and the sound of ice falling into them. He came back with two tumblers of Scotch on the rocks. He handed me one and sat down with the other.

"Alright, spit it out," he said, falling back into the dented cushion and raising his glass to take a sip of cool, amber beverage. I took a drink before continuing.

"That same night, after I apologized my way back into her mother's good graces, Dee mentioned she needed to create a website for a new business venture she was eyeing. She suggested I help her create it, since I've designed a few sites for people already."

"Okay, and?" Eric responded. I took another drink, broke eye contact, and shook my head before continuing.

"So, a week later I'm at home on the couch not doing shit but watching television and I had another brain fart. I turn on my laptop and started searching online for sites like the one she wanted to brainstorm ideas for."

"And?"

"So, I find a few ideas and start taking little notes I can reference for later. Then it happens," I said, pausing again to shake my head in disappointment, followed by another sip from my tumbler. "Let me preface my next few words with *I know now that I fucked up*. I get it. However, in that moment while I was writing up the notes, I was genuinely ignorant of how offensive and dumb what I was about to do was."

"Nigga, what did you do?" Eric said, now leaning forward.

"After I finished writing up the notes for the format, some images, color schemes for creating the site, I started writing up a proposal to document the project because that's what I normally do when working with a client, so in my mind, I was treating her professionally. You know, giving her the same respect I would extend to any client. I wanted to demonstrate to her I'm a professional, annnd…" I paused for a moment, hating the taste of the words forming in my mouth, knowing, especially then, how dumb and naive it was. "I sent her an invoice—"

"You did what?" he said, staring at me intently, face frozen, jaw open.

"I gave her a discount!" I interjected, hoping to cut off his ridicule. "I even mapped out the numbers to demonstrate what I would normally charge someone for this type of project and then displayed a comparison so she could see I hooked her up with a nice, discounted rate—"

"Tarik, if you don't shut the fuck up!" he said respectfully but seriously. "You sent the woman you're dating an invoice? A fucking *invoice*!"

The foolish litany of excuses I tried using, followed by a charming smile, was my father's DNA revealing itself to my college best friend. I was ashamed of myself all over again.

"I know. I said when I started this story, I was dumb. Dumb as fuck!"

"Very fucking dumb! Tarik? Man, what were you thinking?" he scolded through laughter.

"Honestly, I wasn't. In my head, I thought she respected my skill set and was throwing me some work. Until I saw her response and then I knew I really fucked up."

"Tarik, didn't she take a day off of running her own business to drive you around so you could buy a new car when yours died?"

"Yeah, she did," I responded shamefully.

"And didn't she loan you a few hundred dollars to put on top of your down payment?"

"A thousand, but I paid her back. I'm not a freeloader."

Shut up, Tarik! That's not the point!

"That's not the point, Tarik!" Eric followed up my mental scolding with his own.

"She helped you when no one else did or could. Did she write up some contract when she did that for you?" he rhetorically asked.

"She could have, but she didn't. Look, I'm not trying to make you feel worse, but come on, Tarik, what made you think that she would be okay with that? Would you have charged your own family for a site?"

I paused a moment before responding, knowing that despite my best college friend probably knowing me better than most, he didn't truly understand my complicated family dynamic and experiences. This would be the first time I'd give him, or anyone for that matter, a glimpse into how my pack operated.

"Honestly?" I said sincerely. "At that point in time, before knowing what I know now, yes, I would have charged them. My family has charged me money for watching my son, their own kin, while I've been at work. I've been charged by family for them helping me move a mattress and two pieces of furniture twenty minutes away to my new house—"

"What the fuck?" Eric interrupted. His mood changed from reprimand to sympathy. "Hold on for a second, bruh. Don't take this the wrong way, but you do know that's not normal, right? Family isn't supposed to profit off each other."

I took a few moments to ponder whether I should continue to respond honestly about some of the people in my family dynamic.

"Bruh," I said, "I'm not trying to speak badly about anyone that's family to me. I love my family, but some of my experiences don't match the concept of 'what's supposed to happen.' In my family, *sometimes* whatever happens, happens. Rhyme or reason be damned. My family has ruined my credit, my family has stolen from me, my family has stolen my identity, my family had my license suspended, my family has gotten my car towed and left me hanging to come up with the money to get my car from the impound. People in survival mode don't fully process what the weight of pulling themselves up does to those reaching down lending a helping hand."

I paused, fighting the knot in my throat before it cracked my voice. To be honest, I wasn't sure if the knot was due to my revelation about my family or rehashing the loss of Dee.

"My family has repeatedly asked me for a monthly allowance,

simply for being family," I confessed before snapping my head back, throwing the rest of the Scotch to the back of my throat. Eric sat silently, threw back his drink, and reclined into the comfort of his couch as I continued my contrition.

"Again, I know now I fucked up. I'm not going to make any excuses about that. The truth is, at the time, I honestly didn't know any better. Knowing what I know now, I just wish I'd learned this lesson before meeting her. She was the first woman that challenged me and demanded better of me," I concluded.

The truth that I did not share out loud with my friend was, when she and I met, I probably didn't deserve her. Who she was, her station in life, and her understanding of the way the world works was a generation ahead of mine and she knew it. Despite my immaturity and not seeing it at the time, she displayed boundless grace while I stumbled clumsily through our dating until she ultimately saw I wasn't ready to head in the direction she had already been blazing a trail toward. I fumbled her and any chance of a long-lasting relationship we could have had. And that's an error I've had to live with.

part II
PARENTS & FAMILY

chapter 5

"You talk to my wife like that again and I'll kick your ass!"

Those words, on a night like countless, otherwise uneventful nights, would snatch my innocence away from me like a thief would a purse from an elderly woman. My cousin's husband's enraged promise would be my initiation to what level of ferocity could exist amongst those who were previously endeared as family. In my bed, sound asleep, I was startled awake by a voice I'd laughed with over sitcoms and family dinners.

"You better back up before I back you up!" His second threat penetrated my closed door, forcing my rapid heartbeat from my chest to my throat. My 7-year-old eyes finally adjusted to the darkness of my bedroom. I oriented myself, knowing now it wasn't a nightmare fueled by the endless horror movies I'd been raised on. My dry tongue clung to the roof of my mouth.

"Boy! Ain't nobody afraid of you! This is between me and my niece. Stay out of it!" the most familiar voice I'd known, my mother's, raged at her nephew-in-law, her niece's newlywed husband. The two of them had been staying with my mother and me while they saved for their own house after being married only a few months prior. The unfamiliar, dangerous tone of his voice pulled me from my bed. I pulled my door open wide so I could reach the stairs leading to the first floor where the dispute was happening. My feet barely touched the hardwood as I tore down the stairs.

"This is my wife! You're not going to tell me what to do with my own wife! Don't make me kick your ass!" My cousin's husband, a deacon at his church, positioned his six-feet, 200-pound frame between my docile older cousin and the five-feet-five-inch, 115-pound frame of my mother.

"Touch me and you'll wake up in the hospital!" my mother warned, defiant, confident, and in a posture I didn't recognize. She stood barefoot in the living room just outside the foyer, but somehow, she seemed bigger. Much like those animals in nature who spike their fur and broaden their stature to ward off potential predators, instinctively communicating, "Come at me and we'll both bleed tonight." Her ritualistically pristine, straightened hair flared with volume almost like a canine's. She breathed lightly, but her chest rose and fell rapidly, anticipating his attack. She was ready to stand her ground unafraid, no stranger to pending confrontation.

"I said, back up!" he shouted again, this time shoving my mother violently against the hard plaster wall of the living room. She stretched her arms out to grab for anything that would break the momentum, the palm of her left hand smacking against the wall and her right forearm against a wooden, four-legged coatrack. A mix of shock and rage widened her eyes and mouth. Her right hand instinctively grabbed the coatrack to steady herself.

"Stop! That's enough!" my cousin finally said, sheepishly grabbing at her husband's shoulder and waist, distracting him enough so my mother could grab the coatrack with both hands. Before he could whip his head back at his victim, my mother reeled back and swung the wooden rack at her attacker. The muscles in her forearms and biceps flexed as she gathered all her miniature might at his head.

She wasn't strong enough; he grabbed the coatrack midair just before it landed on its target. They both struggled with the rack between the two of them, adrenaline fueling my mother against a more formidable foe, until his natural strength forced her back up against the wall. His force, in combination with her feet sliding against the smooth floor, left her only the option of retreating to the corner of the same wall, that wooden coatrack being the only thing that separated the two of them.

With them fifteen feet to the far-left corner of the living room, I ran down the steps, off to the right, the opposite direction of the fight. Now, under the archway threshold that separated both rooms I grabbed the phone.

9-1-1! Call 9-1-1!

Like they conditioned us to do in kindergarten, I punched the keypad with shaking fingers.

"9-1-1, what is your emergency?"

My cousin saw me on the phone and dashed across the floor towards me in a panic.

"Help! My mom—"

Before I could finish my distress call, my own kin, who had failed to de-escalate the altercation, snatched the phone from my small hands and slammed it down before I could finish alerting the police. To this day, I'm not sure how my mother fought her way out of the corner, back to her feet, dashing past me and into the kitchen, but she did. I faintly heard a rustling in the kitchen but was distracted by my cousin, who had me by the hand, trying to lead me away from the phone to prevent further calls until—

"Get your hands off my son!" my mother yelled, shoving my cousin, her niece, away from me with a shoulder cross-check that would make any hockey player proud. With one free hand, she pulled me in front of her. I looked back to see where my cousin and her husband were while noticing my mother's other hand was hidden along the side of her leg out of my sight. With her free hand, she forced me into the kitchen with frightening haste. The kitchen was dark but she led me to a corner behind the kitchen table.

"Stay here! Don't move!"

I did as she instructed, my butt in a corner, arms wrapped around my knees. She left me there, safe, and returned to the threshold of the kitchen door. I couldn't see past her in the darkness but finally saw why her other hand was hidden from me. Behind her back was a large knife I'd only seen her cut chicken breasts with.

"Oh! You going to stab me?" my cousin's husband shouted emphatically from the other room. My mother's response was cold, short, ferocious.

"How bad you want to find out?"

"Kurt, no! Don't go back there!" my cousin warned her husband. Then from my dark corner of the open kitchen I saw blue and red lights flashing through the house, followed by rapid banging on the front door.

"Police! Open the door!" they shouted. My mother rushed back to the kitchen and threw the knife in its drawer.

"Come here, Tarik," she said, prompting me to leave my corner.

"You did good calling the police," she assured me, grabbing me by the hand and power walking her way past my cousin, shooting an evil look at her husband as we made our way toward the door.

Even as a young child who would eventually have countless street fights in Southwest and West Philly, I knew there was something more insidious about the fight I had just witnessed. Ultimately, my mother put me to bed before returning downstairs to talk to the police officers, who'd come after my cousin abruptly ended my call. The experience left a subconscious mark on my psyche. I didn't know it at the time; I innocently stored the experience away as an anomaly, a one-off where family had momentarily lost its composure, where emotion had gotten the better of them. That was my innocence protecting me from the harshest of realities. I'd soon learn that in packs, pack members fight and not with just harsh words. They use balled fists, wooden coat racks, knives, and, on the worst of occasions, bullets.

chapter 6

My family's American lineage, like many, is rooted in the humblest of circumstances. Despite our present-day urban residence and exterior, we're deep rural Southerners by culture. My South Carolina family name is Mayers. And the Mayers Holy Trinity equates to:

Family is everything.

Land is king.

Our home is our peace.

NOTE: Our bloodline will defend all of the above with whatever weapons are at our disposal.

Family, first and foremost, serves as your first social group. They also double as your first teachers for how to navigate life while also serving as protectors from the eternal dangers of life. Pack mentality at its finest.

My great-grandfather's trinity lesson above governs my family members, both actively and passively. Following the passing of the Thirteenth Amendment, our ancestors, now freed in South Carolina, refused to go back and work the plantations as slaves. Instead, my great-great-grandfather negotiated an agreement with a White planter to sharecrop his land, if he agreed to loan my great-great-grandfather enough money to buy his own plot of land as payment for his effort.

I remember my great-grandfather driving home the point: "Even if your home is the most modest, it ensures a family would always have a roof over its head and never experience the hardships of homelessness and all its traps." It was one of the many lessons passed down to him through traditional African oral stories and histories. Those stories and lessons of survival were passed to him by the elders of his previous generations who had also worked farms, but for free, as the maternal descendants of the enslaved Bubi African tribe native to Bioko Island, west of the Equatorial Guinea coast.

My great-grandfather and his father were bona fide farmers. Once the White planter accepted their terms, they worked the White planter's farm, built a homestead with their own hands, and thrived. Over the course of both their lifetimes, our family would acquire seventy-nine acres of land along a country dirt road in Little Mountain, a South Carolina town with a population below four hundred people—three hundred and forty, to be exact. On that country dirt road, my family's American footprint would be established on the site of that homestead.

I still have living family members, my Aunts Mattie and Malinda, who remember using an outhouse before the homestead had indoor plumbing. The living room doubled as a delivery room and had a wood-burning stove that served both as the kitchen and the source for heat during cold winter months. The farm they cultivated also had livestock, such as hogs, pigs, and chickens. These were the very same animals they'd slaughter to provide their daily meals and sustain their household.

Farming culture dictates that you have many children. The more children you have, the more hands are available to work the land. My family tilled the soil and cultivated mostly soybeans and other staple vegetables like corn, tomatoes, green beans, and spices. They literally sustained their lives off their own land. Not surprisingly, my grandmother carried her father's and grandfather's traditions north. We clung to our large Southern family traditions.

My grandmother and her sister were the first of their twelve siblings to leave their small, rural South Carolina town, for big city living. My grandmother, Edith, left the South after marrying. Originally, she settled in New York but soon after, left the big city for a smaller city in southern New Jersey called Camden, where she bought a house and raised five daughters. My mother and I were the only ones in our generations to have only one child, in comparison to our counterparts, whose offspring numbered between at least three and as many as eleven.

My grandmother, adhering to her father's lessons, worked, saved, and purchased a three-bedroom, one-bathroom, single-family row house for $4,900. This would be the same single-family row house I was raised in that I described in the preface as having no showerhead and only a tub. It remains in my family to this day, where I now house tenants and serve as their landlord. Every member of my family has lived on Trenton Avenue, even my son, at some point in their lives. This home laid the foundation of city home ownership, per my great-grandfather's trinity. Today, almost every member of my large family owns a home, ranging from modest inner-city dwellings to suburban homes up and down the eastern seaboard.

My grandmother also maintained a garden once she arrived in New Jersey after buying her first home. And the children she brought into the world witnessed and learned from her how to cultivate and live off the land once they bought homes with yards. It's no coincidence that even in my generation and the generation after mine, I have family who actively grow fresh vegetables in their modest backyards. Even I experiment with cultivating hemp and cannabis since they've become legal crops in the states I've lived in. Farming, like many other foundational skills that helped form this country, is engrained in the blood of its citizens.

Mine being only two generations removed from a deep rural Southern upbringing, it makes sense why some of the traditions and values I'd unknowingly internalized now manifest themselves. However, these traditions can be both good and bad. The good traditions resemble children in my family being instilled with discipline and respect, so that they answer their parents with "sir" and "ma'am" without exception. Then there are the traditions worthy of being reexamined, such as relegating children to being seen and not heard. The seen-and-not-heard approach teaches developing children that their feelings and opinions are not valid, especially in those pivotal moments when we should listen to them.

Then there are the exceptionally bad traditions where discipline is administered in antiquated methods, such as spankings or beatings using leather belts or switches. Rule of law promoted and regulated through intimidation and fear are archaic forms of disciplining children who knowing or unknowingly disobey their parents.

The first memory I have of my great-grandfather was during the first of many annual summer family reunion trips to South Carolina. I was a child, four years of age, and my great-grandfather's rooster had awakened me from my makeshift bed of folded quilts on the hardwood floor of the very same homestead that was constructed three generations before mine. I peered through the window to see my great-grandfather, in his worn blue overalls, climbing onto his tractor to till the land adjacent to us.

I remember looking around the living room, where a collection of additional makeshift beds lay next to mine, with the slumbering bodies of my mother, my cousins, and my aunts. My oldest aunt, Mattie, was the first of my grandmother's five daughters and the last to be birthed by a midwife within those walls. The same walls where the entire generation before my oldest aunt, a generation of thirteen children who would ultimately become farmers, were brought into this world, none by way of hospitals because of Southern Jim Crow segregation. In other words, their living rooms and bedrooms were their hospitals, since there were no Black hospitals to provide the basic right of medical attention afforded to White citizens of this country.

For those in this country who are "tired" of African Americans referencing slavery, here's an example of why it's our duty to never stop speaking of the systemic effects of racism in this country. Because of Jim Crow segregation in the South, especially in small, country towns with populations below four hundred people, my community of people had to provide its own general medical care because Blacks weren't allowed in White hospitals. We had to cure our own illnesses, birth our own children via midwives, and in the most extreme cases, doctor our own population. A generation living with that expectation culturally develops traditions of mistrust of hospitals and doctors. Especially White ones.

This subconscious practice within my community is evident in the tongue-in-cheek comments made within our own community, where we joke that Black folk don't go to doctors unless we're bleeding out of our eyes and ears or dying. When generations of people are born into an experience where hospitals won't allow them inside their facilities and doctors refuse even to touch, yet alone care for and treat, an African-American patient, I understand now how we didn't know my grandmother was terminally ill until the last few months of her life. Even as a teenager, after coming home for winter break my second year in college, I experienced it when I came down with strep throat, which eventually morphed into scarlet fever. I called my mother at work to tell her about my badly swollen tonsils and the extremely red rash developing on my arms, chest, and neck. Her response was canned and instinctual.

"Take a nap and I'll take a look when I get home from work."

When she arrived home and looked over my body and symptoms, her recommendation was to get more rest and see if it improved in the morning. This was one of the rare instances where I aggressively had to advocate for myself against waiting.

"Mom! I'm itching like crazy! Something is wrong. If you don't take me, I'll walk to the emergency room myself!" I threatened. The genuine concern from her typically reserved son was the catalyst for her listening to me. Three hours later, the doctors at Cooper Medical Center diagnosed me with scarlet fever and commended my mother for bringing me in before the illness spread further and permanently affected my heart with scar tissue.

The generation before mine didn't have indoor plumbing. It was the job of my mother's oldest sister, Mattie, to empty the bucket they kept inside during winters when it was too cold to travel outside in the dark of night to use the outhouse. They cooked over a cast-iron, wood-burning stove that doubled as their furnace to heat the home. Their water came from underground wells the county drilled.

During that very same summer visit as a 4-year-old, I witnessed, by purposeful design, my great-grandfather slaughtering the smallest pig of its litter so it could be prepared for our family reunion dinner the next day. When I say slaughter, I mean I watched my great-grandfather climb into the pigpen with his rifle, shoot Shorty—the name I'd given the little runt—in the head, and fight off the other pigs, who instantly began to eat the blood and brain matter that poured out of Shorty while he shook and seized in the mud, so my great-grandfather could drag the dying animal by its hooves out the pen. In expected Southern tradition, the women in our family gutted, cut, sliced, and butchered Shorty's carcass for its meat on long, wooden, plank tables in the large front yard of the homestead.

That day, I learned second by second where the food we bought from the supermarkets came from. The next day, I ate everything the women in my family prepared, except Shorty. After that summer experience, I didn't eat pork for years. And was thankful I'd never eaten chitlins after watching Shorty's intestines being removed so they could squeeze the waste (pig shit) from inside the intestines so they could be cooked, smothered in hot sauce, and eaten. To this day, the only pork I eat is bacon because—let's be honest—bacon makes everything taste better.

Years later, after returning home from my inaugural Little Mountain homecoming, the Southern traditions of family, the protection gained through our pack mentality and minimalist living were carried north with us, with Edith as our matriarch. She demanded, at a bare minimum, that we retain our disposition of Southern hospitality, chivalry, and protection predicated by our overwhelming number of men. We were taught men opened doors for women. Both the boys and girls alike knew you didn't bring a significant other home to meet the family unless you were seeking our collective approval because a marriage proposal was on the horizon.

But the secluded Southern environment where we cultivated our family norms would eventually be replaced by the hardened, unempathetic disposition of a Northern, inner-city ghetto. And as with any migrating creature leaving its natural habitat, forced to adapt to new and peculiar cultural norms and traditions, we found security in the numbers our family possessed. We never treaded lightly, because we came from a lineage of self-made men relentlessly supported by their women. My family's fortitude was cast in the fires of a majority-White small town where if you saw "Members Only" posted outside of bars or other communal establishments, it was code for "Whites Only." Those "Members (Whites) Only" signs can still be found scattered in the South today, despite it being 2024.

In that small, Southern town, where the total population struggled to match the enrollment of students in my Northern elementary or high school, my great-grandfather and his father stood their ground against White men who didn't want to see them accumulate significant amounts of land and become self-sufficient. In this small town, the norm for "uppity niggers" like my great-grandfather and his father meant a face-off with white-hooded Klansmen would soon become part of their life experience. And in that moment, you had one of two choices: shrink in fear at their presence and relegate yourself as a second-class citizen, or, even worse, sell your land like they wanted while the family retreated to an alternative location to live.

But my family doesn't shrink, we don't know what fear is, and we don't retreat. My family lineage, as directed by our great-grandfather and his father, matches aggression with unrelenting aggression. We prefer summoning our family, grabbing our guns, and standing our ground as free men should. We follow the blueprint of self-preservation my great-grandfather designed, with a shotgun in hand and a pistol tucked in his waistband. We refuse to shy away from conflict. We don't subscribe to fake gangsta games by "flashing" weapons. We pull, aim, and squeeze! We're rooted in the philosophy, "Take as many of them with you as you can" if any adversary dares to trespass on the land or homes we've sacrificed a lifetime for.

You don't touch one of ours without there being retaliation. We're okay with violence. All of us. The family house I grew up in in Camden had never been broken into, despite surrounding neighborhood houses falling victim to home invasion or breaking and entering. The people in my neighborhood knew better and left our house and family alone.

Even to this day, the entirety of Middlefield Road in Little Mountain is laced with my kin, some of whom served this country in the military, so we embrace the Second Amendment. Our protection is reinforced with numbers. Our reputation is solidified via warranted and focused ruthlessness. Plainly stated, we're fucking mean! Wrong us and you're going to have to answer to us. Even our women hold it down.

"He said your mom has chicken lips, Tarik!"

"Who said?" I demanded, instantly triggered by the nonsensical insult. A friend quickly pointed out the perpetrator. I made a beeline for the house, where the door closed instantly behind the elementary school classmate seeking refuge from me. Although Southwest Philly was only thirty minutes away from my family in Camden, my mother and I were alone to fend for ourselves in instances of immediate threat until the cavalry could be summoned. Being an only child, I had to defend and protect myself those initial formative years and had developed a reputation for fighting instantly once someone insulted my mother.

Even in jest, city kids played the game called the "Jones," where we insulted each other's clothes, shoes, hair, homes, parents. "Your momma" jokes were the cornerstone of the insults. However, in my circle, it was understood when insulting me, if you didn't replace "your momma" with "your daddy," fists would fly. I once spit in a kid's face because he didn't want to respect my "your daddy" preference. The fight that followed changed his mind and he used "your daddy" without fail going forward.

And today would be no exception for the classmate who'd just insulted my mother, in my preadolescent mind. I darted after him. My heavy book bag, bursting at the seams from the thick textbooks my Catholic school curriculum demanded, threw my light frame from side to side as my stride and rage reached their peak. I could see the kid laughing and pointing at me safely from behind the locked screen door with Plexiglas at the top half. In midstride, I reached down and scooped from the ground a branch that had fallen from a tree.

Clutching it firmly in my hand, I ran up the few concrete steps, leaving public property, and landed on the front steps of his home. I violently pulled at the locked door, but the modest lock failed to give way. He continued to laugh and point again, and almost instinctively, defying all logic and reason, I smashed the tree branch against the screen door barrier exactly where his face was. The Plexiglas cracked from the blow. He jumped back, startled, his eyes lit with shock and fear.

"You broke my door! I'm going to tell my mom!"

I hit the screen door again, making the crack in the plastic window even worse.

"Fuck you and your mom! I'll see you tomorrow at three o'clock, pussy!"

This time he retreated further into his living room and slammed shut the heavy wooden door behind the screen door. I'd made my point.

chapter 7

Of the five daughters my grandmother brought into this world, my mother was the only one to have just one child. As that lone—and sometimes lonely—child, I would, from time to time, innocently ask, "Will I ever have a brother or sister?" In reality, I honestly only wanted a brother to roughhouse with, and having a younger sister seemed like more worry than fun. One day I asked my mother if she planned on having more children, and her response to my rare request was simple: "When I found out I was pregnant, I asked God for a boy, and he gave me you. So, I never really thought about having more children."

Her flattering answer, suggesting I was the perfect child bestowed upon her by God, always made me smile and reinforced the golden-child perception that beamed down on me like a ray of sunshine during my youth. Such innocence was never meant to last long-term in the environment I grew up in, though. Some may even argue, regardless of my rugged surroundings, that American society would eventually taint any child's innocence, even in the most affluent communities, much like we're seeing now with the rampage of mass shootings plaguing every community in America.

"And as happy as I am you're here," she'd said, "bringing you into this world was not easy, little boy. You were nine pounds and that head of yours split me. Labor was not enjoyable...at all."

"You saying I have a big head?" I joked back, and she only tilted her head and pursed her lips in response. She was nice like that. Never a bad word to say about anyone, but that didn't mean those thoughts didn't dance around in her head.

"Well, my big head came from someone," I teased. Unlike my mother, I was never afraid of speaking the words bouncing around in my head, for better or worse. My mother was the only person I mostly spared my sharp tongue. After all, she did bring me into this world and all the fights I endured in Philly were typically somehow rooted in her defense after someone made a joke or comment I didn't appreciate or deemed disrespectful. So, once I gradually matured and had time to think back on my life, the choices she made raising me, and my choices, either in agreement or in objection to her choices, I tried to make sure to mask any disagreement I had out of respect for the sacrifices she'd made for me.

Those times I purposely muted myself spanned the decade I watched my mother sacrifice her most youthful years dating sparingly because her focus was to educate me properly and expose me to a consistent environment that would nurture my rearing. I'm sure, had my mother made the conscious choice to be less selfless, she would have dated more frequently, found another man to love and marry. That marriage probably would have resulted in more children, and my desire for a sibling would have been granted.

Luckily for me though, my mother's four sisters all had at least three children, with my Aunt Ronnie having the most in her generation with six. My mother was the closest with my Aunt Ronnie and her oldest sister, my Aunt Mattie, who had only one boy, Sean, out of her three children. Sean was older than me by only nine months, so he and I were raised together as if we were brothers. He, like me, was his mother's prince, so we could do no wrong in their eyes, despite our bright smiles and perceived innocence remaining a clever disguise for the mischief we constantly found ourselves in.

Sean and I got into a fair amount of trouble together. Nothing extreme or reform school-worthy, but he and I together were relatively fearless, so we spent our days either chasing or inventing adventure throughout the confines of the four square blocks of Southwest Philly, not too far from Cobbs Creek. Fifty-Fourth and Willows was home base, where we earned the typical scrapes and bruises any adolescent acquired. We loved and protected each other in our own ways. The yin to the other's yang and, in the rarest of moments, the darkness to the other's light. My cousin-brother, whose fearlessness rivaled mine, would also show flashes of cruelty.

Sean and I were at the tender ages of five and four, respectively, when I found myself perplexed by his desire to inflict harm. Many a day I followed behind him as we ventured into abandoned homes and toolsheds of neighboring homes to claim as our makeshift clubhouses. In between the meals our mothers prepared for us, he and I passed the hours outside, exhausting the endless energy adolescent boys have. It was in those moments Sean would transform from my twin adolescent to someone more diabolical when he'd chase, trap, torture, and kill whatever rodent he could.

I'd watch in confusing discomfort as he plucked out their eyes after he'd stomped them to death beneath the soles of his sneakers. For those he chose not to instantly execute and that momentarily survived his wrath, he'd carry their petrified bodies home. Sometimes we believed them to be dead, only to find out they were acting as such or knocked unconscious. That would be until we witnessed them jump to a horrifying consciousness as he dropped them into a pot of boiling water he'd methodically prepared in the same kitchen and pots our parents prepared our meals in.

My childlike mind processed moments like these as him trying to scare me, gross me out, or simply elicit some repulsive reaction out of me for his own entertainment. Most times he would succeed. To this day, I can't stand the sight of rats. Even viewing them on television leaves me averting my eyes before the sight of them triggers an irrational reaction of physical discomfort in which my skin crawls. Despite the many times I remind myself rats on television can't affect me in real life, phobias are irrational fears and I still hate them to this day.

But those terrible acts never compelled me to shy away from weekends where we alternated sleepovers at each other's houses, eating junk food, riding and fixing our bikes, and staying up later than we both should have, unbeknownst to our parents. I love my cousin to this day, despite the moments of cruelty he rained down on vermin in our childhood, a cruelty that would eventually grow as we matured and would spill over onto humans.

Being an adult now and educated more thoroughly about human nature, I can surmise my cousin who was more like a brother to me, has some issues. I'm being polite out of respect for him, of course. I know his behavior isn't viewed as acceptable or "normal" in a "civilized society." I realize and acknowledge that, despite the overwhelming love he received and all the opportunities afforded to him by a loving mother much like mine, Sean is just...different.

I couldn't help but make many observations between his behavior and that of Joffrey Baratheon in the hit HBO series, *Game of Thrones*. My love for him would never allow my lips to speak ill of him. Despite our bumping heads, he and I have never had a physical fight. He protected me and I protected him when we each faced opposition from outsiders. He is the only of my male cousins where we've verbally expressed the words "I love you" in sincerity. However, some would view, categorize, and diagnose his behavior as horrifying.

I'm not a doctor and, I'm going to assume, neither are the readers of this book, so it's not my place to say what Sean is or isn't. All I know is he's my cousin/brother and I love him, flaws and all. However, I'm sure the families of the three people who have fallen victim to his wrath probably animatedly disagree with my Switzerland-like stance. And to them I say, let me remind you of Rule #1 of the Mayers family trinity: "Family is everything," so you're entitled to have your thoughts, but I'd advise you to keep those opinions to yourselves.

"Sean! Tarik! Time to get up! We have to be at church in an hour and a half. Brush your teeth and take a shower. I'll have your clothes ironed by the time you're done," my Aunt Mattie instructed us. Sean and I were at an age where we were still young and innocent enough to share a shower. My aunt had already set the water temperature perfectly before calling us awake. We knew the routine: we each would stand on opposite sides of the tub. One of us beneath the showerhead, relatively untouched by the water, with his washcloth and soap, preparing to rinse off the soap after thoroughly cleaning himself. The other opposite him on the receiving end of the stream of water.

This Sunday morning, I was at the far end of the shower, under the water, rinsing off white, foaming soap. Sean had already rinsed and was on the opposite side beneath the showerhead, readying himself to climb out of the shower. At some point, while I carefully placed my head and face beneath the water to rinse the shampoo from my hair, I couldn't see what Sean was doing. Then it happened.

"*Aaaaahhhhh!*" I screamed out as the most excruciating and unrelenting pain I'd experienced in the four years I'd been alive permeated from the top of my head to my entire upper torso. Thinking back on it now, the only way I could describe it was as if I was receiving a full body tattoo, but these mechanical, piercing needles were glowing red-hot, rapidly piercing my skin wherever my skin had pores. Simultaneously, the skin on my head, face, neck, chest, shoulders, stomach, and eventually, my penis, felt like they were set afire.

My eyes shot open through a painful squint and witnessed my beloved cousin crouched down safely, untouched by the scalding hot water against the opposite wall of the shower from me, his hands turning one of the knobs in the shower. He'd turned the cold water off completely. I was trapped beneath a shower of scalding hot water. Unable to escape the hot water's fury because my aunt's shower did not have a plastic shower curtain, I could have pushed or run through to evade his torture. Instead, my aunt had a sliding glass door and under the shock of these circumstances my panicked young mind couldn't save myself by enduring the pain long enough to slide the door open and escape.

In this instance of fight or flight, I instinctively fought the hot water by covering the parts of my exposed body until my hands couldn't stand the searing water any longer, forcing me to move them and endure the torture with a different part of my body. I twisted, turned, and thrashed my body back and forth against the ceramic tiles and the glass shower door that confined me to a fiery hell.

The experience lasted probably less than ten seconds but felt like minutes, until my Aunt Mattie burst into the bathroom, pulled open the sliding glass shower door, and shut off all the water. I stood at the back of the tub crying and trembling in pain until she yanked me from the tub. She instantly ran cold water in the sink and doused one of our towels in it before pressing firmly against the reddened flesh that spanned my chest to my groin. To this day, I can recall the stark contrast from piercing hot water to the shock of the cold towel against my skin.

"What happened?" my aunt demanded, looking at her son, who was sheepishly poking his head out from the other side of the shower, watching me shake uncontrollably.

"Answer me, Sean!"

"I accidentally turned the cold water off," he responded.

"Why! Why would you even touch it? I already set the shower for you!" she shouted. His response would never make sense to me, no matter how many times I replay that day in my mind. Knowing the God-fearing woman my aunt is and always has been, I sometimes wonder if she periodically experiences the same bewilderment. I say that because Sean finally answered his mother and I'll never forget the expression on my aunt's face as she processed the words coming out of her youngest child's mouth.

It was as if she, for the first time, didn't recognize the child she had brought into this world. Then, I wasn't mature enough to properly interpret her facial expression. It wasn't shock or confusion. Being older now, I can only describe it as perplexed or even mystified, not simply by his response alone but more so by his frank and nonchalant demeanor, when he simply shrugged and said, "I don't know."

We didn't go to church that Sunday and I don't recall if she ever told my mother what happened. What I do know is I didn't tell my mother. I didn't want to tattle on my cousin. I didn't have siblings, but I knew better than to snitch on him. That type of behavior wasn't tolerated how we were raised. He would eventually apologize, but it would be the first of many empty apologies Sean would effortlessly give, despite his remorse for his actions being nonexistent. And that would be the last time he and I ever showered together.

chapter 8

I've danced with death on three separate occasions in my life. Thankfully, with a wink and a nod, the reaper let me know that those three brushes with death were simply a reminder of how fleeting life could be. So, he gave me a pass. He wanted me to know today wasn't the end for me, that my life's purpose hadn't yet been fulfilled. However, remember: death takes no days off.

My first brush with death happened at seven years old. My friends and I, who all attended a church-sponsored summer camp, were at a public city swimming pool in Southwest Philadelphia, not too far from my home on Willows Avenue. The shallow end of the pool was packed to the brim that hot summer day, as most of us city kids didn't know how to swim.

My friends and I created a game where we would see who could jump the farthest into the pool after a running start. However, that proved to be a difficult task for the four of us because, no matter how we tried to time our jumps into the crowded pool, eventually we would land on or collide with another child.

"Why don't we go over there?" my friend Damon suggested, pointing to the side of the pool where no kids inhabited the refreshing water. We all looked at each other and shrugged at what we perceived as a moment of ingenious thinking. Overrun by youthful exuberance, the four of us darted to the side Damon pointed out, our wet, bare feel slapping in rapid succession against the drenched ground surrounding the pool.

When we got to the side, we rock, paper, scissored to decide in what order we'd jump before starting the competition. Damon and I would go first, and our remaining two friends would jump after us once we climbed out of the way. Damon and I took our places just a few running steps from the edge of the pool. We looked at each other one last time.

"Ready?" he asked.

"Yup!" I responded "Ready, set, go!" I sounded off before darting out as fast and controlled as my bare feet would allow. Reaching the edge, I launched myself forward into the air as far as my skinny legs would take me, with Damon airborne just behind and to the right of me. We both landed feet first into the calm, cool water.

"I won!" I shouted as my feet touched down on the tiled floor and I saw Damon disappear into the water behind me. What our inexperience didn't prepare us for was the reason why the pool was less populated there. It was because the floor started to descend toward the deeper end of the pool, the area where only swimmers should venture. Typically, the shallow end of the pool reached its peak at my chest, slightly above my nipples. This time, it reached past my chest, neck, chin and flirted with my bottom lip.

Instinctively, I pushed myself onto the tips of my toes and immediately started turning around with my arm outstretched in a feverish hurry back to the ledge. Suddenly I felt a desperate pull on my arms and Damon's body emerging from under the water with a violent pull that ended with him latching onto my torso. He was shorter than me by only an inch and a half but that inch and a half resulted in his being fully submerged beneath the water.

"Tarik! Help! Don't let me drown!" he gargled in between panicked coughs from the water he'd swallowed. I couldn't respond as he wrapped his legs around my waist and I fearfully inched my way closer to the edge of the pool from where we jumped. My heart raced as Damon's grip grew tighter and tighter, almost choking me. What seemed like forever passed until my fingertips reached the rounded edge of the pool. Damon climbed out as soon as his short arms could reach.

When we climbed out, we both stood as far from the edge as possible with our other two friends looking at us, laughing.

"Y'all dumb asses almost drowned!" one pointed out, nudging the other with his elbows while Damon's and my chests rose and fell in rapid succession. I looked around and noticed that the swarm of kids in the shallow end had not seen what just happened. Neither had the lifeguard on duty. Had we gone a step or two farther down the side of the pool, Damon and I would have jumped into a depth that would have drowned us both.

My second brush with death was instigated by the perversions of a family member. The devil does indeed exist, and his debts are fulfilled via the wickedness of man. I was about eight years old and still living in Philly, but on this occasion, I was visiting my family in Camden, New Jersey. These visits to my Aunt Ronnie's house were arranged so my mom could get a much-deserved break from single parenting. But she also wanted to make sure I'd spend time with my family and nurture those bonds.

But not all family members have your best interests at heart or in mind. My aunt had six children; she also had a job in healthcare, so she spent a lot of time away from home working multiple shifts to provide for her large family. She, like my mother, possessed a head-down, back-bent work ethic instilled in them by their mother, who inherited the same work ethic from her father, Pinkney Mayers, the South Carolina farmer, my great-grandfather.

Her intense work schedule also meant she had to trust her most responsible children to maintain order at home while she was away. In a perfect world, it may not have been fair to ask a teenager to take on the responsibilities of an adult, but sometimes life is only as fair as you make it, so the end justifies the means. During my Jersey visits, my hour-by-hour safety fell upon the collective shoulders of my aunt's children, my older cousins. One—Kevin—looked out for me more so than the others.

This summer visit happened to coincide with a heat wave. This, coupled with the fact my aunt didn't have air conditioning, resigned me to sitting alone on the living room couch watching cartoons, grateful I had the portable room fan blowing directly on me. Meanwhile, all six of my cousins busied themselves with an assortment of distractions, ranging from playing outside with friends to household chores. Everyone knew me being in front of television equaled entertainment paralysis for at least a couple of hours. I was fully enthralled in the show I was watching before *he* came downstairs.

"What's up, li'l cousin?" *he* said. I'm not naming *him* on purpose. Life has already dealt him a harsh enough punishment so there's no need for me to kick him while he's down.

"Nothing, just watching cartoons."

"Word. Whatchu watching?" he asked, descending the remaining stairs, circling around the back side of the couch where I was sitting. Soon as he sat down, he repositioned the fan, pointing it directly toward him. His actions were par for the course; my family didn't shy away from, and sometimes instigated conflict with aggression. I'm sure at some point someone did the same to him, so he was merely repeating the aggressive behavior he'd probably experienced. In my opinion, unless you're a psychopath, human cruelty isn't inherited. It's a learned behavior that, if not stunted in its early growth, will metastasize until it overcomes a person entirely.

This wasn't my first time visiting, though, so I knew the drill. He was testing me, like an adolescent wolf would a pup in its pack. Because I was the youngest of my generation, testing the perceived runt of the litter was commonplace. One of the few dangers of being male is facing those moments in life where you're tested by other men who have taken it upon themselves to determine if you belong or warrant weeding out. It's Darwin's theory of natural selection at its finest. Others may recognize it as today's pop culture buzz phrase, "toxic masculinity." It's moments like these that every man faces and will ultimately determine what type of life he will live—the life of a resolute man or one of timid existence. I reacted accordingly.

"Hey! I was using that!" I responded sternly but not aggressively. The psychological conflict that I would battle my entire life began during those early years. It was textbook "nature versus nurture." On one hand, I clutched the lessons of obedience, goodwill toward my fellow man and especially family, which had been taught to me by my mother and drilled into me by the Catholic teachings I had to adhere to five days a week every school year. Then, on the opposite hand, was learned aggression I'd adopt from countless street fights and interactions like these with those in my community and family who, out of conditioning, thought testing the stranger and/or the perceived weaker was a rite of passage everyone must endure.

"My fault, li'l cousin, I was just trying to get some air, too. We can share it, right?" he said, shifting the position of the fan so he could absorb much of the fan's air, leaving the remnants to sporadically hit me.

"How's that?" he asked sarcastically.

"It's all right, I guess."

"If it's not cool enough for you, just take your shirt off," my teenage cousin suggested, removing his shirt in demonstration. He was already a teenager, as evidenced by the hair in his armpits and the fledgling muscles he'd developed during the workouts he routinely performed upstairs in his room using weights and dumbbells. He'd adopted this daily workout regime after a short stint at a juvenile detention center for a petty crime he'd committed. He'd obviously carried the survival behaviors of juvie back onto the streets with him, now that he was free. In those adolescent gladiator schools, aggression was rewarded and passivity punished.

"Maybe," I responded in a compromise dictated by my kind nature, not knowing it would be interpreted as a sign of weakness. In my mind, it wasn't as good as having the fan's air all to myself, but it was better than before, where only he could feel it, I lied to myself.

It's not that hot. You'll be a'ight, Tarik.

"Go head, take your shirt off," he insisted, sliding over closer to me on the sofa, and before I could even answer, he helped pull my shirt off over my head for me. "See, ain't dat better?"

"I—I guess," I responded, instantly feeling a sense of unease. Without even thinking, I slid away from him until I reached the right-side armrest of the sofa. He then reached in between the sofa cushions, retrieving a concealed butcher knife. Ironically, I was more concerned by his proximity to me than his brandishing a knife. I'd seen my family handle weapons before that were stashed in various places in the home for protection. Unbeknownst to my mother, during one visit, I'd found a homemade gun in a heating vent. During another visit, hidden beneath a mattress, I was shown a starter pistol typically used during track meets, but if flashed, it resembled a small but real handgun.

It wasn't until he slid even closer that my heart began racing. My young, still developing brain acknowledged that my cousin, not the knife, was the real threat. I felt an eerie, unsafe feeling I'd never experienced before.

Fight or flight! Fight or flight!

My subconscious set off alarms I was unfamiliar with processing. I was too young to understand what was going on. He took the butcher knife, carefully, slowly, and sensually moving the tip of the blade across the skin of my exposed torso. My heart leapt into my throat and my hands began trembling.

"W-w-whatchu doing?!" I demanded fearfully as the steel tip of the knife traced imaginary lines on my skin as if he were drawing. My eyes shot back between him and the knife in rapid succession. He never once made eye contact. His attention lay focused on the blade in his left hand as it methodically glided across my bare chest before he slowly placed his right on my shoulder, massaging it.

"*Hey, nigga!*" Kevin shouted from the top of the stairs before thundering down toward us. When I turned around to look back at my predator, he had already hopped up from the couch and was sprinting out of the front door. Kevin gave chase directly behind him, with only a few feet separating them. In my naivety, I gave chase after Kevin. I still try to make sense of why I followed. Perhaps

I felt that the house was no longer safe and I wanted to remain close to Kevin, who had proven himself multiple times before that day that he was trustworthy. Part of me also believes it was instinctual obligation of the pending fight the two brothers were about to have on my behalf.

If one of us fights, we all fight.

As I passed through the screen door and down the steps of the concrete porch, I spotted Kevin closing in on his knife-wielding brother, who had already crossed the one-way street in front of the house. I continued my pursuit, oblivious to the curious kids and neighbors wondering why Kevin was chasing his older brother. The adults shot condemning stares and shook their heads. They'd grown accustomed to the occasional dustup spilling out of the Trenton Avenue home, but they also knew it was better to ignore than to intervene. If you intervened with one of us, you had better be prepared to intervene with *all* of us.

I followed them over the burgundy, brick sidewalk, then between two parked cars and across the one-way street, unaware of the car barreling toward me. The parked cars hid my lanky frame from the driver's vision until it was too late.

All I could remember was a shout.

"Baby, no!" Aunt Rose, a respected elder of the neighborhood, yelled from her house stoop, but it was too late. I had already cleared the parked cars and was in a direct line to be hit by the oncoming car. Finally seeing the large car out of my periphery, I dove for the curb on the other side of the street. My dive cleared most of my body of the car's metal bumper, but my left leg remained airborne and was hit by the sedan. I heard the thud, followed by my body being turned like a helicopter propeller blade. The impact turned me ninety degrees like a watch dial before I landed on the other side of the curb. From my back, I watched the car as it came to a screeching halt, while twenty to thirty feet in front of the car, my sneaker tumbled violently along the asphalt.

Aunt Rose was the first to arrive. Her terrified eyes scanned my body and fixated on my left leg. A gash of skin was missing, and blood ran down my shin and calf, dripping onto the street. My eyes lit up, associating the blood with a broken leg, igniting my pain sensors to pulsate. Tears followed, then came the swarm of children and the remaining neighborhood adults who had witnessed me being hit. Kevin arrived, took his shirt off, folded it multiple times, and placed it under my head so the concrete wouldn't be my pillow.

"Someone call an ambulance! Hurry!" Aunt Rose ordered another parent. More tears came as I reacted to their terrified faces and attempts to fight back tears of their own.

"Don't worry, Baby, you're going to be okay," Aunt Rose said, leaning over me and carefully applying pressure with her fingertips on different parts of my body.

"Does that hurt, Baby?"

"No," I responded.

"What about this?"

"No."

"Okay, good. What about here?"

"No."

"Thank God."

"The ambulance is on its way!" someone shouted from the distance.

"What about here, Baby, does this hurt?"

"No."

"Okay, looks like the car just hit your leg but it doesn't look broken. The ambulance is going to take you to the hospital just to make sure though, okay?"

"Okay."

"Aunt Rose, Kevin?" I asked with a trembling voice, ready to ask the most important question I could muster at the time. "Am I going to have to get a needle?" *I hate needles.*

I would eventually be released from Cooper Hospital later that night. No broken bones or serious injuries. Just an obvious limp accompanied by a large bandage wrapped around my lower left leg.

In fact, I limped two blocks back to my aunt's house with Kevin and the driver of the car that hit me. Yeah, the driver went to the hospital with us to make sure I was okay. He turned out to be a decent guy.

But the alpha in my pack, Kevin, didn't care how decent the driver was. Alphas can't afford civility in a world that only recognizes strength—domineering strength, at that. Kevin's response was short and to the point.

"You're lucky you stopped."

At that tender age, I didn't understand why Kevin responded with a veiled threat to the driver's civility and obvious remorse. Maybe it was the countless turn-the-other-cheek lessons Catholic school had brainwashed me to adopt as typical human behavior. Maybe Kevin, being only a teenager with adult responsibilities, was overwhelmed by the weighted responsibility that wasn't exactly fair to him while still shouldering it in silent resilience. Maybe early adult life lessons had already taught him that being nice and civil never equaled an equally nice and civil return on its investment. Perhaps he'd already learned that age-old lesson of no good deed goes unpunished and saw no reason to be civil. The driver, an outsider, had hit me with his car. Kevin and I are family. Close family. So, by hood logic, that driver had hit Kevin with the car as well. He'd caused my panicked mother to have to rush from Philly to Jersey to come get me, not fully knowing I would be okay. Even my village, Aunt Rose, was affected.

Kevin had worldly experiences I was not yet privy to at my age. Putting myself in his shoes now, as an adult full of accumulated life lessons, I can see how his response was more for me to hear rather than the driver. In a pack where overt expressions of love and concern for one another aren't verbalized, especially from the men, his threat to the outsider doubled as his way of communicating to me the words *I love you* and *I'll always look out for you*.

That's why he chased his own knife-wielding brother out of the house on my behalf, despite his hands being his only weapon. This lesson, like many, I subconsciously absorbed. I walked away from that day's lesson less innocent and naive. I was given one of many premature glimpses into the true nature of the world I was living in. Like my Southern great-grandfather who'd cultivated and passed on his version of the Trinity for Southern survival, my generation was unknowingly drafting our own version, adapted for our survival in American ghettos:

Choose aggression over civility.

Self-defense is the expectation, never an option.

Violence is an acceptable tool to resolve any perceived conflicts.

The driver didn't respond to Kevin's threat. He only kept walking along with the two of us, in silence, until we got back to my aunt's house. Once we arrived and saw the small contingent of my family members clustered on the porch with my mother, he quickly hopped into his car and drove away after leaving his contact information with my mom.

Over the course of my lifetime, I have grown accustomed to witnessing how people responded to Kevin in comparison to others in my family. Everyone likes him. He is blessed with an ability to make seamless and genuine human connections. It's a skill possessed by world leaders, activists, and all those who lead masses. It's a priceless talent. It's an "it factor" that can't be taught or faked. You either have it or you don't. He also commanded the attention and respect of rooms without uttering a word. People equally respect and fear him as much as they like him. He's the perfect storm.

chapter 9

At the age of eleven, I started and managed my first business. My grandmother, Edith Jackson, after seeing me spend a summer devouring Italian water-ice cups whenever I got my hands on thirty-five cents, taught me my first lesson about entrepreneurship.

"Give a man a fish, he'll eat for a day. Teach a man to fish, he'll eat for a lifetime," she said to me.

"Huh?" I responded, too busy to even make eye contact while I scraped a new serving of the snack I still enjoy to this day.

"I can teach you how to make those if you want," she said, with her signature smile that could calm the most savage beast. Without waiting for my response, she went back to busying herself with the homemade cupcakes she had just baked for the downtown family-owned diner she'd hustled into buying her fresh-baked goods.

"Yes, please!" I responded enthusiastically.

"Okay, Baby. Soon as I finish putting icing on these cupcakes."

This was the first summer after my mother and I moved to Camden, so instead of summer camp in a new city, I spent my days with my grandmother while my mother was at work. She took me on her daily errands, which included paying all her bills in person. Grandma was a country girl, so she didn't trust paying certain bills by mail.

"The post office might lose them, Baby, and your grandma pays all her bills on time and keeps her receipts."

My grandmother was an old-fashioned soul. If we weren't running errands or keeping the house in order, we were at her job, where she and a small group of other women worked pressing and steaming dry cleaning. I'd sit in a hard plastic chair trying to busy myself with a comic book, which never lasted long because I wasn't the strongest reader until eighth grade.

Television and movies kept me entranced whenever I was indoors. So, in times like these, when I was left with nothing but idle time, my imagination replaced the cartoons and television shows I was used to watching. For hours, I'd watch these women dressed in the lightest clothes, within reason, labor away in the summer heat with every door and window open so the white clouds of steam could escape their occupational summer sauna. It was literally a sweat shop.

I rarely initiated conversation at that age, so I instinctively became a people watcher. My eyes and their associated thoughts bounced from face to face as my mind drifted off, concocting stories of who they were and were not. I'd wonder if they were married or had children. If this was their only job, or if they had baked goods for sale, side hustles like my grandma. For everything I didn't know about them, my imagination filled in the blanks. By the time my grandma finished her four-hour shift, my imagination had already crafted answers to all those questions.

Back in my grandmother's kitchen now, she asked. "Okay, you ready?" as she gracefully spread the pink strawberry icing onto her last cupcake, wrapped it in Saran Wrap, and placed it in a large, plastic container.

"Yes!" I said, scraping the last of what remained of the water ice with the wooden spoon.

"Okay, so read me the back of your empty water-ice container so we know what that company uses to make it," she instructed. I began reading the words I knew and sounding out the ones I didn't.

"F-filtered water. Sugar! Corn syrup? Ssss-citric acid? There's acid in this? I thought acid burned you?" I questioned.

"There are different types of acid. The one they put in food isn't like the ones you see on TV that can burn your skin. But that's garbage, anyway—we won't be using that for our water ice. Anything else after that?" she asked, cutting off any possibility of my spinning off into a tangent of questions.

"Uh, yeah—"

"Excuse me?"

"I mean, yes there is," I corrected. "Lllemon juice con-con-cen-concentrate? Natural flavor, g-guh-ar? And ex-eeehxan-than and gums," I finished proudly. "What's—?"

"If you can't pronounce it, they're chemicals, Tarik. Don't eat anything you can't pronounce—all those chemicals aren't good for you, Baby."

"Yes, Grandma."

"Okay, so if we get rid of all the chemicals, that leaves us with water, lemon juice, and sugar."

"What about the corn syrup?" I asked, scanning over the list of ingredients to make sure we didn't forget anything.

"That's junk! Food companies make it out of real corn like your grandfather grows in South Carolina. It probably gives you cancer, so we're not using that, either." She gathered the safe ingredients from her cabinets, along with a brown plastic gallon pitcher, filled it three quarters with faucet water, gripped a measuring cup, carefully measured off one and a half cups of white granulated sugar, and poured it in the water. Then, in the same measuring cup, she poured a quarter cup of lemon juice.

"Now, these next two are our secret ingredients," she said, walking over to a cupboard where she kept an assortment of spices and jars she used to prepare her daily meals. From the first shelf, she pulled a single packet of lemon Flavor Aid, the more affordable generic brand of Kool-Aid, and placed it in the pocket of her worn flower apron. Then she reached to the second shelf and slid her hand in between several bottles until midway toward the back, she retrieved a small bottle with a black liquid in it.

"What's that?" I asked with an expression that matched my disbelief.

"Fix your face and pay attention," she said sternly, before retrieving the Flavor Aid from her apron, tearing it open, and pouring the contents into the water.

"Come here," she instructed. I leapt out of my chair, walked eagerly over to the kitchen counter next to her, and climbed up the two plastic steps on the stool in front of the pitcher. She handed me a wooden spoon.

"Now, carefully stir the water until all the sugar at the bottom disappears."

"Okay." I did as she instructed, grabbing the handle of the pitcher with my left hand and sliding it toward the edge of the counter, lightly pressing the pitcher against my ribs to stabilize it. Then I plunged the wooden spoon into the water until it found the slight pile of sugar at the bottom.

"That's it," she encouraged. I steadily stirred the spoon counterclockwise a few rotations before slowly reversing my stir. The sugar gradually disappeared until only a yellow whirlpool of water remained.

"Okay, now for the secret ingredient," she said. Her old wrinkled hands unscrewed the red cap of the vanilla extract. The pitcher of sugar water I'd stirred was finally beginning to calm. She positioned the cap over the pitcher and carefully filled the small, red cap to its brim. When it seemed as if it was about to spill over, she turned the cap and poured the dark vanilla extract into the water.

"This is strong, so you don't need a lot of it. Only use one cap full for every gallon you make, okay? One cap for one gallon," she repeated.

"Got it," I responded, nodding my head.

"Okay, stir that in real good and after that, we gonna pour the water into plastic cups and put them into the freezer and that's it. You have water ice you didn't have to spend your money on. If you try them and they're as good as the ones you buy every day, you can start making pitchers with different flavors. Then guess what you can do?"

"What?"

"You can sell them to your friends and neighbors back at Trenton Avenue. That way, you have your summer treat for free and the ones you sell will keep some extra money in your pocket until you're old enough to start working."

"You think kids will like it enough to buy it from me?" I asked in disbelief. I was just so happy I could make my own for me to enjoy that I didn't consider selling them myself.

"That's up to you. They should take a few hours to freeze. When they do, taste them, and if they're good enough that *you* would buy them, then I'm sure the kids in your neighborhood will like and buy them too," she said, concluding my very first lesson about entrepreneurship.

If it tastes good enough that I'd buy it, others will too.

Four hours later, I'd devoured my homemade water ice. Two weeks later, after asking my mother for $20 to get the supplies I needed to get started, I created a sign on large white construction paper used for arts and crafts and duct-taped it to the railing of my front porch. My grandmother's homemade version of Italian water ice in my neighborhood was an instant summer hit. I sold out more than fifty red plastic Solo cups of a variety of flavors every day for two summers straight before I was old enough to get a traditional job.

It wouldn't be the last entrepreneurial lesson I'd learn from my family of mostly high school-educated men and women. Having side hustles wasn't foreign to my pack—it was expected, almost routine. We all, at some point or another, absorbed directly or indirectly the intricate lessons of producing and selling a product:

Identify a targeted customer base.

Strategize minimizing your expenses without sacrificing quality to maximize your profits.

Sell, sell, sell! Always be closing.

Re-up your supply and pocket your profits.

Repeat.

The winter of that same year, my grandmother taught me another lesson about being an entrepreneur rooted in a steadfast work ethic. We'd been hit with heavy snowfall and she had me help her common-law husband, Mr. Jesse, shovel the snow from the pavement in front of their house.

When Mr. Jesse and I finished shoveling, I went inside and joined my grandmother in the kitchen, where she rewarded us both with a cup of hot chocolate. Once I finished and settled into my seat to remove my boots, she stopped me.

"Tarik, me and Jesse appreciate you helping with the shoveling. We're older so it's hard for Jesse to shovel all by himself."

"You're welcome, Grandma…Mr. Jesse," I responded.

"You know, there are plenty of families in this neighborhood who are also older like us and could probably use some help shoveling their pavements," she suggested, followed by the same intense stare she'd given me before our water-ice endeavor. She was seeing if I would connect the dots and I did.

"Mr. Jesse? Can I use your shovel?" I asked, invoking matching smiles on both their faces.

"Of course you can. Just make sure you bring it back. If you're going to borrow something from someone, it's your responsibility to return it in the same condition they gave it to you. You understand?" he asked, and I nodded. I jumped up from my seat and put on my hat, gloves, and coat before I shot out the door with Mr. Jesse's shovel thrown over my shoulder.

Four hours and six shoveled houses later, I returned to my grandmother's house cold and exhausted. They both were sitting on the couch in the living room watching television. My grandmother smiled as I pulled my snow-wet gloves, hat, and coat off. She rose from the sofa.

"Give me those, Baby. I'll throw them in the dryer," she

instructed. I handed her my items and with numb hands, I reached into my pocket.

"I made $45!" I rejoiced. They both smiled again. "Do you need anything?" I asked, offering to share my earnings with them since I used Mr. Jesse's shovel, and my grandmother identified the opportunity. They both looked at each other.

"No, Baby, that's your money. *You* earned that. That's for *you* to spend on whatever *you* like," she said firmly.

"Oh, okay." I was surprised that they turned me down.

My grandmother, unbeknownst to me at the time, had just taught me another valuable lesson about one of the consequences of earning money. There will be people, both friend and foe, who will enact a sense of entitlement with your earnings. Those same people will accept money you offer or deceptively take money from you despite their not earning it if you allow them to. I didn't comprehend or absorb this lesson at the time, but my grandmother was warning me of the potential oncoming dangers of being successful at earning money. Unfortunately, I didn't absorb that lesson quickly and would eventually have to relearn it later in life. But that's a story for another chapter.

Looking back at both those instances now, wiser from life experience, I should have continued my water-ice business and scaled it into other neighborhoods, starting with my grandmother's. Who knows, maybe I'd have a franchise store or my Edith's Homemade Water Ice much like Rita's Water Ice and/or have my product in supermarkets across the country. Instead, I fell into the same worker's mentality as most of us as soon as I turned thirteen, working a traditional job. I know now that my earning potential was much higher selling my own product in comparison to my summer minimum wage jobs. I'd created a product that was in demand, of minimal expense, and of minimal effort, since the freezer did the heavy lifting. Furthermore, I had my neighborhood market cornered, with no competition.

My target market and my product were conducive to, most

importantly, being affordable, in addition to my neighborhood's homes rarely having air conditioning. My water ices were an addictive, sugary, and cool treat that lined my pockets seven days a week for only two to three hours a day before I sold out my entire inventory. My weekly profit ranged between $95 and $110. However, in contrast to my grandmother's lesson of whatever I earned I keep at her home, in my home, the money I earned was split with my mother.

The first twenty-dollar bill I'd earned hustling my water ice I took from the sneaker box bank I kept in the kitchen. I was going to hang out with friends in the Parkside section of Camden and wanted to flex around my friends that summer day. When I returned home after my mother had gotten home from work, she questioned me about the missing money.

How can the money I earned be missing?

When I told her I spent almost half of it on junk food and giving my friends $1 each out of kindness, she lectured me with a tone reserved for someone who'd stolen. I was confused because her lecture conflicted with what my grandmother, her mother, had said to me the previous winter about money I earned being mine to spend however I chose.

My mother was teaching me another business lesson, in addition to what her mother had taught me. Since our house had two earners now, every morning, she would routinely pull loose change from my sneaker box bank for train fare to her job in Center City, Philadelphia. We never really discussed it; it was just understood that since she and I were on our own financially, we had to lean on each other.

For example, after my freshman year in college, I received settlement money for a civil lawsuit after sustaining a knee injury during a severe car accident I'll go into more detail about in the next chapter. My mother asked me if she could have—not borrow—$1,000 of my $5,000 settlement. At seventeen years old, the remaining $4,000 was still a lot of money to me, so I granted her request. I didn't know, ask, or even care what she would use the money for. It was the first time my mother had asked me for money, and as a newly minted "adult" out on his own at college, I was proud I had it to give her, if I'm being honest. I felt like a man.

Now, back to my mother's lesson: the lesson she was delivering by way of lecture was, my expenses for the products she picked up for me from the market—sugar, vanilla extract, Solo cups, and Flavor Aid—weren't the only expenses that needed to be accounted for. My recipe's main ingredient was water and even faucet water wasn't free. The freezer I placed my assortment of mixed flavors in so they could freeze overnight ran off electricity, and that wasn't free either. Finally, the kitchen I prepared my product in technically belonged to my mother, since it was her house. She paid the property taxes and any other associated costs to maintain it. In the real world, if I didn't have my own kitchen or facility to produce my product, I would have to rent space from someone who did, and that's another expense. All these expenses I overlooked, despite it contributing to increases in her daily expenses.

Once she was done, I understood why she asked about the missing money. It also taught me another lesson about business accounting and balancing your books. What I didn't know was that my mother was keeping a tally of my expenses and revenue I generated to make sure I was profitable. She was also the person who picked up my supplies when she went to the supermarket, and when she got home, the twenty-dollar bill I'd taken was the one she'd earmarked to re-up my supplies, since she was headed to the market right after work that day.

That week, I'd coincidentally started mixing different flavors to create a new mystery mix flavor that was so good I'd eaten many of them instead of selling them. By the end of the week, I'd consumed so many that that $20 was all I had to re-up with. I'd fucked up my re-up money breaking the cardinal rule of hustling a consumable product: *Don't get high on your own supply.*

I'd literally eaten myself into my first week's loss in two years. She'd never lectured me about my business before because the math always added up—until that day. My mother was auditing my product's daily count and it had come up short. Her lesson? Family or not, business is business, and my business was missing money, and someone had to answer for that. Even if you're the owner and operator.

chapter 10

I know that God exists, despite not having any concrete evidence or "visions" or a defining moment or experience where God revealed herself to me. I don't say the following lightly and this will be the first time I've ever spoken my feelings out loud. Although I pray regularly, in private, and despite being saturated with religious doctrine from birth until the age of seventeen, I'd never felt comfortable with the indoctrination of organized religion.

To ensure I received a proper education, my mother insisted I attend Catholic school instead of public. Specifically in the cities where I was raised, public schools did not have access to the resources private and parochial schools already had iron-clad grasps on. So, from kindergarten to my freshman year in high school, I attended Catholic schools. Attending mass, learning and practicing the sacraments, and their associated prayers and hymns were systematically programmed into me before I even fully understood the words I'd been forced to internalize.

To this day, I subconsciously still sit with my hands folded when I'm not actively using them. The rigorous rules of St. Rose of Lima in West Philadelphia and St. Bartholomew in Camden ensured I learned at the appropriate grade level, reinforced the discipline my mother laid the foundation for at home, and exposed me to resources and advancements my public-school counterparts weren't privy to. I was not naive to the fact my education was better than what many of my neighborhood peers received. If I'm being honest, sometimes I exploited it.

All my neighborhood friends knew to knock on my door if they needed their homework done. Now, I didn't say needed *help* with their homework, I said needed their homework *done*. Yes, I did my friends' homework because in my mind, I was helping them, and that help was reciprocated in protection through association, party invites, and being chosen to hang out with the cool kids in those earlier days when I hadn't mastered the art of being a cool kid. In the rarest of moments, it even provided me with a modest ghetto revenue stream that put loose change and single dollar bills in my pocket.

Even though I spent Monday through Friday with the Catholics, come Sunday morning, Catholicism didn't exist. My pack is Southern Baptist. An inner-city, hood Southern Baptist. And that congregation was my true church family. I recognized this flip-flop dynamic early in life. If my mother did this knowingly or not, I'll never know.

My education was my indoctrination of not only the Catholic religion but of the methods one must use to master the game of life. I learned to leverage the resources at my disposal, even if my intentions were not sincere, to my advantage. For most of my elementary and high school years, when I wasn't playing a seasonal sport or working in the summer, I ran the streets with Dawuan and his brother Trilly, who lived three houses over. Trilly was the overweight, unathletic brother, while Dawuan was one of the neighborhood knuckleheads who had good size on him, so he'd earned respect for the few fights he'd won.

Me and Dawuan were cool because me and him used to hang out whenever I visited my Camden cousins while I was still living in Philly. He also looked up to my older cousins, so we never bumped heads outside of the usual shit-talking and cracking on each other that all kids did. They weren't the best of students, despite their mother wanting the best for them.

I'd occasionally do Dawuan's homework for him, especially when it came to math. Every so often he'd come by my house, I'd meet him out on the porch, and he'd hand me the one or two math worksheets he'd brought home from school that day. I'd run into the house, grab a pencil, sit on my porch, and finish it for him so his mom and mine wouldn't see what we were up to. Ten to fifteen minutes later, I'd be done. The first time I did it, he looked at me like I was an alien.

"Damn, Geeksville, you finished already? It would have taken me at least an hour to do it, if I finished it all." "Geeksville" was the insulting nickname he'd given me for being smart and wearing glasses. Despite it being a slight, we both knew it wasn't meant in total disrespect.

"You just mad I can read, Blowtorch," I'd retort with the insulting nickname I came up with after his first girlfriend gave him chlamydia. We would both laugh it off, knowing there was a foundation of mutual respect because we never called each other that when other people were around.

From time to time, that was our neighborhood exchange. I'd do some homework he found difficult because he either missed that class or fell behind after going to juvenile detention for a few months over a petty crime. While he was home though, I knew I had someone I could run the streets with who would throw hands with me when we ventured into other neighborhoods, like 6th Street, where the downtown hustlers and gangstas made their money and solidified their reputations.

Sorry about the tangent. Now, back to me and my family church at New Mickle Baptist Church. On Sundays, that was my true church community. Our service was the opposite of the refined proceedings of a Catholic mass. In my community, Sundays were when my family matriarch demanded and expected our entire family's presence. Grandma Edith was not only a "saved" member of the church, but she also served as a nurse. You know, the ladies who sit in all white at the front of the church to care for those who "catch the Holy Spirit" and fall out, in praise, testimony, and murmuring in undecipherable languages called "tongues." Even at a young age, I recognized the stark difference between the traditions and practices of the two sects of Christianity I'd been immersed in. One served me academically and the other culturally, yet both were confusing.

For those wondering what I mean by confusing, I'll summarize it like this. As human beings, we must get to a place where we think objectively and rationally, and accept the realistic conclusions that our religious affiliations, much like the twisted concept of race, are based on geographic location. In other words, your parents, the region of a country where you live, and that country's location on the globe predetermine your initial indoctrination of religious affiliation. American Christians who have an aversion to Islam would have been Muslims themselves had they been born in the Middle East, where Islam is the dominant religion.

The same goes for those Muslims who have an aversion to Western culture and Christians. Had you been born in the Western Hemisphere where North, Central, and South America are, chances are you would probably be a Christian practicing the very same traditions extremist Muslims rail against.

For those who need me to be even more frank, there is no one true religion that guarantees your salvation above all the others. Every popular religion, for the most part, follows the same rules: don't steal, don't murder, don't covet another's spouse, etc. The only significant difference in religions is their name for their god (or gods) and the traditions we practice worshipping. That's not an opinion; it's not my perspective—it's documented *fact*. A fact that is easily verifiable for anyone who sincerely and objectively cares to learn about other religions and their beliefs instead of trusting the words and opinions of others.

I believe religion, like most things manmade, was created in a sincere effort to better humanity. But man, and by that, I mean we males, taint even the most genuine of intentions from time to time. Especially when those institutions we create reveal themselves to wield power over the masses. Now, I'm not an atheist. I sincerely believe, in my heart, there is a higher power watching, adjusting, and contributing to the human experience.

As I mentioned in a Chapter 8, I've had three brushes with death in my lifetime. This next account would be my third and most traumatic. I remember distinctly the all-too-real feeling of fighting for my life, pressing my hardest to do whatever I could do to survive that moment. That natural human instinct to survive at all costs is real. Those moments when the voice inside your head whispers to you, "Hold on! With everything you got or you're going to die!"

What I'm describing is not paranoia. It's God or your guardian angel or whatever omnipotent being your belief system approves of. Then it happens. You do as that voice instructs you for you to live through and prevail in that moment. You hold on, you fight, you survive at all costs. And for those times when the situation you're caught in is out of your control, God intervenes. Those are the moments that can only be described as miracles because there is no explanation scientists, philosophers, or the most learned person can come up with to explain how you're still living and breathing. The following is my miracle.

During the summer of 1988, I was twelve and my family and I piled into a twenty-passenger van in the Parkside section of Camden, with our destination plotted for Little Mountain, South Carolina. The distance between the two is six hundred fifty miles and, if you adhere to speed limits, it takes ten and a half hours to drive in perfect conditions and with no traffic. The weather was perfect on the day we left.

Once we all jockeyed for the best seats in the back for us younger family members and in the front for our elders, we lowered our heads in prayer. Our devout elders prayed respectfully, asking for traveling mercies while some of us younger family members snuck looks out of the corners of our eyes and snickered at each other, waiting for the long prayer to be over. At the prayer's conclusion, we were off toward I-95 South for what would turn out to be the last overnight group trip we would ever take as a family unit.

I took my seat in the very last row and to the far right of the van by the window, with my cousins laughing and joking about the latest hip-hop albums that were on heavy rotation in the tape decks of our boom boxes. My cousin Speedy, being a DJ, had more elaborate taste in the relatively new genre than most of us. Outside of hip-hop, mostly we recited the punch lines of the new Robert Townsend movie, *Hollywood Shuffle*, that had just been released. We recalled by memory every funny scene of the movie until the sun set and we were at our last pit stop to fill our van's tank. It was getting late so after a quick bathroom break and the elders stretching their legs, we all piled back inside for the last leg of the trip.

"Tarik, you have your seat belt on?" my mother questioned, as my older cousins teased me.

"Taaariiik? You got your seat belt on, little baby? Hmmm?" one mimicked, followed by snickers.

"Momma's boy," they playfully teased, and I shot an angry sneer to camouflage my embarrassment. I unclicked my seat belt as an overt display of defiance only my peers could see. Moments later, we were back on the road for the overnight part of the trip that would have us arriving somewhere between 8 and 9 a.m. Most of us lasted until the early morning hours, when fatigue and the mundane hum of the engine and our tires navigating the asphalt lulled us to sleep one by one. I leaned my head against the window and closed my eyes.

We had been asleep for at least a few hours before we were all awakened by our heads slamming into the seats in front of us and a simultaneous, loud crash. At the time, I wasn't aware of what was occurring and thought I'd been trapped in a nightmare. You know, one of the nightmares where you think you're awake but then realize you're still asleep and must wake again to get back to reality. It took me only a moment to realize I was awake, and this was really happening.

Hold on! Hold on or you'll die!

Amid the most violent crashing and banging noises I'd ever experienced, I watched the ground and clouds switch places over and over and over and over and over...and over...and over again through the large window in the front of the van. During the last roll, I was thrown forward into the middle aisle of the van. Finally, we came to a stop, upside down.

I crawled out from the wreckage on my hands and knees through one of the shattered side windows toward the light and the Carolina grass cascading along the highway gully we'd come to a stop at. Closing my eyes, I play the memory back in my head and it remains the most violent car crash I'd ever witnessed in real life, let alone survived. The only equivalent I can offer is what you see in stunt movie scenes, where the car is purposely flipped onto its side with such velocity it turns as effortlessly as the tires of a car. Bodies of my family members, including one newborn baby, littered the stretch of highway shoulder for approximately twenty to twenty-five yards.

Half of the passengers had been ejected from the van because, like me, many didn't wear their seat belts. Those who had were still inside the mangled van struggling to unlock themselves while hanging upside down. Others were less fortunate and were knocked unconscious from the first violent impact or the multitude of times the van flipped on its sides until finally slowing down and finding its resting place. Luggage, clothes, food, beverages, diapers were scattered in every direction, while cars on both sides of the road stopped so people could run over to offer aid.

"Tarik!" my mother yelled in panic, emerging from what seemed out of nowhere.

"Mom! What happened?" I asked, surprisingly without tears. The human body is a magnificent mechanism. I can recall every detail of the accident, but when I crawled out of the upside-down van toward the grass and sunlight, I don't remember seeing a single body on the ground or in the van. My mother walked us fifteen to twenty yards farther down the shoulder because she was afraid the van would explode like they did in the movies or television. I had a noticeable limp, as if my left knee couldn't maintain my weight, but I don't remember the pain. Once we sat down at a safe distance after a few steps up a hill, I was finally able to take in the full scale of what had just happened.

Only then did I see, for the first time, the bodies of my family members scattered everywhere. I traced the route my mother and I had walked away from the scene, then the path back to the window I had crawled out of, bodies littered the entire way. Call it shock or a continuation of my survival instincts, but I didn't see one of those bodies or their colorful outfits in real time. When I turned to sit on the hill, the original, all-grass canvas my mother and I limped across had been painted. The result was a demented family portrait of carnage.

Most were unconscious, leaving only a few struggling to pull themselves to their feet. I watched as one of my mother's closest cousins, Cyrus, rolled from his back and onto his hands and knees to steady himself before rising to his feet and immediately crashing back to the ground, unable to maintain his balance. As the minutes passed, my shock dissipated, adrenaline wore off, and pain arrived. At the small of my back, a dull ache eased its way from noticeable to drastically uncomfortable from the seated position I held on the hill next to my mother.

She had no visible injuries, probably since she was one of the adults who had kept their seat belts on. My body was begging me to lie flat on the grass to alleviate the stressful position I held, and then a shooting pain came from my left knee. I rubbed it vigorously as the pain grew in intensity. Finally, I gave in to the whims of my body, lying flat on the grassy incline to relieve the mounting pressure on my back. I struggled to find comfort even while stretching both legs out, hoping the pain there would subside as well.

"What's wrong with your knee?" my mother asked, shooting her gaze back and forth from me and the scattered bodies of our family members with injuries that would keep the local trauma center busy for the rest of the night.

"It hurts. My back too," I told her.

"Sit still and try not to move until the ambulances arrive because...we...we're going to sue!" she said confidently.

My heart leapt from my chest to my throat and my brain was still trying to catch up with how my body was processing the trauma of this horrible accident that had pushed the roof of the passenger van down until it rested on the tops of our seats. It wasn't until that moment that I thought about the other car or cars we must have hit before careening into the gully. I looked up the length of the highway, both ways, wondering who had hit us, who we had hit, or what caused our crash. But there were no other damaged cars. The only cars near us were the ones whose drivers had pulled over to help us until the fleet of ambulances arrived to take all twenty-plus of us to the nearest hospital. Then it dawned on me. We didn't get hit by another car; we didn't hit another car. No one caused our crash.

Who are we going to sue, Mom?

Just by looking at the scene—not seeing any other damaged cars, not being awoken by the loud, panicked scream of skidding tires before the initial crash forward that woke me to a spinning world—I knew there was no one to blame. My family had made the mistake of allowing one of our elder family members to take the responsibility of driving during the overnight leg of the trip instead of someone younger, someone more rested. This dilemma was brought on by socioeconomics. The driving assignments were determined by who had the resources, specifically a credit card, rather than by who was best suited for the long-distance overnight driving experience. Not everyone in my family, including my grandmother, mother, and some aunts, had ever confidently driven longer than thirty minutes. All of us kids had no licenses, leaving only a handful of adults who felt comfortable doing it. Unfortunately, we weren't as comfortable as we thought.

You need someone with good credit to possess the credit card needed to rent a van. Then, based on the rental agreement, the person making the rental reservation is typically the only person who can drive the vehicle and is covered by the rental company's insurance. All these small details contributed in their own way to our crash.

We also planned the trip poorly, deciding to leave later in the day rather than first thing in the morning. Our elders should not have had to shoulder the responsibility for any leg of the trip, especially the overnight portion. This is one memorable instance where leaning into my family's Southern-rooted traditions and gender roles could have changed the course of that day.

Unfortunately, at this point in my life, my family had begun showing signs of a rift. The enthusiasm of our family elders stressing the importance of this year's family reunion probably was in reaction to that growing rift. We'd begun to stray away from one another and replaced devotion with mistrust. Jay-Z said it well: "No one wins when the family feuds."

When we were eventually released from the hospital, we all had an assortment of injuries that ran the gambit of catastrophic, such as my Aunt Ronnie being paralyzed from the neck down. My mother and I had only minor scrapes and mine were the worse of the two, with a left knee that would eventually need surgery, but I've never been limited physically and, in fact, played organized team sports until my sophomore year in college. Some family members had broken necks and thick, permanent scars from the glass and twisting metal.

My cousin-brother, Sean, was knocked unconscious, his feet trapped beneath the seats as he hung upside down, until paramedics were able to free him. A mother and her newborn child were both thrown out the windows and miraculously, the child was spared injury because their mother cradled her protectively, taking the brunt of the injuries. The cousin sitting next to me, the same age range and stature as me, hit his head on the bending metal above us as the ceiling crumpled like a tin can. The metal left a gash in the top of his head that ran several inches across his skull.

Me, though? I was largely uninjured. Remember, I took my seat belt off, being defiant, so the only thing *physically* holding me in my seat was me. That's how I strained my back. I twisted my body to wrap my right arm around as much of the back of my seat as I could and clutched it in desperation. I didn't know if it would work or help but it was the first thing that came to me instinctively. During the last turn, I was thrown into the middle aisle, where I landed left knee first, with the van coming to a stop immediately after.

I'd almost drowned, almost been run over by a car, and survived a terrible accident without breaking a bone or requiring one stitch. Being a learned person, I understand that my position in the right corner of the van helped secure me in a pocket of centrifugal force that helped minimize my being thrown around the van during its most violent turns in the beginning of the crash. I understand that once the turns started to slow, with only the strength of a 12-year-old to hold himself in place, these adrenaline-driven moments provided relative security for an additional turn, maybe two.

However, during those last two to three turns, anything or anyone could have crashed into me. Or I could have been one of the first thrown out of the window I was conveniently sitting directly next to for so many turns. Or my slender frame could have slipped up and down against the metal jagged roof like my cousin, who was sitting shoulder to shoulder with me that trip. What I'm saying is there is no scientific, statistical, or logical reason I sustained the least serious injuries among my family. Believe it if you like, or not, but that omniscient voice, thought, metaphysical manifestation, guardian angel, or whatever you choose to call it told me, "*Hold on! Hold on or you'll die!*" And *that* calming voice is who I pray to and who I choose to call God.

chapter 11

My Southwest Philly and Camden roots, despite my mother's sacrifices, wouldn't provide one of the most valuable resources a child needs: a father. As contingency, a consistent father figure would have sufficed, but those are few and far between where I grew up. Don't get me wrong, I'm not going to spout some stereotypical talking point about the lack of fathers and responsible men in my community. Responsible and moral men reside everywhere, even in the ghettos of America, but the unfortunate truth is the few we have are stretched way too thin in my environment.

So thin they sometimes have no choice but to make painful and sometimes selfish decisions. Do they try to save *every* needy young man that crosses their path at the expense and potential peril of their own family, or should they opt to give everything they have to their own family, their own child, to ensure their prosperity? For my development into manhood, I leaned on a plethora of men at different phases of my life when I wasn't left to my own devices to figure things out. My considerably older cousin, Cyrus, was one of those men.

He introduced me to Pop Warner football and Omega Psi Phi Fraternity, Inc. Football introduced me to Coach Drip. Coach Drip believed in my athletic ability, despite my being the new kid from Philly being added to a team of veterans who had already played together the previous year. My success in Pop Warner football gave me the confidence to excel in other sports like basketball, track, and baseball. All these sports kept me out of trouble and off the streets because you can't get into trouble if you're at practice, exhausted from practice, or doing homework when you're not at practice.

Next door to me in Camden was my Aunt Ronnie's house. Yes, my family buys houses not only in the same neighborhoods but sometimes on the same block, and in this instance, next door to one another. My Aunt Ronnie, due to complications from the paralysis caused by the accident, would pass away a few years later. When she passed, she left her house to her ex-husband—we called him "Reds" because he was so fair skinned, with long, curly hair I'd never seen on a Black man before.

My freshman year in high school signaled a lot of firsts I wasn't prepared for. The simplest of adversities would be my transitioning from elementary school clip-on ties to learning how to tie a real tie. My dad wasn't around very often, so Reds taught me how to tie a tie. Three years later, when I got my driver's license, Reds' modest used car was the first car I drove alone without someone else present. He'd watched me take public transportation to my Saturday basketball practices for a month until one day, he simply tossed me his keys on Saturday and said, "Come back right after practice. Right back!"

I simply caught the keys, thanked him profusely, and took my first trip on the highway, up Route 42, leaving Camden to head to my high school in the suburbs of Sicklerville. When I returned home, my mother saw me pull up in Reds' car and her jaw dropped. My mother was too nervous to let me take her car. She was overly cautious like that, but when she saw that Reds trusted me with his car, she let me drive her car whenever I wanted to. His simple gesture of trust spilled over onto my mother, and I've been driving all over America since.

The summer between my junior and senior year of high school, I worked as I did every summer, but that summer, I worked at my first retail job at a clothing store, T&Y Fashion Wear. It was during those three summer months I'd directly and indirectly pick up on the subtle intricacies of being a man from my cousins Speedy and Kevin. Every day, under their tutelage, I absorbed real-time lessons on earning the respect of peers without having to throw a punch. Working at a clothing store also meant I had access to the latest fashion trends and began dressing better. But most importantly, I'd outgrown my shyness. The 15-year-old introvert who started sitting in a corner of T&Y Fashion Wear quietly the first week would develop into a confident young man who could finally hold court with women. It was my best summer as a teenager.

My cousin Speedy's car was the first car I'd driven that had chrome rims and a souped-up stereo system in the trunk. My cousin Curly loaned me his Acura coupe, also with chrome rims and a booming stereo system in the trunk, for my prom. Kevin's car was the dopest, though. A tan Benz tricked out with all the interior features but no over-the-top stereo system that announced your arrival.

Through Kevin, I learned the art of subtlety. About keeping a low profile so as not to draw unnecessary attention. Attention only makes you a target. A flashy millionaire and a boring millionaire are both still millionaires. The only significant difference is the flashy millionaire draws the attention of stick-up boys or the wrath of those who covet what they have. The boring millionaire, however, flies beneath the radar unscathed. Kevin taught me the importance of fostering good relationships with good people and how people liking you will remove many unnecessary boundaries between you and success.

Lesson #1: People do business with people they like.

Lesson #2: Being well liked earns a person extra eyes and ears in this world. Extra eyes and ears keep you safe.

Those rare moments when the streets showed me more than I should have seen, Speedy and Kevin were the guard rails I needed to ensure my exposure didn't sidetrack my ultimate life's purpose.

"There's nothing for you out here. Keep getting good grades and catching footballs," they'd say. "Go home and tell Aunt Sheila we said hi." They'd end the exchange with emotionless eyes before respectfully extending a firm handshake, signaling my time with them had expired. From the outside looking in, it looked and *felt* like a regular handshake, except at its conclusion, I'd have a few perfectly folded twenty-dollar bills tucked into my palm. Kevin always caught me off guard with this sleight of hand. We'd exchange a quick chuckle afterwards because every time, I never saw it coming.

"You see? Subtle." Thus concluding my lesson for that day. After a while, unbeknownst to them, I'd eventually learn that trick.

It's my collection of moments like this that cause me to cringe, however slightly, whenever I hear ladies brag about raising their boys to be men. Now, my visceral reaction isn't a blanket denigration of the efforts ladies must make in the best interests of their children when the men in their lives are inconsistent, if not altogether nonexistent. They are simply doing the best they can with the tools they have. I get it. However, the truth is, ladies know as much about navigating life as a man as I have knowledge about navigating life as woman.

Allow me to elaborate. I can expose myself to countless books, documentaries, educational videos, interview thousands of women, and at the end of the day, I will never be able to fully appreciate what the female experience is unless I've actually lived it. I can intelligently speak to what menstruation is but until I've physically, emotionally, and psychologically experienced the shedding of the lining of uterus walls, I will never be able to fully comprehend and navigate that experience. I will never know the feeling of a human being growing inside me, centimeter by centimeter. I will never know the sorrow and horror of miscarrying a child, or the painful beauty of birthing a child into the world.

As much as I desire to empathize with women, no matter how much I educate myself on their experiences, I will never fully comprehend the second-by-second experiences of women.

Unfortunately, my environment provided limited access to college-educated men for me to mimic. In the generation before mine, my family had one male college graduate, my cousin Cyrus. My generation produced two, me and Cyrus's second son. That meant there was only one person to guide me and another cousin toward our aspirations of becoming college graduates. Luckily for my cousin, that one graduate in the generation before ours was his father. But my exposure to his father wasn't consistent because he had his own children to raise and a son to prepare for undergraduate matriculation, a career to manage, fraternity obligations, and a football team to coach.

That's not a slight, for the record. I love my cousin. In fact, he is the sole inspiration behind my pledging the greatest fraternity in the world, Omega Psi Phi Fraternity, Inc. I'm merely acknowledging that there are only twenty-four hours in a day and one man can only do so much with his time. And unfortunately, one man cannot be everything to everyone.

So, that leaves us with an abundance of college-bound young men needing guidance but only a few willing and able to provide that guidance. As nature dictates via Darwin's theory, everyone can't be saved, so many will fall through the cracks due to this lack of college-educated men sharing the lessons they've learned on how to navigate this experience called life. For those with no guidance, some will have to navigate life's gauntlet of trial and error before figuring it out on their own—if they're lucky enough to figure it out.

The first college-educated male role model and intellectual I had access to consistently, day in, day out, would not arrive until I was twelve years old. Unfortunately, my teacher—we'll call him Mr. Jacobs—would set a very low bar for what a mentor should be. Despite his shortcomings, he would show rare flashes of influential moments. To his credit, he introduced me to the joys of reading and writing. He made sure my classmates and I were exposed to the academic tools we needed to be successful in his classroom and beyond. He would be my first example of someone who graduated college, but that accomplishment would not translate to him being an effective mentor in the classroom.

A military veteran whose service to his country I fully acknowledge and respect, Mr. Jacobs was also mean, a bully, a womanizer, and a drunk. He was the type of educator who played favorites. Especially if you were one of the prettier girls in his class. Now, before your imagination runs wild, I am not suggesting he was inappropriate with his students, but the pretty girls did win favor with him more easily and their grades reflected it.

Now, before anyone goes on some tangent about me suggesting pretty women can't be smart—please stop it. I'm *not* saying that at all. I've had the pleasure of working with some of the smartest people in this country and most of them are women. In fact, I prefer to work with women in corporate America because they get shit done! They've worked too hard to get where they are and they're not going to let anyone ruin that for them. I respect that! I prefer to work with people like that! *But*—I know favoritism when I see it. And Mr. Jacobs had his favorites in my class, both male and female.

And for a student who was not female and whose mother refused his advances, I was not in his circle of favorites. The truth was, if you were a boy in his class and he didn't recognize the same fever for academic prowess and achievement he had himself, you could easily fall by the wayside. I would equate his behavior to that of a good doctor with an awful bedside manner. He knew he was intellectually exceptional and with that power, he rarely empathized with those he deemed intellectually unworthy of his time.

Even at an early age, I could detect the selective disdain in his tone when he addressed me. Or the moment he threatened not to promote me. He drew some odd pleasure in having that power over his students, a cocky arrogance I equate to college coaches who dangle the threat of revoking athletic scholarships over their players' heads, knowing they're trapped with limited options for a better life. All of what I'm claiming became evident the night of my eighth-grade graduation.

Approximately twenty-five students waited anxiously to receive our final report cards from St. Bartholomew Catholic School. This night would signify our last time all being together. There would be no more nuns proudly hanging thick, wooden paddles in front of the classroom as a disciplinary deterrent (with the permission of our parents, of course).

We boys had, for the last time, worn our light-blue dress shirts, khakis, and penny loafers to school. The girls could now retire the plaid navy blue and gray dresses they wore every day. But we all donned bright smiles during the modest reception in the basement of St. Bartholomew Catholic Church on Kaighn Avenue. I and my eclectic collection of friends for the last four years could finally celebrate with our parents, family members, and loved ones over light refreshments. It was one of those exceptionally happy days…until it was ruined. Not just by Mr. Jacobs, but also by the other man in my life, who should have been primarily supportive of me. My father.

First up at bat to ruin this triumphant evening was Mr. Jacobs. He couldn't even let me enjoy a final night with my friends to celebrate our accomplishment. He enthusiastically walked over to where my parents and I were huddled, greeted them, and introduced himself to my father, this being the first time they'd met. He handed me my final report card, shook my hand, and in the same motion, wrapped his other arm around me in the customary way Black men in my community developed as a masculine version of a hug. As he bent over to embrace me, he whispered in my ear. It could have been a perfect opportunity to leave me with a final word of encouragement or well-wishes in preparation for high school, but he failed me yet again with his final sentiment of hurtful words.

"Luckily for you, I don't fail Black students," he whispered so my parents couldn't hear, and ended our embrace with a false smile aimed at me before walking away. Once he turned his back, my mother rolled her eyes before turning her attention to me and my report card. I wished Mr. Jacobs hadn't come over. I didn't want her to open my report card; it wasn't one of my best. I wished my dad had heard what he'd said to me and punched him in his mouth. I wished my older cousins were there so we, me included, could stomp him into the linoleum floor until blood was shed.

Although I knew I passed, as evident by my wearing a cap and gown, I also knew I'd struggled throughout the school year in his class. Even worse, this was the only time my father had come to my school, despite only living thirty minutes away. I knew the moment I passed my parents my report card, the revelation of mediocre grades would follow.

"Let's see what you got," my father said. He grabbed the card from my hands and unfolded it. His smile immediately faltered.

"What is this?" he exclaimed. "You barely passed." Then he turned to my mother with a look of confusion on his face. "You want me to help you pay fifteen hundred a year for high school and these are the type of grades he's getting?"

"Kenny, not here. We should go outside," my mother said through clenched teeth and tight, painted-red lips. My dad stormed outside. My mother turned to me, placed a hand on my shoulder, and quickly rubbed my upper back before leading me outside, dejected and embarrassed. Luckily, we were the only ones outside. As soon as the heavy metal door closed behind us, my father went on a tirade.

"These grades are terrible!"

"Lower your voice! People may hear us," my mother said, cutting him off. "He still graduated, Kenny. He had a rough year, but his grades aren't usually like this. I wouldn't suggest sending him to Camden Catholic if this was the norm," my mother said in my defense, while I stood silently looking down at the ground and my freshly shined shoes that peeked from the hem of my graduation gown.

"I'm not paying for these types of grades. And I'm not going to dinner, either. There's nothing to celebrate." That was the last thing he said before making an about-face, without any goodbye or even a lukewarm hug. He gave us both his back and headed to the car he'd borrowed to come to my graduation.

"I'll do better next year! I promise!" I shouted, finally breaking my silence, hoping my plea would encourage his return. It didn't. He unlocked the car door, climbed in, quickly turned the ignition, and pulled off into the night. That night, my mother and I went to dinner by ourselves.

"Don't be mad at your father. I'll talk to him," she reassured me, but the damage had been done. And that quickly, that seamlessly, I'd been altered.

After my graduation night, my dad and I wouldn't talk again until a week before school was set to start. A few weeks earlier, I'd received my acceptance letter to Camden Catholic High School. There would be no athletic scholarship like my teammate and friend JC had received. There would be no economic hardship grant either, because although we were poor, my mother had steady employment. As an academic insurance policy, my mother took out a $10,000 home equity loan on our house to cover my four years of high school tuition and expenses. It was my guess that starting school soon was the reason my father was calling.

"Your mother told me you got accepted to Camden Catholic—congratulations," he said.

"Thank you," I nervously responded, recalling his disappointment months earlier.

"I'm going to give your mother money to help pay your tuition, and you better get good grades," he ordered.

"I will, Dad, I promise," I responded, just happy to hear from him and to hear he was going to help my mother out.

"Damn right, you will. And when you start working this summer, you're paying me back the money I give her, too."

"Oh...oh, okay," I said, unsure of what else to say.

"All right, I gotta go. I'll talk to you later," he concluded before hanging up the phone.

The moment the line went silent, I felt a strange, slow, festering burn in my heart for my father. I can only imagine the same emotion must have spawned itself in my mother at some point during their time together. The typical feeling of sorrow was dulled and replaced by anger. My brain, fueled by disappointment, flooded my memory with a culmination of extended absences, missed birthdays, football games, basketball games, track meets, talent performances, and countless weekends where he was supposed to visit but instead performed disappearing acts.

Even worse were the times he'd called me from a bar where I could hear the music and chatter in the background just before he could fix his lips to say, "I can't make it to pick you up tonight. I have a bad headache."

A fucking headache? Nigga! I can hear the music in the background!

Much like the stereotypical, unwilling television wife who had no desire whatsoever to show affection to her husband, my father chose not to show up for his son. The slow burn intensified. My maturing mind drew its own conclusions.

He doesn't want to endure me, just like those wives don't want to endure their husbands. Fuck him then!

My transition away from unconditionally loving my father had begun. From that day forward, I wouldn't allow myself to feel disappointment at his absence. The longing that was once reserved for my father would slowly die like a neglected potted flower, one that is not watered and is left to slowly wither.

My father had failed me initially, and the next influential African-American man, my first Black male teacher, had also failed me and others. Yeah, Mr. Jacobs, if you're reading this, my evaluation of you is not an exception. Most of the young men from our eighth-grade class have remained friends to this day. And we've had discussions about you, now that we are reflective adults. And although none of us believed or expected you to be responsible for replacing our fathers, you did have a responsibility as an educator to make the students who passed through the threshold of your door better, not worse.

Now, I don't believe Mr. Jacobs to be a petty man. I simply believe he didn't or still doesn't fully grasp the weight of his behavior and how it affected some of us. I don't believe him to be some sadist drawing pleasure out of targeted belittlement of his students. Maybe in some twisted way, he felt that was his form of tough love, what young Black men needed to prepare them for life in America. Or maybe, in a momentary lapse of objectivity, my kind spirit chooses to make excuses for him because I don't want to honestly believe that the first Black male teacher many of us had was equally an intellectual and an asshole.

Mr. Jacobs had a propensity to prejudge which of his students were worthy of his exemplary college credentials. His career as an educator landed him in an inner-city elementary parochial school as a stepping stone. I believe he aspired to be among those educators at the more critically acclaimed institutions, such as Camden Catholic, Paul VI, and Bishop Eustace, teaching AP English to overprivileged kids so he could prove he deserved to educate them and belonged in their intellectual circles.

I recall Mr. Jacobs saying one afternoon. "I brought something I wanted you guys to see," he said. We broke our attention away from the assignment he'd just given us before he began rifling through his briefcase. "This is one of my report cards from college." He held it up in the air with a very apparent sense of pride. "This is just one year but all my report cards looked like this," he added, stopping at the front desk of the aisle closest to the door of our classroom. Each student took a few seconds to unfold the sturdy card before passing it to the student behind them.

When it reached me, I scanned it and was admittedly equally impressed and jealous. Not spiteful jealousy but a wishful type of jealousy. I'd never gotten straight As. Not even close. I worked hard and earned respectable grades, but I was an average student at best.

"I graduated college with honors with a degree in English," he boasted. "I'm a military veteran, and yet these things didn't guarantee me a job. I had to earn everything I have and so will you. I once had a job interview where I called the person who would be conducting the interview, and we had a good conversation. Then, when I showed up at the interview, he was shocked I was Black," Mr. Jacobs said. His face grew tight, sharing this story that served both as a cautionary tale to us and a moment of vulnerability for him. "My interviewer didn't admit it, but I could tell by his expression. It wasn't the only time this has happened to me, either," he warned. "While I have them on the phone, they love me. That's because they only hear my voice, how I talk, my mastery of language, and my accent. They think I'm White. Until I show up in person for the interview."

It was moments like these where Mr. Jacobs shone—these cautionary tales that came when he was laser-focused on seeing us collectively succeed. Those moments where he shared his experiences of being a Black man in America and the methods he used to successfully navigate the classrooms and the world. He introduced us to Shakespeare and algebra ahead of schedule, knowing the knowledge would prepare us for our freshman year of high school. The summer we graduated, he handpicked students to participate in an advanced math program where they'd be paid to learn the equivalent of AP math classes to prepare those deserving few for the rigors of advanced high school academics.

He Mr. Jacobs was the head basketball coach my sixth-grade year; that's how we first met. But after a mediocre season, he was demoted to assistant coach. Making the demotion worse, he was now reporting to a man who wasn't a better basketball player, wasn't better educated, and who made an honest living as a truck driver. Mr. Bernie Stout, our new coach, loved his team and his cigars. He was old and wasn't the best player of the sport, but that man could motivate and coach some kids. We played our hearts out for Coach Stout, and under his leadership, we excelled the next two years with the exact same players.

From one perspective, it was great developing into a winning team our predominantly White private school contemporaries now hated playing against. Then the not-so-great other perspective was the backlash directed toward those of us on the team who excelled on the court but not in his classroom, despite our most genuine efforts.

I wasn't the only person to experience Mr. Jacobs' wrath. The most talented athlete at our school was named Edgar Banks but we called him JC. JC was a star quarterback for the city's Pop Warner team, the Centerville Simbas, during football season, and St. Bart's point guard the following basketball season. He and I weren't the closest. He reserved that honor for Fatar, another classmate and member of our basketball team who shot from the corner three-point line like Larry Bird. Unfortunately, we would lose Fatar to the streets during our high school years after someone shot and killed him.

JC and I were friends; we just had moments where we would occasionally bump heads,. Eespecially after he stole a girl I was talking to. I can't blame him, though. At the end of the day, she chose him over me and that's how it goes sometimes. Now, back to Mr. Jacobs.

Mr. Jacobs would regularly point out JC's academic shortcomings in front of the class. "I don't care how many touchdowns you throw or how many points you score. If you don't take my class seriously, you won't amount to anything," he once belted out after JC didn't turn in a homework assignment. In fairness, I can understand now, as an adult, the lesson Mr. Jacobs was trying to convey. But again, his bedside manner and delivery technique left a whole lot to be desired. Especially when you're smart enough to recognize we didn't have much exposure to intellectual men up to that point.

We instinctively wanted to draw nigh to Mr. Jacobs. We instinctively wanted to appease him as an educator because he represented the life experience and wisdom we were lacking in our lives. Instead, his behavior had an adverse reaction. He repelled us. Why do you think we played so much better for Coach Stout than for him? Coach Stout loved us without even having to say it. Coach Stout had our backs, so we happily played ourselves to death for that man. Mr. Jacobs, not so much.

If a young man like JC is continuously embarrassed in public by an older version of himself because of his academic shortcomings while being showered with praise for his athletic prowess, which of the two do you think he'll gravitate to and invest the most effort in perfecting? JC was an eighth-grade all-star, praised by his peers and high school coaches alike because they saw him as a tool to help them win their next conference and state championship.

Mr. Jacobs, on the other hand, interpreted JC's struggles in his classroom as disrespectful and as misplaced effort. Coach Stout built us up when we fell short and could convince us that a setback was an opportunity we could learn from.

I don't have one negative memory of the two years I played for Coach Stout, and he at one point benched me midseason for another player. I didn't like being benched—no one does—especially when I was replaced by one of my best friends, Kelly Collier. But here's where the genius of Coach Stout revealed itself and why he will always be my first basketball coach and not Mr. Jacobs. The following is a testament to how coaching style and delivery can make all the difference.

"I heard Kelly is off academic probation," I said to Coach Stout after a practice once rumors of my best friend's return to the team had circulated.

"Yes, he got his grades together after I talked to his parents and ensured them we'd keep him focused on school going forward," Coach said.

"So, he's taking my spot?" I asked Coach, knowing Kelly was a better player than me.

"Kelly is going to have to earn that spot. I don't promise playing time. But I'm not going to lie to you either, Tarik. If I do decide to start Kelly, you're first to come off the bench," he said, trying to soften the blow of the pending change we both knew was coming. I played basketball with Kelly every day in Parkside and had never beaten him one-on-one. I knew it was just a matter of time. Coach Stout obviously saw my disappointment.

"I still need you, Tarik. If you do come off the bench, that means I need you to captain the second-string guys. There are a few new guys on the team, and you can teach them the new plays and you'll be their point guard. You're calling the plays; you're running the offense when your team scrimmages the first string. You need to help make those guys better. Can you do that for me?"

Suddenly I didn't feel so replaceable. I would still receive significant playing time but no one wants to lose their starting position. Coach Stout though, even if it was a clever Jedi mind trick, stayed true to his word. I was sixth man before I even knew that term existed, and I captained the second-string team. He even announced it at the beginning of our very next practice.

That's why we loved Coach Stout: he was hard, but he was also fair. Without any formal training I'm aware of, Coach Stout accomplished turning my demotion into a lesson about adversity and identifying opportunities in that adversity. He showed me even in demotion I could still develop a new life skill. What did I learn? Perseverance and leadership.

Comparatively, Mr. Jacobs preferred the scorched Earth nuclear approach. This one instance with JC, instead of in private conversations like mine with Coach Stout, Mr. Jacobs, for some reason, opted for public humiliation when he lashed out at him in front of the entire class yet again.

"I hope you break your leg and lose your Camden Catholic scholarship!" Mr. Jacobs yelled during the middle of a class session. JC didn't respond. We were Catholic school kids, and despite the predatory rigors of the streets we shared with criminals and adults whose hopes and dreams were permanently deferred, we never disrespected our teachers. We didn't disrupt class. The structure our parents afforded us also provided safety, discipline, and compliance with rules. The truth is, some of us relished the fact we were in a safe environment for seven hours out of the day where fights rarely happened, over-aggression was nonexistent, and we were treated to a healthy environment perfectly conducive to learning, unlike our public-school counterparts.

So, we tried to make sense of why Mr. Jacobs, a college-educated Black man, would be filled with such ill will. Even now, as an adult, recalling these moments, I struggle to piece together why one would purposely wish failure upon a younger version of himself. Was it simply because too many of us didn't fit the academic mold he envisioned for us? Or do I dare to ponder a deep-rooted problem outside of his control that we kids couldn't fully comprehend?

During the exercise of extracting these traumatic memories, I've been forced to accept human behavior is obviously complex, especially in response to the intricacies of a constantly changing world and its vices. Perhaps Mr. Jacobs had struggles unseen by us, demons that some who have served in the military were hesitant to acknowledge.

Perhaps those days I detected the smell of beer on his breath coincided with the instances of his outbursts. Loosening his tongue, revealing an inebriated, uninhibited truth—as an adult, I am far too familiar with these. Could it be alcohol ultimately revealed the true feelings of an academic overachiever who'd been relegated to teaching, boyz in the hood, when he'd much rather be among those he thought were more deserving? I haven't seen or spoken to Mr. Jacobs since my eighth-grade graduation, so I guess I'll never know.

chapter 12

I learned that my father had been to prison during casual conversation with my mother, awaiting the arrival of guests for our annual Thanksgiving dinner. At forty-six years of age, with my 22-year-old son in his senior year of college, I had the unceremonious honor of adding my dad to the tally of men in the Jackson/Moore clan to the rank and file of convicted felons. This revelation was yet another disappointing fact about a father who'd left much to be desired.

With much reluctance, I admit that collectively sixty-three percent (yes, I did the math) of the men of the Jackson (maternal) and the Moore (paternal) clan have, at some point, lost their freedom to incarceration. They have been placed in shackles, stowed away from their families, stripped naked before armed men for inspection, and deloused, the letters of their names converted to serial numbers logging them as property, and their freedom stripped away. That's over half of the namesakes of my pack domesticated to serve a master. Nearly two-thirds of my bloodline returned to bondage.

However, the long-term effects of incarceration are much harsher. That's sixty-three percent of our entire family left unprotected, relegated to fend for themselves emotionally and financially because the men had been removed from their families' homes. Once you become a convicted felon, your way of thinking and functioning in "regular" society changes, much like war veterans who return home shell-shocked or with PTSD due to the horrors of war.

Once stamped with *that* designation, "convicted felon," once you must check *that* box, your options of maximum earning potential essentially disappear. Like a rudderless vessel at the mercy of unforgiving tides and nature's elements, you only hope God or fate will intervene. If you're lucky, the universe will be gracious and violently run you ashore. But these new shores hold no promises that your new location will be welcoming or sturdy enough to support the new foundation you wish to lay. It never promises to provide enough sustenance for you to survive, let alone thrive.

Those recipients of grace, the rare success stories where felons beat the odds and have extraordinary lives worthy of acknowledgment and praise, are the exceptions. But let's be honest—they are the one percent. They are the rarest and most valued, diamonds forged after withstanding the deepest and darkest depths of pressures deemed unsurmountable. They are not the norm. They are the gladiators of old. The Hannibal, Shaka, Achilles, Alexander, and Hercules of legend whose names are carried on the backs of history, so we'll continue to sing their praises, never forgetting their names. The reason we call them heroes.

As for the rest, the ninety-nine percent of men the American industrial prison complex systematically annihilates, never was its objective to rehabilitate. Forever was its design to emasculate self-worth and profit from the housing of their broken spirits, lest we forget the proceeds gained, returning them to slave labor. Now I knew my father was no exception and among that ninety-nine percent with no hero's story.

Unfortunately for my mother, my father would be her downfall. Distracted by his rugged good looks, bright smile, and infectious charisma, she failed to see the two of them were not evenly yoked. I once, momentarily, found myself in a rare, uninhibited conversation with my mother.

"You must have thought he was really handsome," I said, devoid of a smile. I wanted it to be clear this was not a moment of jest. She paused for a moment before responding.

"Yeah, when we met, he was the fun party guy everyone loved being around"—she allowed herself to smile— "aaaannnd he *was* really cute," she admitted. We both laughed. "Where'd that come from?"

"Honestly?" I pondered before continuing. "I was just thinking how you two are literal opposites of each other. You're extremely nice. Only see the good in people, completely ignoring the bad. And he's extremely selfish. You two were a terrible combination." That brief exchange is the most honest conversation my mother and I ever had, our first equally adult moment of unbridled honesty. My father is as selfish and unambitious as he is charming. And my mother fell in love with his charm but would dislike him in the end.

At the age of twenty-one, my mother brought me into this world. Shortly after I was born, my father became a statistic, selling narcotics to undercover law enforcement while attending Temple University. My mother, armed with only a high school diploma yet a superior work ethic, began the next stage of her life without my father.

Once my father was released from his short stint in prison, he tried to be in my life. However, his participation in rearing and protecting his child came and went at his own sporadic leisure. He was what pop culture now deems an absentee father. In fairness, there are moments where I have fond memories of our times together. Most of those times are relegated to my prepubescent years. Then there's a span of a consistent decade where he and I reconciled and made mutual efforts to redefine our relationship. The NFL football season and our fervent love of our respective football teams—his, the Cowboys, and mine, the Raiders—helped rekindle my love for my father.

However, being a steward of candid, no-nonsense communication, I would be insincere if I didn't admit those years he was noticeably absent, from my teenage to young adult years, while living in very close proximity to my mother and me, were detrimental to my appropriate evolution into manhood. In other words, I know his absenteeism was *not* due to a lack of resources or circumstance. His absence was due to a lack of desire to be a father after an unplanned pregnancy. So instead of a son, I was an obligation, one he couldn't even afford.

"Tarik where are you going?" she asked her now-independent, 15-year-old son.

"I'm going to Philly to spend the weekend at Aunt Rita's house with Will and Bob, remember?" I said, pausing at the threshold of our Camden row home.

"Oh, I forgot. You have money? Clean underwear—"

"Ma! Seriously?" I responded with a manufactured smile to offset my tone so she wouldn't perceive me as disrespectful, but still asserting myself as a responsible young man who'd come into his own years ago. "I have everything I need. Besides, it's not like this is the first time I'm going there. I've made this trip plenty of times. New Jersey Transit to Center City Philly, then hop on SEPTA all the way up Broad Street until I get to the pizzeria on Cheltenham Avenue. From there, it's a three-block walk to Aunt Rita's house."

"Make sure—"

"To call you soon as I get there," I said, finishing her sentence, followed by a wink and a smirk.

"Tarik! Your mouth!" she reprimanded after I interrupted her.

My mother knew her child. My mouth had gotten me into trouble before I could even remember being alive. My unbridled innocence, when verbalized, could be in one moment adorable and embarrassing the very next. Even now, as an adult, I make a conscious effort to manage my words so my passion won't best me whenever it short circuits the filter between my brain and mouth.

My mother once told me of an instance where 3-year-old me and my uncanny talent for "speaking my truth" mortified her in public. As the story was told to me, she and I were on a SEPTA bus line headed somewhere unimportant. I was sitting on her lap in the front of the bus. Then two to three stops later, the bus picked up a passenger, one who had some type of deformity or facial burns, which startled me.

At the sight of the passenger, I didn't cry or avert my eyes. Instead, in childlike innocence, I pointed and said, "Look, Mommy, a monster." The entire bus heard me. Other mothers gasped and threw my mother disapproving, judgmental looks. A group of teenagers laughed at my unperceived cruelty. Even though I was too young to remember it, I still carry guilt for how I made the passenger feel.

My mother said she apologized profusely but to no avail as the man strode past us to the back of the bus and sat by himself, obviously upset. My mother then rushed off the bus before it closed its doors and we waited for the next bus to take us to our destination rather than endure the humiliation I caused.

"My bad, Ma—I mean, sorry, Mom."

"Mm-hmm, I'm not one of your little friends in the street. You don't talk to me like that. Honestly, I don't know why you insist on speaking slang at all. You know better," she reprimanded. "If people can't accept you for who you are, how you look, how you speak, then they don't belong in your life."

That was one of her rules, that I spoke "properly" when at home and to adults. Especially adults! Remember, we adhere to rural deep Southern family culture. Speaking out of turn or improperly initially earned you a wicked stare. Repeat offenders got a backhanded pop on the lips, leaving them momentarily numb. She'd worked two jobs at times and taken equity loans against our house to pay the tuition of the Catholic schools she insisted I attend. So, it was an expectation that I demonstrate the benefits of the education she afforded me. Even if it meant enduring being ridiculed by my peers, who relished speaking truncated English, also known as slang.

If you're wondering, yes, I was called a White boy, a geek, a nerd, and any other variation of insult reserved for inner-city kids who didn't speak broken English religiously. At one point, some in my friend circle thought the nickname Geeksville should be my street name after overhearing me and Dawuan insulting each other in jest. A light slap-box punch in the mouth for one of the less-respected knuckleheads in my circle put an end to that idea. No need to feel sorry for me; I proudly proclaim that I'm a geek who likes technology, reads books over a thousand pages long, and played video games way too much growing up. Yeah, I was that kid.

But I was never one dimensional. Like a chameleon, I seamlessly fit into multiple social circles. I was also lucky to be one of the few naturally athletic kids from my neighborhood. And in a small city that revered its athletes, I got a pass from most grief, especially while I was winning football and basketball games and accumulating track medals.

"You are correct, Mother. My grammatical shortcomings won't happen again while we converse," I responded sarcastically—yet respectfully.

"Boy, be on your way before I throw something at your head. And tell your father I said hello and I hope he's doing well," she said.

Oh yeah, I forgot to mention. My dad only graduated high school. And since he did time after becoming a felon for selling drugs while in college, he couldn't find steady employment after he was released. So, mostly he worked sales jobs in furniture stores or car dealerships when his personality overrode his conviction history. But in those jobs, he only earned money through commission, so if he couldn't manage to make any sales, he was broke. At this point in my life, he'd recently lost his job at his most recent car dealership, couldn't pay the rent at his apartment, and had to take up residence at his sister's house, my Aunt Rita. Since my Aunt Rita, her two sons, and her daughter occupied the three bedrooms upstairs, my dad was relegated to the living room couch.

So those weekends spent with my cousins doubled with some time spent with him as well. That's how I learned to play poker. I'm sorry to admit, poker is literally the only thing my dad taught me how to do my entire lifetime. But to his credit, I'm a pretty good poker player now.

"I'll let you know when I get there!" I shouted as the screen door slammed behind me, placing an exclamation on my last words to my mother before I would return Sunday night. An hour and a half later, I was knocking on the door where one of my favorite cousins lived. Their mom, Aunt Rita, was a home care aid and spent most of her time working in the homes of the people under her care. This meant me and my cousins Will and Bob, who were three to seven years older than I respectively, had our run of the place, as long as whatever we did didn't kill anyone or cause the neighbors to call the police.

We stayed up extremely late, watched R- and X-rated films, ate pizza, hoagies, and Chinese food for breakfast, lunch, and dinner, and occasionally had a girl over for make-out sessions. The first time I saw cocaine in real life was there. My cousin Bob had a period of one year where he and a friend would put coke in their cigarettes and smoke it. All the stories our teachers lectured us on in school about the dangers of drugs never matched up to what I saw in real life.

Bob never did anything crazy, or I never felt in danger. When he smoked cocaine, all he and his friend did was blast their music obnoxiously loud and dance all night. And their smoking and drinking never spilled over to me. He never once offered or suggested I indulge in anything like that. He knew better and so did I.

So, I looked forward to my weekends with them. Despite being left to our own devices, we knew we couldn't do too much coloring outside the lines, mostly because Will and Bob's little sister, Kim, was the eyes and ears for Aunt Rita. She was our moral barometer. If she made a fuss about any of our activities, it probably saved us from landing in a juvenile delinquent facility.

Like the time I told some kids talking shit to us during one of our many trips to McDonalds to "shut up and suck my dick." Word got back to my dad after Kim told her mom what I said and that was probably the only time my dad sat me down to have a stern disciplinary talk with me. Kim said something because I was being reckless in a neighborhood I wasn't familiar with, but the truth was I didn't care. I didn't like what was being said to me, so I responded how Southwest Philly and especially Camden taught me: to return the energy you're receiving.

To her credit, that was the only time she "snitched," but in hindsight, it was the right thing to do. I put her in an unsafe situation popping off to someone I didn't know, even if it was in retaliation. The same goes for months later when she told my aunt about another night Bob and his friend were smoking coke. Seeing him repeat the behavior told her it wasn't a one-off and she was legitimately concerned for her oldest brother. The next time I visited, Bob didn't live there anymore. Aunt Rita told him he had to get his own place if he was going to do drugs.

"What's up, y'all? What we gettin' into this weekend?" I shouted the moment the solid wood door opened to Bob, Will, and Kim's single-family row house. The three of them greeted me from the living room. It had hardwood floors and mirrors spanning the entire living room wall on one side, making the space seem larger than it was. I looked past them at the living room couch and saw it was empty. The wear and tear of my father's six-feet-three-inch frame had taken its toll on the cushions the two years he'd been squatting unemployed with them.

"Where's my dad?" My inquiry threw the energy off instantly. Will was the reserved and shy one. Bob the rebellious, outspoken one of the two, followed by the youngest and only girl.

"He don't live here no more," Kim blurted out. "My mom kicked him out because he stole Will's gold chain and pawned it. My mom not talking to him right now. She's pissed. Everybody pissed."

I looked at Will and he immediately broke eye contact. He did it so fast I wasn't able to gauge if it was out of anger or some other type of emotion. He was hard to read sometimes.

"Kim talkin' bout the gold name chain you couldn't find a few months ago?" I asked.

"Yeah. Last week we got mail from a pawn shop not far from here. It had your dad's name on some slip that said he had fifteen days to come and buy some jewelry back or they were going to put it up for sale. The mail even had descriptions of the jewelry. It listed a gold chain and a gold watch. Yeah! That nigga, yo daddy, went in my room while I was at work, stole my stuff, and pawned it after my mom let him stay here. She even bought him food so he could eat. Your dad is fucked up. We not fucking with that nigga."

This was the first and only time I'd ever seen Will angry, and rightfully so. His mother had bought him that name chain and gold watch as high school graduation gifts. Last time I visited, he'd been stressing about losing it because he didn't want to have to tell his mom and disappoint her. That his uncle, my father, was the thief never dawned on any of us.

"I'm sorry, man," was all I could say. Even though I wasn't responsible for my father's character, I still felt shame.

"It's all good. We went down there and bought my stuff back from the pawn shop before they sold it. I just won't be leaving my shit out no more," Will said.

"What you hiding it for? Ain't none of us gonna steal it," Bob chimed in.

"I know and I trust y'all," he said, looking at me specifically. "But still, I ain't leaving it out. I know better now."

I visited my cousins in Philly almost every other month from my teenage years until I went off to college. And after that weekend, the only time I saw that chain and watch was when Will retrieved it from whatever hiding place he concocted to wear it on rare occasions. He trusted me; I know he did. He just never trusted, in general, the same way again. If family could steal from you, that meant anyone could. And he was right. A few years later, I discovered my dad had stolen money from a joint savings account my grandfather, his dad, opened for me.

There is a genuinely sincere part of me that wants to believe my father doesn't lack a moral compass. He came from a good home. His father, my grandfather, was amazing to me and everyone else I knew who knew him. My grandfather didn't drink or smoke, worked hard every day until he retired, and lived modestly the rest of his days until the age of ninety-six.

My father has sisters with whom I developed deep, loving bonds that are much stronger than my relationship with him. His sisters always made me feel loved and appreciated. They reminded me without even saying anything that I was not a mistake, despite not being planned. I loved spending time with them.

My father, like too many others, has had a life filled with small miscues, errors, and bad judgment calls that have culminated in a life I fear will have a difficult time being celebrated. The trail of damage he's left resembles the path worthy of a wrecking ball instead of a man and father. Simply put, my dad is a nigga with a propensity for doing nigga shit!

chapter 13

Although I grew up poor, we were never on public assistance and never lived in public housing or experienced days where we had no lights. We were never *that* poor, but the only pair of sneakers I owned were whatever was on sale, and at times, we had beans and rice for dinner. When my growth spurts kicked in during puberty, I routinely wore high-water pants because my mother's income couldn't keep up with my height. I never walked around hungry, but I could tell we were low on money if my mom grabbed a box of Fruity Os instead of Froot Loops while grocery shopping.

When you're poor and part of a big pack, you quickly learn that sharing each other's resources is how to survive at times. I'd worn family members' sneakers that didn't fit me but were newer than the ones I had with holes developing in the thinning soles. Hand-me-down clothes weren't foreign to me either, and sometimes I even looked forward to it, especially when the clothes came from family members who "hustled" and had a better sense of style than I did.

Fast-forward a decade: once I was established in my tech career, the roles of the provider and the receiver reversed dramatically. I gave family members money to help them make ends meet. I paid some family members to watch my son instead of sending him to day care. I did it because I wanted him to establish the same bond I'd had with my family and experience that feeling of kinship that came with it. I'd drop him off in the mornings to play with their children, his cousins, instead of sending him to diverse summer camps in the affluent communities where I worked.

I saw it as an opportunity for family to develop bonds, especially considering Jason would be my sole addition to our pack. Unfortunately, a select few interpreted my generosity as an opportunity to put extra money in their pockets. I once let a family member live with me for six months to help him get back on his feet because he was in the middle of a divorce. Unfortunately, that same cousin, Leroy, would violate my trust.

"Driver! Turn off the ignition and place your hands outside the window where I can see them!" the police officer who'd just pulled me over ordered. The flashing blue and red lights lit up the inside of my Honda Accord sedan. My heart raced while cars sped past me on Route 42 North in Camden, only five minutes away from home. I found myself turning my head, avoiding making eye contact out of some misplaced embarrassment with those passing vehicles.

All these people are probably thinking the worst about me right now.

I squinted my eyes, trying to locate the officer in my side-view mirror. The muscles in my shoulders began to feel the effect of my having to suspend them awkwardly out the driver's side window. I heard him drawing closer to me from the gravel and rocks crunching beneath the soles of his black boots. When he finally reached me, he shone a flashlight into my eyes and then into my empty car.

"Everything okay, Officer?" I asked in a steady tone, purposely lowering the bass of my naturally baritone voice, seeing his other hand was softly placed on the handle of his holstered firearm.

"Any weapons in the car?" he asked as he continued to inspect the back seats and floorboards.

"Not at all," I responded.

"Then you won't mind opening your glove box to show me

there isn't anything in there? You know, for my safety."

"Sure, Officer. But I'm going to have to reach over and do that," I said, being overly cautious and overcommunicating my intended actions.

"Place your left hand on the steering wheel and keep it there and slowly reach over and open the glove box with your right hand. Slowly," he emphasized.

"Of course," I reassured him and slowly followed his instructions as I noticed his grip on the handle of his still-holstered gun was no longer loose but gripped tightly, ready to react. I opened the glove box and its interior light shone brightly, revealing two pieces of paper. My car registration and insurance card. "Okay if I grab my paperwork?"

"Go ahead," he said. "Whose car is this?"

"Mine," I said, handing him the two slips of paper.

"License?"

"It's in my wallet in my pocket."

"Go ahead and get it. Slowly!" he emphasized again, and I complied with growing disdain as I retrieved my wallet from my left front pocket and pulled my license out to join my other documents in his meaty fingers.

"Stay here and I'll be right back."

Stay here? Where do you think I'm going? You have all my documents, you fucking moron.

Minutes later, he returned. Something about his mood had changed.

"You're driving around with a suspended license. Did you know that?"

"What? I mean, that's not possible. My license has never been suspended," I assured the officer.

"That's not what our system says. You didn't pay a ticket from three years ago. Early on New Year's Day, just after two in the morning. I'm going to have to impound your car."

"Wait! Three years ago, I was in college in Baltimore. I didn't even have a car. Neither did my roommates. No way I got a ticket," I insisted again. The cop stared me in the eyes as if trying to gauge whether I was lying or not. Before he could respond I went into my wallet, retrieved my old student ID, and showed it to him so he could see the range of years I attended the school, proving I was in college.

"This ticket three years ago…it was issued here in Jersey?" I asked.

"Yup," he responded.

"I'm telling you, Officer, I didn't get a ticket. I just got this car a little over a year ago. I couldn't have gotten a ticket. I didn't have a car to drive. You checked my registration and insurance, right? Everything is on the up-and-up. Don't impound my car. I'll go to the DMV tomorrow and straighten everything out."

He pondered quietly for a moment.

"Dispatch. Cancel that impound," he said into his shoulder-mounted radio. Then he turned to me. "Today's your lucky day. I'm going to let you go and get this sorted out. If I pull you over again and it's not taken care of, I'm impounding your car and you'll be walking until you sort it all out. Understood?"

"Deal! I really appreciate it," I said sincerely, now regretting thinking of him as a moron earlier. He handed me back my license, registration, and insurance card.

"You have a good night and get that license taken care of, Mr. Moore."

The next morning, after driving the most cautiously I had in my entire life to the local branch of the Department of Motor Vehicles, I sat in my parked car waiting for the facility on Mt. Ephraim Avenue to open. An armed security guard approached and unlocked the glass front door, initiating a mad dash of power-walking drivers slamming their doors closed, including mine. We all reached the door in rapid succession before heading toward the welcome counter for customer number assignments.

"Number three, please head to window number four," an employee announced over the intercom.

"Good morning, how can I help you?"

"Good morning, I was pulled over yesterday and the officer told me my license was suspended due to an unpaid ticket I received three years ago while I was in college in Baltimore. Can you pull up my driving record and confirm what he said is true?"

"Sure, just let me have your license and I'll pull up what I can find," she assured me. I retrieved my license from my wallet and slid it to her across the countertop. She looked at my license while beating multiple keys on her keyboard. After a few clicks of her mouse, she quickly glanced up at me and my license then back at me.

"One second, sir. I'll be right back."

"Okaaaay, sure? Um, is everything okay?"

"I'll be right back," she repeated, but my gut was setting off alarms. Something was wrong. I tried positioning myself at an angle, hoping to get a glance at her computer screen to see what had caused her sudden exit to the back office. She returned a few minutes later with a taller, older gentleman who clearly outranked her, based on his style of dress. He joined her side to look at her computer screen. He looked at the screen, then me, and finally my driver's license.

"Sir, can you confirm your mailing address and date of birth for me, please?"

"Of course," I replied, before reciting them both.

"Okay, I'm going to need you to come with me to my office to get this straightened out."

"What did you find?"

"We should discuss this in my office, sir, so she can help the next customer," he insisted, sliding my license off the counter and motioning toward an area where I could access his office. I nodded my head and complied, making my way behind the desk partition, through the doors of his office, and taking a seat in front of his desk.

He plopped down in his worn, cushioned chair, placed my ID on his desk, and beat the keys of his keyboard efficiently and smoothly.

"So, you came in because you found out your license was suspended for an unpaid ticket?"

"Correct. Just like I explained to the officer last night and to the young lady I spoke with before you, I wasn't even driving when the ticket was issued. I was in college."

"I did find the ticket. It was a moving violation…a speeding ticket on New Year's morning."

"What year, specifically?" I asked.

"January 1, 1998, at 2:34 a.m."

"New Year's 1998, I was with my roommates in Baltimore. I wasn't even in Jersey. It couldn't have been me." Then he swung his screen around so I could see it. On the screen was my name, address, date of birth, a scanned copy of my Philadelphia birth certificate, and a small box that contained a color photo.

"Okay, so tell me who's the person pictured on my screen?" he asked while revealing a picture of my cousin Leroy with a big smile on his face.

"I don't know who that fool is. Obviously, they're impersonating me. So, shouldn't you drop the ticket and reinstate my license?" I said, knowing my upbringing had taught me better than to snitch. Especially on family.

"We can't just drop a ticket. It must be paid if you want your license back," he said, going quiet and looking at me for what I'd do next. I shook my head, let out a deep, disappointed sigh, and pulled my wallet from my pocket to retrieve my debit card to pay the fee for the violation and reinstatement of my license. In total, getting my license right cost me a few hundred dollars that Leroy would never pay back.

"Thank you. I'll be right back after processing the payment," he said, rising from his seat and exiting his office. The heavy door slammed behind him. I sat quietly, pondering how I had ended up here. Then the doorknob twisted and he returned with my card, a small receipt for me to sign, and two pages of white paper. One was my driving record abstract. The other was a form, which he placed in front of me. It was prefilled with my information.

"Now that the violation has been paid and the person in the photo is obviously not you, we'll reinstate your license immediately, but you have to tell me one thing or I'll have no choice but to open an investigation," he said, doing his best television cop impersonation. "Tell me who's the person in the photo and why you gave him your documents to make a fake license under your name," he demanded in a stern voice, staring me in the eyes.

I returned stoic eye contact and responded simply, "Good luck with your investigation." I grabbed my receipt and left his office.

He must think I'm stupid.

I knew damn well he wasn't going to investigate anything if he hadn't already done it the past three years my license had been suspended. Besides, even if he did, my cousin was a career criminal. He'd never track him down.

chapter 14

One of the consequences of a one-parent household where the parent has only a high school education is facing the reality that you're probably going to be stuck in an existence of living paycheck to paycheck. Survival mode will be your normal. Savings are minimal, if there at all. When emergencies arise, your only option is to maintain the same lifestyle with fewer resources by tightening your belt and eliminating anything extra or extracurricular. The basics—food, water, shelter, and love—you'll have and fortunately, that is all that is required to sustain you.

One of the possible effects of someone stuck in the rut of financial survival is it potentially leaves no room for financial literacy improvement. I was fortunate that my mother always had good credit, despite her meager earnings. Banks never shied away from giving her loans. They knew Ms. Jackson would always pay them back. But that still meant we ate food that wasn't name brand and shopping for new clothes was extremely rare and was routinely done at thrift stores. My mother leveraged her good credit to finance my early education, and that strategy paid off.

However, once I achieved the status of having a successful career, I had no idea how to properly manage the money I made because I was never taught financial literacy. I knew from watching my mother to always pay your bills, but the fine intricacies of money management had evaded both her and me. It would ultimately be up to me to learn the sensitive intricacies of managing my money through self-educated trial and error. What I needed was a financial management education proficiency exam, much like the writing and speech exit exam every student had to pass before Morgan State University would award their cap, gown, and degree.

Despite it being a hassle, I would later appreciate Morgan for this gauntlet of real-world preparedness. The writing and speech proficiency exit exam was excellent preparation for the barrage of job interviews I would soon face. One of the exam's objectives was to make sure we enunciated when we pronounced certain words like "ask" and didn't lazily say "axe." They ensured we understood and could articulate the grammatical differences between the words "their," "there," and "they're." The university made us jump through these hoops of foundational skills to ensure we didn't embarrass them or ourselves once we were out in the real world after graduation.

But that lack of financial literacy led me down a road of wasting money through a plethora of bad decisions that ruined my credit twice in my life—once in college and again shortly after graduation. When I applied for financing for my first car in 1999, I had no idea what my credit score was, not to mention who the three credit bureaus were. In fact, I didn't even know they existed. When I graduated, it was the height of the internet dot-com boom, so my technology degree put me in a place to earn plenty. What to do with the money I earned was another story.

My first six to seven years after graduation, I paid my bills but ordered takeout food regularly instead of cooking at home. My savings were minimal. I faithfully contributed to my 401(k) but just the minimum four percent so I could earn the company match. I paid off my student loans early, but I carried too many credit cards that all kept maxed-out revolving balances. I partied at clubs and lounges every weekend, frequented strip clubs, and regularly treated friends who were less fortunate.

Then, one day a coworker and I were having lunch in the office. I'd purchased lunch, approximately at $10 per day, from our company cafeteria for months—of food I could have easily cooked for dinner and packed for lunch the next day. Ten dollars per day, $50 per week, $200 per month, $1,200 for the first six months of my employment eaten and shitted out.

"Tarik, I'd like you to go home tonight and pull your bank statements for the last six months and add up all the money you've spent on takeout food," my coworker said in the most sincere and genuine sentiment I recognized only in mothers. "And I'm not just talking about here during lunch but on the weekends when you go out, for dinner when you don't feel like cooking. All of it." So, when I got home, I went through my bank statements and tabulated all the money I'd wasted. The number shocked me.

I'm not naturally an emotional person, but before I went to bed that night, I wanted to cry. The total amount I'd spent eating out, partying, treating my friends, and spoiling my family equated to an amount that could have, if redirected, paid the thirty-year mortgage on my first home in seven years instead of the sixteen it would eventually take me.

The worst revelation was the amount I spent on my family. When you're one of the few "successful" people in an entire generation, the less fortunate of your family will instinctively lean on you for help. If you have a large family like I do, combined with a good heart like I do, it's difficult to say no. You're inclined to help, especially those who've made sacrifices for you to reach the level of success you have. You turn a blind eye to the fact that their early contributions didn't match what they would eventually ask you for when they expected the favor returned.

Eventually, requests for help become more frequent, and more significant. One lesson I've learned is no matter how generous you are, no matter how much you help, it will never be enough for some. The worst part is the moment you say no, you find out who is really in your corner and who the takers are. I remember a cousin who had just been released from prison visiting me four months after my graduation.

"You were in college as long as I was locked down. I was wondering if you were ever going to graduate," he sarcastically joked. If you're wondering if that was a backhanded compliment, it was. "Now you got yoself a good job and all, whatchu gonna do with all that money you makin'?" he asked.

My cousin didn't graduate from high school. He'd been in the streets hustling ever since I could remember. He was completely ignorant that the path to completing an undergraduate degree could span anywhere from three years, if you're ambitious, that the average is four years, and up to six years if you wanted to drag it out like I did. In my defense, I never went to summer classes until my last semester in college and that summer session registration was only because I'd run out of financial aid. The spring semester before that summer session, I'd taken twenty-one credits because I had to graduate. Anything other than earning my degree would have been a disappointment for me and my family.

When my elementary and high school peers attended summer school, it wasn't out of choice. It was a punishment for not doing well during the regular school year. I had never been to summer school before college, and I refused to go now that I was out on my own and paying my own way through school. Yeah, that was a rude financial awakening as well. My mother made the miscalculation that my respectable grades and being a minority interested in studying engineering meant merit and financial hardship scholarships would fall out of the sky in abundance.

There would be no merit or academic scholarships because my GPA and my SAT scores weren't high enough. There would be no economic hardship scholarships for being poor, but we soon learned when I applied to the United Negro College Fund that those scholarships are for people living below the national poverty line, which we weren't. My mother's income was literally $3,000 a year above the threshold to qualify.

My graduating senior year at Morgan State University, I went to the bursar's office to settle my bill. The financial aid counselor then informed me I'd exhausted all my financial aid allotment. I honestly didn't even know that was possible. I thought if you were enrolled and making progress toward graduation, you could take as long as you wanted, since you were only borrowing money you'd be paying back once you started working after graduation.

While I was in high school and it was finally time for me to decide what college I'd attend, how to pay for it, where I'd live, and any other logistical details, I had to figure that out on my own. My mother always supported my decisions, but unfortunately, she didn't have the experience and subsequent wisdom to properly guide me there. And she never pretended to, either. It was an unspoken understanding between the two of us: she would support my decisions but ultimately all those life decisions were up to me to figure out on my own. I was in uncharted territory and as a result, my first two years in college, I ended up at a state school called Jersey City State College. It's a Liberal and Media arts University now, just a stone's throw from New York City where Jersey's aspiring artists, actors, and directors attended undergrad.

It was only after I was enrolled at Jersey City that I discovered my new institution of higher learning didn't have engineering, computer science, or any other major related to technology. They didn't even have elective classes with the word "computer" in them. Originally, before the Jersey City fiasco, I'd applied to Rutgers University's School of Engineering in New Brunswick. Naively, I thought graduating twenty-fifth overall in my senior class and possessing a letter of recommendation from my Computerized Electrical Technology instructor would ensure my acceptance. I was wrong.

Instead of a letter of acceptance like I'd received from every other private school I'd attended, Rutgers sent me a thin envelope stating I'd be placed on their wait list. The news was demoralizing. It would mark the first time I'd ever locked onto a goal, did the work, followed the rules, and failed to attain my objective. Immediately after, I filled out and mailed applications to schools all over Jersey and the only school where I beat the application deadline was Jersey

City State College. Honestly, I think I could have sent them my application the first day of school and they would have still accepted me. I was just a butt in a seat paying tuition and putting money in their pockets.

I knew my first day of stepping onto the school's campus, I would not be staying at the school that literally spanned one city block and at best, had ten buildings. My first two weeks of classes, I was routinely stopped by security asking me to prove I was a student there by showing them my ID. After sitting down with my class registration advisor, we both determined and agreed I was at the wrong school and the best thing for me would be to complete as many core general studies classes that would transfer over to my new school over the course of the next one to two years maximum.

So that's what I did. For the next two years, all I'd register for were core classes, learn to drink, smoke weed, meet women, and play division III football before transferring to a historically Black university, Morgan State University in Baltimore, Maryland. Morgan would be significantly more expensive, since I would be attending a university out of state, but it was the best decision to make. I had no college savings, and tuition and room and board cost $9,000 a year. Financial aid would only approve $5,500 to $7,400 per year. So, I made my first strategic adult decision by not using the money I'd borrow from the government to pay for my room and board. All my financial aid would go toward my tuition. I would live off campus in my own studio apartment. Instead of deferring to pay my cost of living until graduation, like most who leverage student loan money for dorm rooms and student cafeterias, I paid those expenses as I went along in the form of rent and cooking at home to feed myself.

That decision also meant I had to find an apartment, a roommate, if possible, and a job that would cover all my living expenses while still allowing time for me to attend classes and study. I was also still holding onto the pipe dream of playing division I football at Morgan. All those years living in survival mode with my mother would now be put to the test. I cultivated my own version of a minimalist lifestyle now that I'd be officially on my own.

The summer before I would attend my first semester at Morgan, I worked one full-time job during the day and a part-time job during the evenings. I got my first beeper and dipped my toes into the world of "hustling." I earned and stacked all my money those three months to minimize how many hours I'd eventually have to work while in school. I found a studio apartment for $509 a month on the ground floor of Goodnow Apartments off Moravia Road.

I had no furniture except the bedroom set I brought from home and a dining room table and chairs my mother found at a discount store. There was no sofa, no television, or living room set. My box-spring and mattress had no bed frame. I simply stacked them on top of the new carpet in the farthest corner of my "bedroom." When I wasn't in class or studying, I worked. I had countless jobs. I worked at a convenience store called Wawa, did telemarketing at MBNA and Dial America. At one point, I even delivered pizza for Pizza Boli's until I landed a really good job doing bill collection for Bally Total Fitness. Yes, I'm the guy who would call you if your membership dues were late. I'm the guy who woke you up early in the morning and interrupted your family dinner to collect your payment over the phone. The Bally job was perfect for me. Not only did it pay $10 per hour but if I hit my collection goal for that month, I'd earn an end-of-the-month bonus as high as $1,200.

I had declared an Electrical Engineering major at Morgan and knew the course load would be strenuous, so I cut out everything that I deemed not necessary. That meant division I football wouldn't happen for me and neither would a social life. The first party I went to was halfway through the semester, after midterms, during homecoming. I once had two friends from Camden, Tyrone and Keneisha, who also were students at Morgan, unexpectedly come to visit my new apartment halfway through the semester. After only fifteen minutes of small talk and pleasantries, I told them they had to leave.

They were understandably confused and I'm sure they had some choice words for me while they drove back to campus, and rightfully so. Truth was, I'd just gotten home from work and was behind on my reading and studying for a Chemistry for Engineering exam I had in the morning, and I was *not* doing well in that class. Had it not been for my laboratory work, I would have gotten my first D ever in life instead of the C that I scratched and scraped for. Sorry about that, Tyrone and Keneisha. Love y'all, but my mother was haunting me the entire time you were there.

"Earning a D is mediocrity in this house, Tarik. If you're going to do something, do it right." That's a Ms. Jackson quote from my childhood, after getting my first C at St. Rose of Lima Elementary school in West Philly. I put all my effort into everything I do. It's a borderline unhealthy obsession, if I'm being honest with myself. My therapist also agrees. But it's historically worked for me. I can count on one hand how many times I've failed at something and still have fingers to spare. I lock in on a goal and I become relentless, sometimes overbearing, because I refuse to allow myself to fail. Even if it means not sleeping, not socializing, not doing anything that doesn't bring my objective to fruition.

Despite the money I saved over the summer before matriculating to Morgan, and the twenty to twenty-five hours a week I worked at Wawa, there were nights in between paychecks where all I had to eat was white rice seasoned with pepper and salt and Baltimore city tap water to drink. I never invited people over out of embarrassment. Maybe for some subconscious reason, that's also why I hurried Tyrone and Keneisha out of my poor man's apartment. They and two other people would be the only visitors I'd have in my apartment my entire freshman year at Morgan.

Toward the end of my first semester, Wawa reduced my hours to ten hours a week. The cushion of money I saved over the summer quickly dried up. At one point, my lowest financially, I couldn't even afford rice. Which meant I had to do something I'd never done before. I applied for food stamps with the city of Baltimore. It was embarrassing. I didn't tell my people back home I was struggling. I didn't want to borrow their money—that's *if* they had it to loan.

When I was approved for food stamps, I remember being so elated that Baltimore didn't use paper food stamps but instead, a card with a pin code like a debit card.

The $228 a month the city approved me for saved me from becoming a criminal. Well, a full-time criminal. What I mean by that is, for the week it took me to apply and get approved and receive my card, I literally had no food in the house. Zero! I had money to get to campus so I could go to class and come back. It would be five more days before my card would be ready and I hadn't eaten for almost two days. It wouldn't be for another three years until Earl "DMX" Simmons would release his song "The Convo," but he and I were already kindred spirits. It's one of the reasons I gravitated to his music and still listen to him this day. DMX got me through undergrad.

"...thou shall not steal but I will, to eat..."

And that's exactly what I did *to eat* those next five days until my card arrived. I stole. I cased the Giant supermarket just down the road from my apartment. I scoped out what times had the most customer traffic so I could blend in. I scoped out what time frame had the security guard with the beer belly in case I had to outrun him. I knew they didn't pay those guys enough to chase you but just in case, I'd rather it be the fat old guy rather than the youngster with something to prove. And most importantly, if security did chase me, or by some bad luck the police got involved, I needed an escape route that didn't lead immediately back to my apartment. I needed a contingency plan, a place to hide out for an hour or two until I lost them.

When I couldn't distract myself from my growling stomach any longer, when the countless cups of water I drank to fool my stomach that it was full no longer worked, when every ounce I drank simply ran from my mouth, through my empty digestive tract, and I urinated into my toilet like a waterfall, I made my move on the Giant supermarket. I put on one of my fashionably oversized sweatshirts, tucked it into my jeans, and tightened my belt so whatever food I slid down my sweatshirt wouldn't fall out.

Once I got to the store and grabbed a few staple items, I neglected to remove a sensor from one of the items and set off the alarm near the door. It caught the attention of a security guard. We locked eyes.

"Stop!"

I didn't stop. I put my four by four hundred relay track speed to work. He honestly never had a chance. I lost him after turning a quick corner and disappearing through a wooded area near the supermarket I figured he would never follow me into. I got away with a small bag of rice and frozen thin-cut chicken strips and never returned to that Giant again, not even when my food stamp card arrived three days later. I'd shop at a different Giant grocery store in another neighborhood the remaining years I was a student.

With my food insecurity issue resolved, I still needed to find another job, and quickly, to cover rent, utilities, and other living expenses. Luckily, due to a lawsuit settlement, I had bought a car the year before, so I started delivering pizzas for Pizza Boli's to bridge my rent gap and keep my utilities on. That's how my first year at Morgan would go until I found two roommates my sophomore year, so my last three years at Morgan, I was splitting living expenses instead of carrying the load myself. And I was elated that I could get off public assistance after getting rid of my car and taking public transportation to and from school and work.

Those initial years after graduating from Morgan and securing my first job as a network technician and administrator, I celebrated and splurged excessively. I was a regular at the monthly party called Philly's First Friday. Whether I was with friends or alone, I hit every party, bar, club, and lounge along Delaware Drive and Center City. I told myself as long as I was contributing to my 401(k), I deserved to spend the money I'd worked so hard to earn. Having my bills paid for that month was my measuring rod of being a responsible adult.

When 2 a.m. rolled around and there were no women left to chase during the let out, I'd drag myself back across the Ben Franklin or Walt Whitman Bridge. I'd grab food at a local pizzeria or chicken spot to consume whatever deep-fried garbage I immaturely categorized as food. I'd routinely see the same faces from the city who were also habitual partygoers. Among my circle of friends, I'd developed a stupid reputation of being the best driver when under the influence. It's not something I'm proud of.

In fact, the very first time I got drunk, at age seventeen, I also drove. At seventeen years of age, I'd never had a drink, despite being exposed to it routinely by friends and family on my father's side. On my mother's side, in accordance with my family's Southern tradition, dictated by my grandmother and adopted by my mother, alcohol was never in the house. If you were to entertain or invite people over, which was rare, then cases of beer and bottles of cheap wine would be purchased and consumed that night. Once the party was over, the house went back to being dry, so I never had access to makeshift bars in the homes I frequented growing up in Jersey.

When I did party, I did what people coined "buzzed driving." I've even been pulled over by police while "buzzed" and passed their sobriety checks. Now, had any of them asked me to blow in the Breathalyzer, I'm sure I would have failed. I'm not sure if it was my naturally calm and laid-back demeanor that translated well with the two or three officers who'd checked my pupils with a pen flashlight off the Ben Franklin, trying to gauge if I was drunk or not, but I made it home every night. Maybe it was my presentation as a glasses-wearing driver who'd mastered vernacular code-switching as a corporate survival technique that put these officers at ease when conversing with me. Or maybe I was just lucky. We'll never know, now that I don't buzz drive anymore.

But the partying and being frivolous with my money didn't stop, as evidenced by a summer night out with an old friend I'd grown up with from Camden. We hadn't seen each other since high school, when we played a basketball game against one another in our senior year. It was good catching up with him, but I didn't care for his friends much. Even after hanging out and buying rounds of drinks for us all to throw back, I never warmed up to them.

I knew when we left that Philly club and headed back across the Ben Franklin Bridge to Jersey, the next time I'd run the streets, I'd be content with it being just myself or just my friend and me doing our own thing.

"Aye, yo, let's hit up Crown Fried before we call it a night. I could fuck some wings up right about now," the most obnoxious of my childhood friend's buddies blurted out.

"Cool, but y'all have to eat it in your own rides. I'm not trying to find crumbs and shit in my back seat after I drop y'all off," I told his friends.

"Man, ain't nobody gonna fuck up your car."

"I know you're not because you're not going to eat in it after we get our food," I reiterated. I purposely ended my comment with a laugh to lighten up our drunken moods. Practically speaking, no one ever gets into someone's car and intentionally spills a drink or drops food, but when it does happen, it's the owner who ends up having to deal with the fallout. Now, my car wasn't anything special. It was a practical Honda Accord that didn't even have a leather interior or any special features. But it was mine and I take care of everything I own, which means keeping it clean.

That night, I got lucky and found a parking spot only a few feet past the seedy chicken takeout storefront. We all hopped out of the car and joined the loitering contingent that had either already placed their orders or were waiting to do so. Besides the partygoers were the usual vagrants and drug addicts hustling their way into people's hearts to acquire loose change or a dollar bill or two, if lucky.

"What up, cousin!" a familiar, raspy voice called out from the crowded, dingy storefront. My eyes locked in with the only other person as tall as me. He approached me; I instinctively smiled just before we clasped our right hands and slapped each other on the back. Instantly, I could smell he hadn't had a proper shower recently. Through drunken eyes and a delayed mental capacity, I slyly looked him over and took inventory of the shabby, oversized clothes eclipsing his frail frame.

He's getting high again.

"What's up, cousin!" I responded with another smile, despite his appearance. I was genuinely happy to see my kin, who'd given me my first boxing lesson in front of the house I grew up in and was now the owner of.

"I'm good, you know, doing what I do and maintaining," he responded, but I was unsure if he was trying to convince me or himself. The smell of his breath and the color of his teeth told me everything I needed to know. "You look good, little cousin. I've been hearing good things about you. We're proud of you. All of us, nah mean?" he congratulated, and I sincerely received and appreciated it.

He was one of the kinder-hearted men in our pack. He and I were a lot alike in that respect. We both shared a moral compass of never chasing conflict. Instead, we preferred harmony, considering our upbringing amongst chaos. However, when confronted, we never ran from it, ever. We knew retreat went against the unwritten rules of our pack. Our approach of traversing Camden's streets would eventually lead us down separate paths in life, but he would always remain someone I respected.

He'd missed his calling in life as a recipient of inherited musical talent. His mother possessed a powerful contralto voice the residents of my block could hear before you could see her, especially after a few drinks. My aunt's genre of music was R&B. For our generation, it was hip-hop. As an adolescent, I stayed at my grandmothers until my mother got off work. He'd lived in my grandmother's basement since his release from a juvenile facility, as he had nowhere else to go.

I'd go down into the basement and shoot the shit with him, and he'd playfully tease me about my Catholic school uniform, and I'd tell him he was just jealous that I could read, but it was never out of spite. Just the dysfunctional way members of our pack joked with one another while also demonstrating you wouldn't allow someone to disrespect you. I'd listen to him burn countless hours reciting rhymes over beats he played on a boom box. I was with him the first time I witnessed a battle of aspiring rappers in the city. He'd gone up against another rapper who showed up at my grandmother's door and challenged him on the front steps to a battle.

That's when I fell in love with hip-hop and later purchased my first cassette tape, *Criminal Minded* by Boogie Down Productions, led by KRS-One. Even his name, KRS-One, spoke to me: Knowledge Rules Supreme Over Nearly Everyone. KRS-One was one of the original conscious hip-hop artists and I fucks with that. Like every little boy in my circle, I dabbled with being a rapper while in grade school. Musicality is one talent I do *not* have, so my rap aspirations were extremely short-lived, but I did win my first and only elementary school battle.

Unbeknownst to my musically inclined cousin, I won that battle and performed in my school's talent show using his two-verse rhyme called "The Situation." It was the first time this shy only child experienced the feeling of being the center of attention and a cool kid. And for the new kid who'd transferred from Philly, that acceptance helped me a lot. The first verse to that rhyme has been burned into my memory.

> *The situation that I'm in when I grab the mic*
> *I have to say all the rhymes that my people like*
> *I know you want to shut me off like I'm a machine*
> *But I know you just jealous cuz I'm making that green*
> *That cold cash money that you have to earn*
> *Cuz I'm the only MC that has money to burn*
> *Each time I walk down the street*
> *I reach the top of my peak*
> *Cuz I get paid EVERY DAY*
> *And not every week*

Yes, back then, every day was payday for my cousin. He hustled.

He was one of many in our pack whose sole income came from hustling. He and others did time for it as well. Outside of my mother, these are the members of my pack who protected me, schooled me about real life, not the make-believe kumbaya bullshit I saw on television. They raised me to see the world as it really was, not what so many naive American citizens hoped it to be.

But a lot had changed since then. Now, here he was living the consequences of breaking the cardinal rule of hustling, the same lesson I'd learned selling water ice as a kid: never get high on your own supply. He took the panties off that bitch, crack cocaine, for a taste instead of pimping her out like the whore she was. Now he was in love with the whore and she had the upper hand.

"For real doe, cousin, how are you? You need anything?" I asked, cutting past the small talk. That's the thing about family. Our pride, sometimes shame, can convince us that the front we're putting up can camouflage the distress signal our shared DNA is sending.

"I'm good, man, nah mean? Just happy to see you," he continued.

He can't bring himself to ask you, Tarik. No matter how wide you're leaving the door open for him, his pride won't let him walk through it. You're going to have to drag him in.

"Oh shit, my bad. You want something? I'm about to order food to soak up this alcohol so if you want something, I gotchu." I didn't wait for him to respond and reached into my pocket to retrieve the money I had left over from partying that night.

"Yo, Tyreek! Fuck that bum! That nigga need to get a job," the asshole from my back seat said, emerging from Crown Fried Chicken, butchering my name and shoving french fries into his mouth. My cousin looked over his shoulder to see who hurled the insult. I craned my neck, doing the same. My cousin and I locked eyes, his embarrassment restraining his anger.

I looped around my cousin and shot a stiff left jab to the asshole's eye. His head leaned back, and french fries fell from his mouth. I followed the stunner with a right cross that landed his jawline, knocking him off balance. No words needed to be spoken.

One of us fight, we all fight!

My cousin, in defiance of his frail frame, instinctively dropped his center of gravity, widened his stance, pivoted, and readied his fists. Fists that were decorated with the darkened and scarred knuckles of a seasoned warrior.

The back-seat asshole, shocked by my assault, never saw my cousin's second-pronged attack. A crashing left hook to the body landed and crumpled our victim. His hands dropped his bag of food to protect his midsection, bending him over to the perfect level to meet my cousin's combination left hook that rocked his jaw and body back toward me as if we were playing table tennis with his face. But there would be no return volley from me. My cousin would win this point, finishing him off with a clenched right before I could even reset my stance for another power punch.

Our victim's body went limp, and he crashed onto the block to join his chicken box and fries. Onlookers laughed, some pointed, and others shrugged it off as par for the course for a Saturday night in Camden. My cousin and I broke out of our fighting stances and looked at each other. He looked me up and down as a stranger would when sizing someone up before we exchanged smirks. We'd both underestimated each other. Seeing his frame, I didn't think he had the power he'd just displayed. He, remembering my protected golden child persona, didn't realize a lot had changed since the early days I followed my rapping cousin around.

"Okay! I see you, cousin," he said simply, until our victim's snoring interrupted our exchange.

"I had a good teacher," I replied, nodding to him in acknowledgment. I shook my right hand in the air to relieve the throbbing developing in my less-seasoned right hand. I placed it in my pocket, fumbling around for a few seconds before taking it out to clasp my right hand with my cousin's again. This time I held him a second longer than our initial greeting, now oblivious to his hygiene. I wanted him to know he was loved. I needed him to know I had his back, regardless of his condition.

"Your boy? He gonna be a'ight?" my cousin asked halfheartedly.

"Fuck that nigga," I said nonchalantly. "We ain't boys. You and me though, we family."

I finally released him from my embrace. This time I'd be the cousin leaving the tightly folded twenties neatly tucked in his palm. He looked at me with the same surprised expression I'd given the cousin who first showed me that magical, sleight-of-hand exchange.

"Subtle, huh?" I repeated, mimicking the lesson the alpha of our pack had taught me so many years ago.

He didn't verbally respond to my gesture. He didn't have to. His eyes spoke the words of gratitude then and in harder times that followed, when I knew most of the money I'd give him would never see the inside of a cash register. Sometimes we're financial fools for our loved ones.

From time to time, but never habitually, that same cousin who gave me my first boxing lesson would knock on my door in dire straits, for a couple years after the night we took turns reconfiguring the back seat asshole's face. To his credit, he would only do so when he had no other options to feed his addiction and I never refused him. Now, there may be some who believe my generosity only encouraged his behavior, even enabled his addiction. From your perspective, that may seem logical to you but here's a perspective you may want to consider. The perspective of a ghetto bastard.

Whether I gave my cousin the money or not, my cousin was going to get high. He didn't have the strength and support to beat his addiction at this point. He only came to me when he had nowhere else to go. That means he was at his most desperate, or at least on the verge of it. Had I refused him in his time of need, he would have employed whatever methods at his disposal to take from you, everyday citizens, what his addiction demanded. And I just showed you what his hands are capable of. Now imagine him with a real weapon in the commission of a crime, whether that be assault, robbery, or worst-case scenario, even murder. Life and writing this book also taught me that the totality of a person and their journey aren't confined to a particular stage of life—especially the worst stage of life.

My cousin finally kicked his habit and has been clean for over a decade now. He's happily married and has never seen the inside of a prison cell again. I don't know if the money I sacrificed to him on multiple occasions helped with his recovery. I'll never know for sure if the tens of thousands of dollars I'd forfeited across multiple family members at my own financial expense contributed to helping them out of whatever jam they were in.

The truth is, I honestly don't care. I've never desired congratulations or acknowledgement. I shy away from being the center of attention. The good deeds I've performed from childhood to the present day have always been genuine. I don't give with a premise of hoping and wondering how it'll come back to me. The deeds I perform are done out of love, including the money I surrendered. And as far as I'm concerned, instances like these are some of those rare moments I was happy to forfeit those funds as money well spent because, honestly, in the most extreme of circumstances, I've probably saved your life or the life of someone you know and love. Now, excuse my passion speaking for me when I say, "You're welcome, America."

chapter 15

I, like many, am admittedly a creature of habit. My routines and habits, especially the good ones, have always created a mirage of stability in my life. My process of manifesting success was as simple to me as arithmetic, as direct and thoughtless as one plus one equals two. However, familiarity and comfort can breed complacency, and I'd become complacent in old habits. As my life changed, I didn't modify my approach to life in parallel. I didn't make the necessary changes to antiquated habits to fit my new lifestyle.

So, despite my methods of old serving me well at those prior points in my life, I had to make a conscious effort to self-correct, force myself and my habits to evolve and match my ambitions. Up until that point, what I'd failed to recognize is those methods that had delivered the outcomes I've always desired hadn't evolved to match my new socioeconomics, circle of friends, and lifestyle overall. The old habits I clung to were developed and thrived in my past lifestyle, rooted in a survival mentality. That antiquated mentality of survival, if maintained, would inevitably morph into self-sabotage.

I'd been born into an existence where everyone I knew and interacted with was in survival mode. I hadn't met an affluent person, let alone one who looked like me, until I attended Morgan State University. So, for the first nineteen years of my life, the habits I formed to navigate life were rooted in struggle. My choices in literature, the amount and genre of television I absorbed, the type of women I pursued, even the management of my finances and relationships with family members were developed under the distress of survival. For me to transcend to my next stage in life, all of that had to change.

But sometimes, despite your best efforts and intentions, life tests you. People make plans and God laughs. I'd made the decision to revamp how I would manage my life. However, I didn't have the wisdom to know yet that I couldn't do it effectively without the guidance of someone who'd already done it. I, like many, needed a coach or mentor to guide me from missteps and mistakes as I adjusted to my new learning curve. Someone trustworthy to give hard but fair advice to stop me from entertaining old habits destined to collide with my new goals. I had to acknowledge that I couldn't figure everything out on my own.

"Tarik Moore speaking," I announced in a measured, professional tone. That was my typical greeting when a phone number I didn't already have saved as a contact flashed on my caller ID.

"Hey, Baby, it's your auntie. Can you talk for a bit? I need to bounce something off you," my father's sister asked, prompting a smile to grace my face. My Aunt Rita and I had been close for as long as I could remember. I'd grown up with her two sons, Bob and Will, and her daughter, Kim. Her children, my cousins, were the only relatives on my father's side that felt like siblings to me.

On weekends when my dad hadn't failed to pick me up, it wasn't unusual for him to drop me off at their house when he didn't invite them over to his apartment for the weekends. I developed a genuine bond built out of love for them and we spent as much time together as possible. My aunt looked out for me, fed me, bought me birthday and Christmas presents, and paid for annual summer trips to amusement parks. I even stood as a groomsman in her wedding. I love her.

"I don't have a meeting for another thirty-five minutes. What's up? Everything okay?"

"Yes, Baby. I'll make it quick and won't take up much of your time. I know you're busy."

"I'm never too busy for you. What's on your mind?"

"Well, I'm looking for a house with more space now that I'm a foster parent. My three-bedroom is too small for all of us, so I found this new four-bedroom house with a fully finished basement, but my credit isn't good enough to qualify. I make enough with my salary and the state money I get for foster care to cover the mortgage. And Will still lives with me and he chips in with the money he makes. It's just my credit. I need help getting approved. So—"

"So, you need a cosigner for the mortgage?" I concluded.

"Yes, Baby. Would you be able to help me with that?" she asked softly. I could detect her hesitation and wanted to make her ask easier.

"What are you going to do with your house in Cheltenham? The three-bedroom house?" I asked.

"I have two tenants who want to live there. The house is paid off except for an equity line of credit I took out to remodel the kitchen. That's only about $400 a month so they can cover that easily between the two of them."

My newly formed instincts of changing my spending habits pleaded emphatically with me to respectfully and regrettably decline her request. I'd read enough books and heard enough cautionary tales to know better than to attach my name to anything I wasn't paying for. That's what my brain said; my heart, on the other hand, crept in to remind me that this was Auntie. I had a lifetime of witnessing her work ethic. The same went for her son, Will. He had only graduated from high school, but they had always maintained jobs.

My relationship with her and her sisters were what I'd wished I'd had with my father. My aunties were better parents than he was. When my father was unemployed, she'd let him live in her house.

She was one of the nicest people I knew. My heart wouldn't allow me to tell her no. So, I didn't.

Two days later, I'd met her real estate agent, toured the newly renovated house, was approved for a loan in my name alone, and we closed a month later with the understanding that she would live there. I'd be the landlord; she'd pay me rent to cover the mortgage—everyone wins. Or so I thought.

For the next two years, like clockwork, my aunt deposited the money she promised to cover the mortgage into the bank account I'd set up just for that purpose. She did her part, and I did mine. We both kept our word to each other. But her tenants did not.

"Hey, Baby, you gotta minute? I need to talk to you about something important." In my life experience and almost everyone I know, any conversation initiated with those dreaded words "I need to talk" typically means bad news is soon to follow.

"What's wrong, Auntie? Everything okay at the house?"

"Yes, everything is good here. It's my house in Cheltenham that's the problem."

"Okaaay? What happened?" I asked, bracing myself.

"Those damn tenants haven't been paying rent. I'm behind on my equity loan and property taxes." I reclined backwards into my seat, laid my head back onto the top of my ergonomic office chair, and stared up at the ceiling. The survivalist in me instantly began processing how to remedy the situation. Then something out of the ordinary happened. I stopped myself.

This isn't your problem to fix, Tarik.

I turned off the emotion of the conversation and processed my aunt's information with logic and reason.

"Well, now that you know, can your tenants pull enough money together to cure the account and become current? Or how fast can you evict them and get new tenants in there? Or do you and Will have enough money cure the account?"

"C-cure the account?" she asked.

"Sorry, I mean can they catch up on the payments?"

"Oh, okay. I asked them that, but they said they don't have the money. I'm going to have to pay for it all myself or lose my house," she said before going eerily silent. "That also means I'm going to have to use all the money I had coming to pay you rent for this house, and since I can't trust them to pay rent, I'm moving them out, and I'm going to have to move back there. I can't afford to catch up there and keep living here."

"I see," I responded as the wheels in my head spun out of control. "When do you plan on moving out? I need to find another renter or put the house up on the market for sale. I can't afford to pay that mortgage on my own," I told her. The truth was I did have some savings but that would only get me through two to three months before I started feeling the weight of carrying two mortgages. In my naivety, I didn't anticipate this worst-case scenario and had made investments with most of my discretionary funds elsewhere.

"I'll move out as soon as I can, but I'm definitely going to miss this month's rent because I have to pull all my money right now to pay the bank to get caught back up so I don't lose my house. Once that's taken care of, I'll need another month to get everything together here to move back to my house."

"So, we're talking two months before you can move out?" I asked.

"Yes. I'm so sorry but I can't lose my house. I've had it my whole adult life," she said emotionally. I felt her pain and was enraged her tenants couldn't manage the measly rental amount between the two of them. Then my mind shifted to calculate the numbers behind it all. The mortgage was over $2,000 a month, which I'd have to cover on top of my own mortgage in Jersey. Then I'd have to get the house ready for another tenant by making minor repairs, cleaning, and painting before I could even show the house to potential renters or buyers if I chose to sell the house instead.

Ultimately, my aunt, her youngest son, and her foster children lived in the house for two months before moving out completely. Once I saw the condition of the house and my limited funds to do the repairs to freshen it up for a new tenant, I decided to put the house up for sale. Then the recession of 2008 hit. The housing market crashed, and buyers were scarce amid the subprime mortgage bubble bursting.

People plan and God laughs.

A month later, in the middle of the recession, Fortune 500 companies I'd worked tech projects for tightened their belts. They reduced the money they typically invested in new IT projects, and I was laid off from Accenture, the consulting company I worked for. It was the perfect storm of adult life challenges, and I was underprepared financially to weather it. Ultimately, my aunt couldn't save her house. The house in Philadelphia I purchased in my name to help her and add to my real estate portfolio was foreclosed on. My credit would be ruined for the next seven years.

People plan and God laughs her ass off.

That same year, the transmission on my Accord died on the New Jersey Turnpike. With a foreclosure on my record and now working a government job making sixty percent less than I had only months earlier, I couldn't get approved to finance another car. I spent the next year taking public transportation to and from work. I lived thin, only paying for the necessities. I stopped going out, buying new clothes. I turned off my cable. I literally just worked and went home, cooked at home, prepared leftovers for lunch, and went to bed so I could save enough money to offset my bad credit with a larger down payment. When the time came to make my purchase, the roles had been reversed and I went to several family members who I'd helped and looked out for over the years when I was doing well. I asked them to cosign on a modest used car. Just like my aunt had asked me three years prior. It was ironic that I was now delivering the same story she had provided me. I explained how I had the money, steady work, my expenses were reduced to minimalist standards, but I just needed a cosigner to get me over the top. They all said no…like I should have said to my aunt. It was hard enough asking and even harder hearing no after no. It was a hard lesson to absorb but I did, and I learned from it.

It's during times like these that you discover who really has love for you. It was during those two painful years I discovered who I could rely on in both days of joy and years of pain. My mother and two of my fraternity brothers helped in those times when I needed them most. My dean, G. Lee, and another one of my chapter bruhz, Charles "69" Solomon, each, at some point, loaned cars to me temporarily after discovering I was walking to the grocery store and taking the bus to and from work.

My mother did what mothers do. She was supportive and bore the brunt of my venting sessions of disappointment, first in myself for making a bad decision. Then at others who disappeared the one time in life I requested their help.

People plan and God determines her lesson was learned and ends our suffering.

Several more months passed until the time came that I had stacked enough cash and my credit had recovered enough to where I no longer needed a cosigner. God stopped laughing long enough to intervene.

I crossed paths with a young lady I'd met years prior. She's a private person so I won't put her name out there, but I call her Dee whenever we converse. She was then and remains the most successful businessperson I've met in my lifetime. She's intelligent, which is evident by her finishing high school a year early and attending one of the best universities in the country. She has great natural instincts when sizing people up and carries an opinion I both respect and value. And she's down for hers; she isn't intimidated by and doesn't shy away from that hood shit.

Her words are direct, her value in herself is uncompromising, and when her mind is made up about something, that's what it is. She doesn't sugar-coat shit! If you did something stupid, she tells you, "That was fucking stupid. Don't do it again." In my lifetime, only she and Kevin remain the most intuitively intelligent people I've met whose advice and counsel have yet to fail me.

When Dee discovered I had no transportation, she took a day off from running her business to drive me to a dealership so I could buy a modest Dodge Durango. She instinctively participated in the negotiation and loaned me $1,000 to add to the money I'd already saved to ensure I would be approved. To this day, outside of my mother's deeds, it was the most selfless and loving act I'd experienced in life. As the years after my buying the car passed, I made sure to thank her on the anniversary of its purchase until the car died 210,000 miles later. The progress I've made thereafter in my tech career, entrepreneurship, and ultimately in life can be directly attributed to the days that followed the purchase of that Dodge Durango. I'll forever be in her debt because, Dee, you a real one.

chapter 16

My community, and my family in particular, was never fond of law enforcement. The fact that in 2008, the police killed my younger cousin, Leroy Jr., only helped fuel our disdain for police. Ironically, one of my mother's longest-lasting relationships was with a law enforcement officer, a Camden County Sherriff who worked at the courthouse in Camden. When the day came for him to meet my family, the meeting was received better than expected.

"Well, if you think about it, cops have guns and so do we," one of the funnier of my cousins said in jest. "I guess he'll fit in all right." We all laughed in unison, the officer not so much. If I were to not generalize and instead speak specifically about my personal experience with law enforcement, it would be a different story from the cookie-cutter speaking points embraced by those shouting to defund the police.

But don't get it twisted; I'm adamant in my stance that law enforcement—especially cops on the local level—are out of control. A lot of police officers, *not some*, are woefully out of their intellectual depths when it comes to the skills required to properly police a community. My book before this one titled, *I AM...*, under the name T. H. Moore, is literally centered on police brutality and their vicious shortcomings. I unapologetically and metaphorically drag corrupt cops through the street in the same fashion and fever as Achilles did Hector in *The Iliad*.

But I digress; many of the men in my family, on both sides, have had unfortunate experiences when it comes to the justice system, resulting in incarceration. On the contrary, two of my younger cousins have gone against the grain and are sworn police officers. They're my idea of what a good cop, born and raised in the community they police, looks like. In addition, three of my best friends are in law enforcement. One is a correctional officer, another is an ICE agent for the Department of Homeland Security, and the third, after serving in the military, policed in a narcotics unit and eventually transitioned to the Secret Service, where he worked both then vice-president Biden and afterwards President Trump details.

I have a multitude of fraternity brothers I don't know personally but who are also in law enforcement. So, I've seen both the good and bad sides of the spectrum from a civilian perspective. I've seen and experienced the dark side of policing where the power they wield is abused. I've been profiled and pulled over by squad cars where obviously nervous officers approached my vehicle, their hands already gripping their holstered weapons, their left foot forward, their right foot a step back, ready to draw as if we were at the precipice of a Western showdown at high noon.

Moments like that infuriate me because I'm placed in a position where I must shrink my normal self and assume a docile state of being to defuse their unwarranted, perceived fear of someone they've haven't exchanged one word with yet. I emphatically resent having to play the court jester with officers by conjuring a quick joke and an exaggerated, forced smile to someone who shouldn't be afraid of me in the first place. American civilians shouldn't have to morph into shucking and jiving coons to make it home safely.

In one instance, I sped past an unmarked police car on a stretch of straight highway. The moment I passed him, he jumped out of the middle lane, gave pursuit, and switched on his lights.

Fuck! He got me.

I pulled over safely onto the shoulder, and when he arrived at my car, my window was already down. My license and registration were already in my left hand and protruding out the window in an admission of guilt, ready to receive my citation. From my side-view mirror, I could see him craning his neck to inspect my empty leather back seats. His right hand rested comfortably—too comfortably—on the handle of his firearm. He displayed nervousness with a slowing approach led by tactically bent knees. I spoke loudly from my open window.

"Hello, Officer! So, let's be honest. If you hadn't turned on your lights, you think you could have taken me the next quarter mile?" I saw him fight back a smirk and his posture lightened up. He instantly became less aggressive.

"If I wasn't on duty, I definitely could have taken you," the crew-cut officer quipped in return. Removing his hand from his firearm, he took my paperwork with a slight chuckle.

Now, I don't want my readers to think that I operate under the impression that I believe the burden of de-escalation is the burden of American citizens. To be frank, that's law enforcement's job. It's your job, law enforcement officers, to not assume you're behind enemy lines when interacting with the citizens of your own country. It's your responsibility, law enforcement officers, to carry the burden of defusing and de-escalating your overly anxious aggressiveness, not ours.

It's your job, law enforcement officers, to ensure we citizens feel safe and make it home safely. That is literally your job description: to uphold the law and protect innocent, law-abiding citizens from criminals. Not to assume all citizens, especially the Black and Brown ones, are criminals. The burden of proof is not on us. The burden of jumping through your hoops of submission to prove we're worthy of living is not on us.

Your demand of unquestioning compliance with every command you bark at us with mindless profanity and intimidation is nothing more than an exercise of forced citizen submission. It's no wonder we resist. America was built on the principle of freedom in opposition to tyrannical British rule, yet you expect us free Americans to reduce ourselves at your beck and call. Go fuck yourselves! You're not special! You're doing a job like the rest of us. You're *not* soldiers.

Many of you cops are only high-school graduates, which equates to your education level being average, not advanced. That's why we don't see the same killing sprees at the hands of federal agents, because they're required to have a college education to even qualify for employment. Now, I'm not trying to sound like an educational elitist. I understand having a college education doesn't instantly make you a better person. What it does do, especially for those who leave home to attend college, is expose to you a world and culture outside of what you've been accustomed to the first seventeen years of your life. You meet people from all over the country, sometimes even different countries. That life experience, even if you flunk out and never graduate, indirectly teaches you that the world is much larger than your hometown.

In comparison to Feds, local police officer education is mediocre. Yet too many of you, *not all*, only wish to create an environment of faux superiority so you can feel good about yourselves. It's asinine and your tactics of insisting law-abiding citizens in their own country *comply* to your undereducation and superiority complex is how insurgencies are created. I repeat…you are *not special*; you're average at best. Except my two cousins, love y'all, y'all da beeest! (DJ Khalid voice).

Breathe, Tarik. Don't let your passion rule you. Whew, talk about a rant. My therapist is going to have some choice words for me when she reads this part.

Despite my instinctual disdain for another person imposing their will on my life, I'm also not going to go out of my way to put my life in jeopardy. Especially knowing there is a contingent of unscrupulous police officers who enjoy abusing their power. They approach and instigate conflict in hopes they can act on their bigotry. And whether some of my readers choose to accept the following as legitimately confirmed fact or not, there are some morally corrupt individuals who harbor ill will and contempt for people of color and have purposely infiltrated law enforcement, knowing it places them in a position to exercise their prejudices and bigotry with impunity.

This country has, up until recently, sent a message that there is no consequence or recourse for the wicked behavior of law enforcement officers. Simply stated, police law enforcement has morphed into gang mentality, where beating, maiming, and murdering are acceptable outcomes for citizens. This gang mentality is upheld by our legal system, which provides an endless supply of "get out of jail free" cards to police simply because of the colors they wear. And much like gangs who flash hand signs to rep their set, police flash their badges. That's the flag they fly.

Aware of the nuances of law enforcement I've described, I decided at one point in my life to leverage my career in information technology to enter the field of law enforcement. Yup, there was a time when the Philadelphia branch office of the Federal Bureau of Investigation was heavily recruiting techies to bolster their Cyber Division. This branch was developed in response to the statistical spike in crimes being perpetrated via the internet now that the world wide web was in full swing.

Over the course of six months, I applied, passed their standardized test, attained a physical fitness test score that qualified for their SWAT team training track, and passed their panel interview and drug screening in D.C. I was on track to reach Quantico in two months, but first, I had to pass my first-ever polygraph. Before the polygraph, I needed to gather additional information that would be used for my background check. Much of the information was standard, but the bureau also wanted information on all my immediate family, both maternal and paternal. My maternal side was easy, but to collect my paternal information required me sitting down with my father, so I called him and we set up a parley for the next day.

"Hey, Dad," I said, greeting him as he opened the door.

"Hey, son," he responded more enthusiastically than I. For me, this was the equivalent of a business trip. I never have and never will be disrespectful to my father, because my mother didn't raise me that way. However, in a previous, candid conversation we had while I was in undergrad, I'd made it clear that I didn't respect him as a man or father. After that conversation, I excommunicated him.

By the time of our sit-down, I had my own son to raise, a career to manage, and entrepreneurial goals I'd set for myself that would require a certain level of selfish focus to attain. Simply put, if he wanted to cultivate a relationship, then he would have to initiate it and I would accommodate it if my schedule and time permitted. Eventually, he would reach out and consequently, our relationship would improve. However, it would take a few years before I reached a point where I could honestly say I had forgiven him enough to make space to love him again.

Some people take the word "love" for granted. It shouldn't be tossed around haphazardly. Even if you were to examine the root meaning of the word as it fits in the English language, love is not just an emotional feeling; it's a verb. Love is an action word. It's performed and demonstrated intentionally.

So even in the most rudimentary form of the English language, to *love* someone is to perform an action that demonstrates that emotion. Simply saying you love someone cheats the meaning of the word if there is no real action behind it.

Up until this point in my adult life, I had no evidence that my father loved me. He didn't provide for me, he didn't teach me anything except poker, he was absent for many birthdays, and would rarely even call. I had no sustained collection of actions where my father demonstrated love for me. My list of his *did nots* were staggering in contrast, though, resulting in an extremely uneven scale of his life's work demonstrating, by logic, that he did *not* love me. I would even cringe when he said he loved me. I would, out of respect for my mother, reciprocate the gesture, but my response wasn't sincere, and if I am to be completely honest…I lied to him.

So, that evening I was cordial during our initial pleasantries, removed my coat, took a seat on the couch opposite him, retrieved the packet the FBI provided me, and began my information collection. I treated it as a preliminary practice interview for whatever future criminal interviews I'd have to conduct once I earned the title of Special Agent. In my mind, the government needed questions answered and I was there to collect those answers.

"This may take a while. The Feds have a lot of questions I don't have the answers to for me to continue in my screening," I warned.

"Okay, I don't have anywhere to be, so I'm all yours. Shoot," he responded with a smile that suggested he was simply happy to spend time with his son after so many years.

"Okay, first question. Do you have a middle name?"

"It's Lawrence."

"Okay, when is your birthday?"

"August 10, 1953."

In case you're wondering, yes, these are the questions I had for the man who had lain with my mother and eventually brought me into this world. Our interactions were so limited I didn't even know his birthday or how old he was until that night. I knew nothing significant about the man. I continued the questioning.

"I already have my aunt's names, their addresses, and birthdays, so I'm good there. But what about any other children you've had, my siblings? I already talked to Tiffany and got her information, but I remember you having another child I haven't met—a sister, right? What's her name?"

"Nyarah," he responded.

"I'm assuming her last name is Moore as well, but correct me if I'm wrong. Also, what's her address and date of birth?" I asked and suddenly his face went blank. His eyes redirected their focus to the ceiling, searching his mind for an answer that would never come.

"Uhhhhh. Uhhhhh. I don't remember right now, but I can find out and get that to you," he said, but my dad stutters when he's flustered. I role-played and didn't relent, like the special agents I saw on television or in movies.

"If you don't know her most current address, just give me the last known address. That'll be good enough. There's mail forwarding so they'll be able to find her using that."

"That's the thing. I don't know…right now. I can find out for you, though. My, my…memory isn't so good right now—you know it's kinda late and I'm getting old," he joked. I wasn't amused. I tilted my head to the side like the family dog when it doesn't understand a command.

"Any address, Dad. All I need is any address. Even her mom's old address will do."

"I'm sorry, Tarik. I just don't know."

"You don't know where my sister is, your daughter?"

"I'll get it, though," he reassured me. Shame began washing over him. Disappointment slowly rose in me like an unattended bathtub with the faucet left running.

"Okay, just get it to me as quickly as possible because I have to turn this information in no later than a week from today, and the Feds don't do late. Okay?"

"No problem," he assured me, readjusting his position on the sofa.

He's uncomfortable.

"Okay, next question. What is Nyarah's date of birth?"

"Uhhhhm, I not sure. I'll have to get that to you, too."

"You don't know when she was born?" I said with condescension. "Okay, do I have any other siblings, because if I do, I have to list them. They're using this information for a background check. Anything I omit, intentionally or unintentionally, I'll have to answer to, or it may jeopardize my continuing the screening process."

"No, I don't have any other kids."

"Okay, your stepson. Does he still live here?"

"No," he responded and then I paused before asking him the question I'm sure both of us knew was coming.

"What's his date of birth and what's his address?"

"I don't know."

Respect your elders, Tarik. Respect...your...elders.

I had to gather all the self-restraint and invoke the voices of my mother and grandmother in order to not curse my own father. He'd had three children with three different women and hadn't played a role in raising any of them. He didn't even know them. He lowered his head and broke eye contact with me.

Welp, this was a waste of time.

I closed the packet, displaying the bureau's seal on the top page. The once-rising disappointment began to subside and was replaced by a new emotion I'd never experienced for my father: I felt sorry for him.

Sorry, because despite the struggle my mother painstakingly endured, she managed to raise a child on her own who, by most accounts, had made a decent life for himself. She also, in turn, made a decent life for herself. My sister, Tiffany, whose mother I remember being equally gracious, beautiful, and nice, married a man after my dad had failed her as well. My sister's mother had carved out a good life for herself with a man who would raise my sister as his own.

That night, I left the house my dad's wife owned. I drove my car back over the Ben Franklin Bridge and called my mother once I got back home to Woodlynne, New Jersey.

"Hey, Ma, you busy?"

"No, just watching TV. What's on your mind?"

"I just came from my dad's."

"Right, you had to get some information from him for the FBI."

"Correct," I responded shortly.

"He get you everything you needed?"

"Uh, yeah, for the most part. Some info he has to hunt down, but I have a week before it's due, so he has some time to pull it together." I purposely selected those words. I didn't want to disappoint her more than I had to. To her credit, my mother always sees the good in people despite their repeated displays of character flaws. Over the years, she'd insisted I reach out to my dad, develop a relationship, and forgive him. To her credit, she never once uttered a negative word about him. She left it up to me to formulate my own opinion. She didn't want to force her experiences on me. Or perhaps she hoped he would rise to the occasion, and we would have a better relationship than he had with her. She literally championed him despite his not deserving it.

She and I are different that way. I take people for who they show me they are. I place them in the front row or the balcony cheap seats, if that's where they truly belong, or deny them admission in totality to my life's show. In the construct of nature versus nurture, nature won in developing my personality. Had nurture prevailed, I'd be more like my mother, but the world would have eaten me alive if I had.

Tonight's debacle would only reinforce my evaluation of where my father belonged in my world. I denied him entry to my life's show for the next two years until he met his grandson for the first time. Nurture would prevail in this instance. Much like my mother, I wasn't going to punish my son and his grandfather by not allowing them in each other's lives. I would make sure Jason knew his people, his family.

"Ma, tell me something."

"Okay?"

"My dad—you two are literally polar opposites of each other in personality and character."

"Is that your question? Sounded more like a statement," she corrected.

"You're right. What I'm trying to say is, you deserved better than him, Mom. I just wanted you to know that."

Two weeks later, after I got the information my father promised, I turned in my packet for my background check. This would be one of those times I'd mentioned earlier about being able to count on one hand the number of times I failed when I failed my polygraph, and my pursuit of a federal badge would come to an unceremonious end. For the record, I see why polygraphs aren't admissible in court. I'm not making excuses and blaming the machine for my failure. The polygraph administrator did his job honorably and the test detected two untruths out of the ten questions during the test. The interviewer, on the other hand, did his job extremely well and worded his questions to where I'd have to be a choir boy to have passed. But maybe that's the point. Maybe the Feds prefer choir boys and I'm not that. My past isn't pretty and sometimes my nails got dirty. The two cleverly worded questions by my interrogator that I failed were:

Question #1a: Have you ever smoked marijuana?

My response: Yes.

Question #1b: How many times have you smoked marijuana in your lifetime?

My response in my head: *Who duh fuck counts how many times they've smoked weed? Tarik, he's staring at you, reading you, trying to detect lie indicators. Say something! Guess!*

My response: Uhh, twelve.

This machine is going to blow up when it hears your answer.

Yeah, I panicked. He had me sitting in an "interview" room. An interrogation room is the more appropriate description. And I'd never had any run-ins with law enforcement, so he caught me slipping and I folded under the pressure.

Question #2: Have you ever falsified information on a mortgage application to get a loan?

Response in my head: *Where the fuck did that come from? Of course not or I wouldn't have been approved. They don't just hand out loans to people who look like me. Do you know how many hoops I must jump through to get approved for a loan?*

Response: No.

That was the end of my pursuit as Special Agent Tarik H. Moore, and it would also be the first time I'd failed at getting a job I really wanted. It would also be the first time I'd shed tears as an adult.

chapter 17

I grew up in a family and home where love was assumed or demonstrated through action, rather than speaking the actual words. I can count on one hand how many times my mother initiated the statement, "I love you." Displays of affection, like simple hugs, were even more scarce. Despite my accumulating academic and athletic achievements, my mother, at times, competitively compared me to my peers. Specifically, those who consistently earned their places among honor roll students when I had failed to join them in those accolades.

Her praise of me, in my presence, was also rare. I'm not sure if it was a calculated tactic to keep me humble or not, but it did drive me. To her credit, she did keep a scrapbook of newspaper articles I appeared in after winning football championships, track medals, student government appointments, and ultimately, the National Dean's List as an undergrad, so I knew she was proud of me. But actually hearing those words, "I'm proud of you," still evaded me.

As an adult, I initiated expressions of love, but even then, I could detect uneasiness in her retort. It's almost as if she'd never received or experienced love in its verbal form, so her response to its expression was wrapped in awkward disbelief, shyness, or surprise at hearing the words. Despite overt expressions of love being denied to me, her devout demonstration of love through her responsibility to me was ever present. My mother always maintained employment.

When her money was stretched thin, she secured part-time jobs to make up the difference.

The latest fashion and footwear never found themselves at home in my closet and sometimes my lack of funds was on display as an overdue haircut. We rarely ate out because she religiously prepared meals daily as her demonstrative routine and parental love language. I'd never experienced our utilities being shut off due to nonpayment. Unlike some of my friends who experienced disappearing acts by their water, heat, and electricity providers, those experiences were foreign to me. My mother and I had never been on public assistance, while one of the functionally illiterate neighborhood kids who would secretly come to me for help with their homework showed me what food stamps looked like.

The home my mother provided was the epitome of stability. We never experienced eviction or foreclosure like my friends three doors down from me. I had everything I needed but the fulfillment of wants was extremely rare. The only exception to the governing rule of needs over wants was for items or activities that fed my love of technology. If an experience offered me a leg up to learning a skill not privy to everyone, my mother found a way.

When I was six, my mother bought me my first personal computer. I wouldn't be able to afford my first desktop or laptop computer until I was twenty-three. I didn't realize it at the time, but that "computer," a keyboard with eight megabytes of built-in memory, with a serial cable that plugged into an adapter so our living room television could serve as a monitor, unknowingly introduced me to my professional destiny before I'd realize and appreciate the significance of that moment.

The first clear memory I have of my mother saying "I love you" happened when I was thirteen. It was my freshman year at Camden Catholic High School. I didn't assimilate well into the school's privileged, predominantly White, Cherry Hill culture. Being greeted by a lunchroom table of five strangers as a "nigger" my second week of school let me know instantly this school was not the place for me. My sadness, perhaps depression, was obvious to my mother. She'd sensed I needed an out-of-the-ordinary expression of support, so she uttered the words. I returned the sentiment feeling better but was disappointed it took her stumbling across the words "Life sucks and then you die," which I had doodled on my bedroom wall calendar, to verbally express her love. Being called "nigger" was my only outright racist experience while at Camden Catholic my one year of attendance, but there would be a consistent slew of other coded phrases and microaggressions from classmates and even the dean of students that I don't care to recount. All I knew was I wasn't wanted there, and I wasn't going to stay there, no matter how good the school's academic reputation was. But convincing my mother to approve my leaving would require more than my saying, "I don't like it here."

I'm sure some of you reading this may demand evidence to support my claims because that's the world we live in now. It's not enough for an adult to call out discrimination; American social justice demands we relive and make account of our traumas, so I'll oblige you just this once. But don't get sensitive when rehashing these memories changes the tone of text as the anger awakening inside me is revealed. You can't ask for an accounting of wickedness and expect kindness from the person reliving it. So, with that said, *fuck* Camden Catholic!

The semester before my application and acceptance to Camden Catholic, I was a student at one of the only two Catholic elementary schools in the city of Camden. My eighth-grade year, the principal of my elementary school, St. Bartholomew, arranged a visit from representatives of Camden Catholic to introduce us to the school. Afterwards, if our interests were piqued and we desired to continue a parochial school education, we were given applications for consideration and acceptance into the following year's freshman class.

The Camden Catholic visit was scheduled during a regular class period so we could utilize our cafeteria before our school's lunch session would require use of the room. It would be my first meeting of their dean of students, accompanied by an additional four to five students from their senior class. Each student gave an oral presentation of the school and answered questions we had about its academics, facilities, athletic programs, and other extracurricular activities. The seniors' presentations were flawless, blaring testaments to the quality of the education there, and they answered all our questions.

Out of all the questions we asked, the one we all had reserved for the dean of students, at the request of our teacher Mr. Jacobs, was the most important.

"Why doesn't Camden Catholic have a single Black teacher at the school?"

We saw the lone Black student representative among the high school seniors smile in approval of our question. The dean answered with expedition, "None have applied," with conniving confidence like a debate-prepped politician. It was my introduction to how a person could be so untrustworthy by deliberately lying to children and his potential student body. It demonstrated that he didn't care for us, only the money our tuition provided and the diversity quota his job description mandated he fill.

With matching conniving, our eighth-grade teacher had presented his updated resume to Camden Catholic's dean of students when they initially arrived. Our job, as instructed by Mr. Jacobs before we went to the cafeteria, was to put the dean on the spot and force his acknowledgment and confirmation he'd received our teacher's resume.

"But our teacher applied," one of my classmates debated.

Gotcha!

We all celebrated in nonverbal unison, stealing glances at each other with slight smirks, thinking we'd scored one for the home team. But our celebration would be short-lived.

"You're absolutely right," the dean instantly admitted, preempting his counterattack. "He literally just gave me his resume this morning." The dean slyly pulled our teacher's folded resume from the inside left pocket of his suit jacket. "I'll take this back with me, and his credentials will be considered," he continued with a smirk and the air of this obviously not being the first time he'd been challenged with the criticism.

The dean had prevailed in Mr. Jacobs' strategic sparring session, leaving his classroom of minions without any further, canned, follow-up questions. Our question-and-answer session of Camden Catholic's visit ended.

But the visit was not over: up next was a private session with the assistant coach of their basketball team. A successful visit to the hood wouldn't be decided by the number of minority students added to their ranks. No, this visit would not be deemed successful if the coaching staff couldn't persuade some of the best players on our team to join their middle-tier program.

For the last two years, our team routinely dominated the elementary ranks of our parochial league. We wouldn't know until the conclusion of the summer how many of our collective would find ourselves trading in our St. Bart's navy-blue and yellow-gold colors for Camden Catholic's fighting Irish green and white. When the final word came and we tallied our numbers, only a handful of our twenty-plus classmates and teammates were accepted into their freshman class. And of course, our two best players, Edgar "JC" Banks and Errick Thomas, would be their prize admissions for the basketball program.

To say my freshman year there was turbulent would be an understatement. Assimilating into a culture and environment where it was obvious we weren't welcome was admittedly difficult for me. We did our best to close the ranks of our tight-knit group, to fit in, and make friends who didn't look like us. Four years later, in the spring of 1993, after enduring the same culture shock and similar hardships, fewer than half of us who entered Camden Catholic's doors would leave as alumni of the school.

I enthusiastically transferred after my freshman year, JC also left after his freshman year without playing a single season of basketball, and Errick left for California to spend more time with his father, who was a retired NFL football player. Melissa DeShields left after her freshman year and transferred to Camden High School. Of the original six St. Bart's crew who'd been accepted, two—Shawn Whyles and Kimberly Gaines—would be the only alumni of Camden Catholic High School.

I never quizzed my friends about their experiences at Camden Catholic. Through loose conversations where we periodically reminisced about our time there, I did discover I was the only one called a nigger. I also quietly endured the snide comments by White students claiming my acceptance into the school being a case of tokenism or affirmative action because they assumed I was an athlete, despite my not participating on any of their athletic teams. The truth was, I was sent there to take full advantage of the school's academic prowess. Sports, despite my being naturally athletic, were never my priority. Especially there. For the first time in years, I lost interest in playing sports. I didn't want to represent *that* school or wear *their* colors. I hated it there.

I honestly played sports to break up the monotony of school and fight off boredom. My laser focus was on academics at Camden Catholic and was also driven by my desire to prove wrong those who thought me intellectually inferior. Physically, I knew I could mop the floor with these coddled prep kids. I also knew they didn't live by the same no-snitching rules as Camden kids. The moment we laid a hand on them or even threatened to beat their asses until their eyes and ears bled, the Cherry Hill police would have us in handcuffs and a juvenile corrections facility would have soon followed, as most of these kids' parents would have been delighted to make an example of any of us.

That's why the kid who called me a nigger didn't wake up in the hospital that day. Even at that age, I knew the dangers of letting my anger determine my future in their world. He would have woken up battered and bruised and I would have been in handcuffs in the back of a police cruiser, instantly regretting the pending creation of my criminal record. My momma didn't raise a fool.

Midway through the school year, Camden Catholic would show me and my friends from St. Bart's that we had been conned by a system that didn't care if we were successful or not, as long as we padded their pockets with our tuition and helped them win championships. It was after the conclusion of midterms when the school published an issue of the school paper. This publication included a Q&A section where questions submitted by students were answered. One of the questions asked was the same question we'd asked six to seven months prior during their visit to St. Bart's.

Question: Why aren't there any Black teachers or administrators at this school?

Answer: None have applied.

They lied to us again, but this time it wasn't confined to one rogue administrator working outside the realm of decency. Reading the same canned response in the school's official publication parroted to us months ago gave us our first verifiable glimpse of purposeful discrimination, bigotry, and willful ignorance. I received my first lesson on how, not only could an individual purposely lie and deceive about fair play and equality but, even worse, I'd now witnessed and had proof that an entire institution would support this systematic practice of exclusion.

It was at that point, at the age of thirteen, that I would make an adult decision not to continue my education there, even without my mother's approval. Despite their storied reputation of undergraduate acceptance to premiere Ivy League schools, I resigned myself to the fact I now despised the institution my mother had to work two jobs and take out a $10,000 loan against our house for just to afford my attendance. I would reject this institution, its Christian-rooted curriculum whose moral compass had degenerated into a proven practice of lies, deception, and athletic exploitation I'd expect from Satan, not Christ.

They condemned these behaviors in the light as sins unworthy of God's approval, yet in the dark, they revealed their true selves as selfish and wicked, like the devils they were. It was at that moment

I knew nothing good would come of my allowing them to manage my education. I was resigned to the belief that organized religion, Catholicism specifically, was a fraud. A practiced fallacy leveraged to control the masses, and I would no longer have any part of it. And don't get me started about their obsession with raping children. That's right, I said it. The Catholic church is a profiteering, organized criminal institution of child molesting and raping pedophiles.

At the end of my freshman year, I'd covertly connived my way out of Camden Catholic, unbeknownst to my mother. To his credit, during the previous year, Mr. Jacobs did spark my interest in reading. Reading initiated a mental exercise foreign to me until then, and my mother noticed. She brought home the book *Roots*, by Alex Haley, for me to read. Those 1,100-plus pages sparked an unrelenting inquisitiveness in me. I started questioning everything, especially human behavior.

After completing *Roots*, I read every book Malcolm X had written, starting with *The Autobiography of Malcolm X*. I became a mental revolutionary. I took the lessons he taught and started practicing civil disobedience whenever I experienced an injustice. Some battles I won and others not so much, but the lessons I learned from each experience opened my mind to a consciousness and knowledge of self I never knew existed. Then it came to me: the only way I could instigate my exit from the school.

I knew my mother would never willingly agree to transfer me to another school if I simply asked, especially while still getting good grades. She didn't care if I didn't like the school, the teachers, or the administration. She didn't care how many in-school suspensions I accumulated in the dean's office because I refused to assimilate to Camden Catholic culture, now that I was inspired by the intellectual, measured defiance Malcolm had taught me via his books and speeches. I had read too many similarities in his experiences that matched mine. I now had a blueprint for how to navigate America, and it was liberating.

She didn't care how many times she had to endure their

parent-teacher conferences, during which they attempted to shame and embarrass her for not being able to afford the embroidered sweaters with the school's name on them. They ridiculed her for not buying me the hard-bottom shoes they deemed appropriate instead of my bargain brand rubber-bottom shoes. She endured their socioeconomic criticism until her next paycheck, when she could afford to buy me the shoes and embroidered sweaters they deemed appropriate.

Personally, I wanted to wipe the school off the map of Cherry Hill, New Jersey, for disrespecting her.

Remember, the only times I habitually fought were in defense of my mother's honor.

I fought back the urge to share the humiliation with one of my more unscrupulous cousins who didn't give two fucks about life. A cousin who would *not* have hesitated a second to roll with me up to that school to wreak havoc had I confided in him how they'd treated the aunt he revered as a second mother. I entertained fleeting thoughts of slicing the dean's tires for summoning my mother to the school to endure the humiliation. Nah, fuck the tires. I should firebomb his whole luxury car with a Molotov cocktail. Why stop there? Torch the whole fucking school, dressed in all black to avoid detection, masked up to hide our faces from cameras, gloved up so there were no fingerprints, and on a weekend to ensure the school was empty. Yeah, that'll show 'em not to fuck with my mother. Yeah, I thought about it…very carefully.

Obviously, I didn't go through with it. The school still stands there today, unscathed. My mother didn't send me there to start a war. She showed me what grace looked like. She endured the conferences with humble dignity, knowing she was doing the best she could, and no embroidered sweater or hard-bottom shoes purchased in the *short term* would change the fact that I was there to take advantage of their academic rigors for my *long-term* advantage. She knew how to play the long game. One of the most important lessons I learned from her: patience.

Instead of violence, I separated myself from the school. During my freshman year's final exams, I purposely failed my language elective, French, so I'd guarantee receiving my first D for a final grade while passing all my other classes. I knew when my mother saw that grade, she wouldn't dispute my attending another school she didn't have to pay $2,500 a year for.

I would transfer to and eventually graduate from a STEM-focused high school of my own choosing, thus marking the second adult decision I made on my own without adult guidance. I never shared the hardships I experienced at Camden Catholic with my mother. I didn't even reveal that I wanted to transfer until after she saw my final grades and I slyly manipulated her into thinking it was the best option for me personally and her financially. I closed the deal with, "Mom, it doesn't make sense for you to waste your money on Ds, and I can get an education in exactly what I want to do for a living in Sicklerville Technology High School."

"You know what, that's a great idea," was her only response and the only time we discussed it. Reading her body language, though, I saw a slight hint of what could be interpreted as disappointment. She was proud when I'd been accepted to attend school at Camden Catholic. Entrance was not guaranteed. She had been so set on seeing her child walking across the stage of such a prestigious school instead of this school she'd never heard of, twenty minutes farther out of the way in the wooded sticks of South Jersey.

The other reason for her melancholy mood may have been her facing the reality that I was becoming a man and needed to learn how to make my own important decisions without her. That this was a time in life where a young man needed a father or father figure for guidance. It also ushered in a new realization that she could no longer protect me from a country that no longer viewed me as a child but instead as a man.

Her naturally coy and reserved instincts would not match up well when squaring up against men like the dean. Maybe she thought, had a man been by her side, the dean would not have taken so many liberties, subjecting her to those demoralizing conferences, because the very presence of a man by her side would have checked the dean's tone and choice of words.

My time at Camden Catholic was my introduction to facing worldly issues that were once masked due to my small-city, insular environment. Now, in high school, with life taking me to the world outside Camden, I'd have to navigate this world as it saw me now: a tall, deep-voiced Black man whose lack of smiling gave them an excuse to label me as angry, aggressive, or dangerous. I learned at an early age, even though I didn't know it at the time, that my interactions with White men would be complicated. That there would be times when my mother wouldn't be able to protect me from them, that there would be situations where only men could deal with other men. To the world, I was no longer a child. I was becoming an educated, well-read, and prideful man. By American standards, I was becoming a threat.

"Ms. Jackson!" the receptionist beckoned, announcing it was our turn to see the optometrist. This would be my first pair of glasses after a routine eye exam provided by St. Bartholomew the spring before my acceptance to Camden Catholic revealed I no longer had twenty-twenty vision in my left eye.

"Come on, Tarik. We're up," my mother advised. We both rose from the mismatching plastic waiting room chairs to meet the doctor who would be administering another eye exam in preparation of fitting me for my eyewear.

"Mom, I want those flip shades like Dwayne Wayne," I said, invoking the name of the main character of my favorite sitcom, *A Different World*. He was smart, a geek who bragged about having scored perfectly on his math SATs. He'd successfully wooed the prettiest girl at Hillman College, a fictious HBCU, and was studying engineering just like I wanted to do. He was the perfect representation of who I was and wanted to be in the future, in living color.

"We have to see if they have them first, but if they do, I'll get them for you," she reassured me with a smile.

"Okay, so we have you down for an eye exam and your first pair of glasses today?" the doctor asked, and my mother nodded in response.

"Well, let's get him up in the chair and see how his vision is." I hopped my lean, growing frame into the cushioned seat with a device in front of me I'd never seen before.

"Rest your chin there," he instructed, and I complied. "I'm going to change a few lenses in the device, and you just have to tell me if the letters on the wall are better or worse." In the excitement of it all, my attention was all over the place. My ADD was on tilt. The geek in me was enthralled by the sophisticated eye device I'd just rested my chin on. I wondered how it worked, how much it cost, if it was a computer or not. The doctor slowly moved the device in front of my face and closed the sides around my nose.

"Okay, we'll start with the right eye, and you tell me if words in front of you are better or worse. Okay, first lens. Better or worse?"

"Neither," I responded. The doctor flipped another lens in the device. The prescription in the lens became stronger, making everything blurry for my right eye.

"What about now? Better or worse?"

"Neither."

"Really? You sure? You can't see better or worse?"

"No."

"All right. Let's try one more." He flipped the lenses two more times, and the magnification was so bad I had to move my head from the device because it caused discomfort in my right eye.

"That's the strongest lens. You must be able to see better or worse now."

"Nope. It hurt my eye. I couldn't see any words at all."

"Wait, that doesn't make sense. I set the lens to the strongest magnification. If you couldn't see a difference, how did it hurt your eye? That means the strength of the lens is so strong it blurred your vision. So, yes or no? Did your sight *become* worse?" he asked with a perplexed look on his face.

"Oh, I thought you meant I had to look for the actual words 'better' or 'worse' through the lenses. The words on the wall never changed so I said no," I explained.

He looked at my mother and asked her, "Seriously, lady, how dumb is he?"

My mother froze in shock but failed to reprimand him. She failed to defend my misunderstanding his instructions. She failed to walk us out of the doctor's office she was set to spend her hard-earned money in. We didn't leave to find another optometrist who would show us the respect we deserved as customers of his medical practice.

"Ask him again. He just didn't understand what you meant," she politely replied, seated in her chair.

"Okay, I'm going to start over and this time when I change the lens, you tell me if the words on the wall appear to look clearer to you…or…more…blurry…to…you…okaaaay?" he exaggerated in an insulting tone. I shrank in the chair as his insult weighed even heavier on me. I looked at my mother once more, waiting for her to intervene. As a child taught to never talk back to let alone disrespect adults, my hands were tied, despite the accumulating pile of profanities I wanted to spew in his direction. Despite my wanting to spit in his face. Instead, my mother and I sat quietly enduring his demeaning eye exam, despite my dying inside.

"I understand," I responded in embarrassing compliance. When the exam had concluded, I jumped out of the chair, ready to leave immediately. But I couldn't; we still had to pick the frames the glasses would be placed in. He didn't even have the Dwayne Wayne flip glasses, so I couldn't even claim a moral victory for enduring the humiliation. I angrily chose the first frames I saw to expedite our exit. My mother paid the doctor for the visit, eye exam, and frames before thanking him before we left. I was ashamed for her and me as we exited his office.

"Why didn't you say anything when he called me dumb?" I asked, fighting the lump developing in my throat and the rage boiling in my veins.

Honor thy mother and thy father.

"You're right. I should have said something," she admitted and that was it. She didn't say another word while we continued our fifteen-minute walk home. I already knew she should have said something. My question centered on her thought process, her reasoning for not saying anything. I wanted an explanation, but I knew all along I wouldn't demand one, not from my mother. She didn't owe me that; she had given me life.

I was unsure what to even say to drive home my disappointment without using those exact words. My level of communication wasn't mature enough to articulate how I was feeling at that moment, the way I can now as an adult. I knew what the optometrist had said was wrong and disrespectful, but my mother had just taken it. Even worse, she'd just padded the pockets of the man who had insulted her only child. I knew from that point on, when it came to people in a perceived sense of authority, I'd have to protect and defend myself and her as well. My mother was too kindhearted, forgiving, and docile to defend me or herself when pitted against men. That day, I became the man of our house, and it was my job to protect us both from men like that, regardless of how I was raised.

That moment initiated my evolution in embracing being mean when matched against men—*especially* White men. I would never let my mother or me feel that way ever again.

part III
VIOLENCE & RACISM

chapter 18

Much like love, hate is an equally purposeful and powerful emotion. I don't use the term "hate" haphazardly, either. In fact, I use it rarely. As rarely as people claim to see aliens or Bigfoot.

With that said, I hate racists. I'm not talking about the willfully ignorant, unconsciously biased, culturally insensitive, or even brainwashed children raised in homes of hate, unbeknownst to them. I'm referring to the purposeful, inherently evil, morally corrupt, hate-embracing racists who sincerely believe another person is inferior simply because of their ethnicity or skin color. *Them!* I hate those people!

If I'm being honest, as I strive to be, I would be content spending the rest of my days on this earth exterminating them. I know that's dark, and some may even draw comparisons to Hitler's philosophy and approach toward the Jewish population in Europe. But I and any other human being with common sense would be able to dispel that notion as a false equivalency. Racists have proven themselves to be of no earthly good to humanity. Their extinction would be nature's perfect execution of Darwin's theory of natural selection. Nature's punishment in response to a pathetic subculture of human beings who refuse to evolve or are incapable of doing so.

Can you imagine a world devoid of racists? I can, especially considering the countless lives they've ruined. They didn't ruin my life, but they did soil my innocent perception of the world and its inhabitants when I was six years old.

"Mom, where are we going?" I asked as we jostled back and forth, side to side, balancing ourselves with only the help of the strategically placed metal bars of the SEPTA bus. It was almost noon on a perfect summer Saturday afternoon. By the time we'd reached our stop, it was standing room only. With every acceleration between stops and the wide turns around corners, she and I danced to the rhythm Philly's dilapidated streets and potholes dictated.

"South Philly, Tarik. One of my coworkers is selling me his car. So, we're headed over to where he lives so I can buy it," she answered. My eyes lit up with excitement and a smile enthusiastically graced my face, so bright I could feel my cheekbones accentuate.

"Yup, no more walking nine blocks to the grocery store and back," she said with matching exuberance. Moments later, we arrived at our stop. She paused for a moment and looked up at the surrounding street signs before grabbing my hand to lead us three blocks from the bus stop. I looked around, taking in a part of the city I'd never been to.

Despite that, I did recognize the youthful exuberance of neighborhood kids chasing each other. They swerved and hopped back and forth from the street and sidewalks, playing the familiar game of tag I played with my friends in my neighborhood. All the while, adults sat on their front porches or stoops, equally enjoying the sunny day and keeping a watchful eye on the kids. Before I realized it, my mother came to an abrupt stop at a house. I, not paying attention, crashed into her.

"Tarik," my mother said, and I instantly defused her would-be scolding stare with a giggle.

"Sorry, Mom."

"It's okay, just pay attention," she said, turning her gaze back to the house in front of us. Without hesitation, she ascended the four modest steps to ring the doorbell. We waited only a few seconds before we heard the doorknob turn and the door swung open. A round-bellied, average-sized man looked at my mom and then me before greeting us with a smile.

"Heeey, Sheila, how ya doing?" he said, coming down the steps to greet my mother.

"Hello, Stephano," she responded, giving him a one-arm, polite hug with a pat on the back.

"Come on now, we're not at work. It's Steph," he said taking a noticeable once-over of my mother before turning his attention to me.

"And this must be Terry," he said.

"Tarik," I politely corrected, snatching my hand from my mother and extending it for a handshake.

"I'm sorry, big guy, Ty-reek."

"Not Ty-reek. Ter-rick," I enunciated. "Put a *T* in front of *Eric*."

"Ahhh, got it! Tarik."

"Yup, that's it."

"That's a nice name ya muddah gave you." He turned his attention back to her again with flirtatious eyes and a grin. "You want to test drive the car again, or you ready to just buy it and get it over with?"

"I'm ready. Got the money in my purse," she said, looking over her shoulder at a green, two-door, Datsun hatchback. "That's the car right there, Tarik." She pointed behind me.

"You're it!" a kid from the group I saw earlier shouted before sprinting in the opposite direction. One of his friends, a chubby kid, tried his best to give chase but was obviously struggling.

"I haven't moved her since you drove her last, except to fill the tank up with gas so she's ready for you. Come on in and we'll get this done and you can be on your way with your new car. Well, new to you, but like we talked about before, she's in good condition. I take good care of all my cars. I change my own oil, rotate tires, tune-ups, brakes—I do it all," he reassured her, gesturing for her to come inside. She walked up the last two steps, crossing the threshold before realizing I wasn't following, as I was fixated on the kids playing. I had no interest in watching them do whatever adults did to buy or sell a car. It was a Saturday and I wanted to run circles around those kids like I did my friends at home.

"Come on, Tarik, you'll have plenty of time to play once we get home."

"If he wants to play while we finish out our business, he'll be fine for a few minutes. It's a safe neighborhood. We look out for one another around here," he reassured my mother before shouting down the street. "'Ey, Leo! Come 'ere, want you meet somebody!" He bellowed loud enough for the whole block to hear. Two of the kids came running down the street without question at full sprint. They were fast but not faster than me, from what I gauged. When they arrived at the stoop I looked up at my mother, giving her that familiar head-tilted look I routinely gave when I wasn't ready to come inside during the summer, begging for some grace.

They'll never catch me. Let me run circles around these kids.

"What's up, Uncle Steph?"

"This is Ms. Sheila, and this little guy is Ter-rick."

"Hello, Ms. Sheila, nice to meet you."

"Nice to meet you guys too," she responded.

"You said your name is Derrick?"

"No, Tarik," Steph corrected. "Put a *T* in front of *Eric*, ya numb-skull." Steph gave me a wink, instigating a smile from my mother. "His mom is buying my car, so he might as well hang out with you guys while we finish up."

"Hey, don't leave this block. Understand?" my mom directed.

"Come on, Tarik. My friends are waiting," Leo said, taking off down the block back toward his young crew of friends.

"Thanks, Mom!" I said before darting after Leo and his quiet friend. Only two steps behind the two, I gave them all a preview of what they had to deal with. I switched gears from a jog into a full sprint, splitting Leo and his friend, making a beeline to the reaming three. Halfway there, I looked over my shoulder back at the two and smirked.

Yeah, try to keep up.

"You're fast!" Leo said, feverishly pumping his arms, trying in vain to close the gap. I reached the other kids a second before Leo and his companion caught up with me. I extended my hand to Leo's three acquaintances, making use of the time while they caught up.

"I'm Tarik." The slow, chubby "it" kid from the game of tag I had just seen didn't reciprocate the gesture, leaving me there hanging.

"'Ey, Leo. Who's da new guy?" he questioned while also introducing me to what suspicion looked like before I even knew the meaning of the word. His body language evoked an unfamiliar emotion from me, one that was eerie and uncomfortable. I quietly tried to process his response because it was the opposite of all the social norms I'd been exposed to when greeting someone new. I'd experienced being the new kid on the block in Southwest Philly. I'd been the kid from a different state visiting my cousins in Jersey. I'd been taught the proper etiquette of greeting someone by my Catholic elementary school, but everything about this chubby kid didn't line up.

"This is Tarik. His mom is buying Uncle Steph's car. Did you see him? He's fast, isn't he?" Leo said, patting me once on the back and smiling. The "it" kid looked me up and down. Despite my social skills being bewildered, my instincts alerted me to something that was off.

"You're not moving here, are you?" the chubby "it" kid asked.

"No, I already live somewhere else," I responded, confused. I had no idea why that was even relevant. I just wanted to play tag.

"Good! Because Black people don't live around here," the chubby "it" kid declared. "Come on, y'all, let's go to my house." He motioned for the other two kids I hadn't met to follow. The quiet acquaintances of Leo quickly followed, leaving just me and Leo looking at each other. We both were trying to figure out what to say next.

"Come on, Leo. We're going to my house," the chubby "it" kid persisted.

"But what about—?"

"Come on, man, you know he can't come."

Leo looked over at me, uncomfortable and embarrassed, but the draw of pressure from his friends pulled him along into their orbit like a moon to a more powerful planet.

"Sorry, man. Your mom should be done soon, so maybe I'll see you around?" he said, extending his hand once more as we slapped five unceremoniously before he darted up the street to join his friends. I walked slowly back toward Stephano's house. Coincidentally, as I touched the first step, the door swung open.

"Oh hey, I was just about to come get you. You have fun?" she asked before she could recognize my mood was off.

Steph's flirtations injected themselves into the conversation again. "Enjoy the car, Sheila, and if you have any issue, just let me know and I can take care of it."

"Uh, sure. Thanks, Steph. I'll let you know," she responded cordially, not being a stranger to men's advances. She walked past me toward the car and unlocked the passenger door for me. Seconds later, she was seated on the driver's side next to me. She waved once more at Steph, who was standing in the doorway.

She placed the key in the ignition, stepped on the clutch, and reacquainted herself with the stick shift. I stared aimlessly out the window in front of me.

"First, second, third, fourth, and reverse…reverse…ugh…reverse. There it is," she said triumphantly. "Finding reverse is tricky." She finally noticed I was melancholy, considering the joyous occasion.

"You okay?"

"Yeah." I was unsure what else to say.

"No, you're not. What happened?" she demanded in a protective tone. "Tarik, tell me."

"Uhhh…" I paused before continuing. I was unsure how to explain what happened and how I was feeling. It was all so foreign to me, but I knew it didn't feel good. "Mom?" I questioned hesitantly.

"Yes, Tarik?"

"What's Black people?" I asked and my mother's posture shrank instantly. She looked sad. I don't ever remember seeing an expression of sadness on my mother's face before that day, and it burned an impression in my memory. I'd never forget it, like I'd never forget the chubby "it" kid and his mysterious dislike of me. My mother looked down the block in the direction Leo and I had run, only to find it empty. She then ducked her head to look out my passenger side window, seeing Steph still watching, smiling, gawking at us.

She shifted her gaze on the adults sitting on their porches and stoops. For the first time, I noticed they all had eyes on us. Her sad eyes became piercing. Her sadness morphed into anger. She took a noticeably deep breath; her chest rose and fell as she let out a deep sigh.

"I'll explain to you when we get home. First, let's get out of here," she said with a sense of urgency.

chapter 19

I'm of the latchkey generation. By the age of eight, I took the bus to school alone. I'm not talking about those safe, yellow, school-sanctioned buses. My school didn't have those. What I did have in Southwest Philly was the SEPTA G bus stop four blocks from my house on 58th and Willows Avenue. That's where I stood with other children, some with and some without their parents, rowdy high school teenagers and adults on their way to earn a fair day's wage.

Every day, I trekked the ten-minute walk from my front door to the bus stop, followed by thirty minutes on the bus until my stop at Fifty-Seventh and Media Street. From there, it was another six-block walk before I reached my Catholic elementary school, St. Rose of Lima in West Philly. On some days, I'd run into other classmates who also traveled alone on the bus, and we'd make the trek together, but there were plenty of days my education required me to navigate these streets alone.

"Fifty-Seventh and Walnut! Everybody off!"

"Fuck you talking 'bout? This ain't my stop!" a large passenger in stained maintenance overalls complained, startling me out of my inadvertent nap. I feverishly scanned my surroundings until my foggy mind cleared and I remembered I was still on the route to school. A line of passengers shuffled past me and off the bus.

"Sorry, folks, the bus is having mechanical problems. The next bus will arrive in ten to fifteen minutes," the driver announced, ignoring the cutting glances thrown at him just before passengers descended the steps leading to the filthy city curb. Sometimes life tests your mettle to gauge if you've been forged properly. To deem your place in nature's spectrum of natural selection. Beginning in kindergarten and ending at the conclusion of my promotion to the second grade, my mother and I took this bus route together. She kept me alert, making it a point to identify certain landmarks, occasionally warning me.

"I'm preparing you for the day you're going to have to do this without me," she'd remind me on days I'd forget to dictate, out loud, what street I should turn onto next between our bus stop and my Catholic school in West Philly. Her lessons were life lessons meant to complement the arithmetic, science, and English taught at St. Rose of Lima. The dos and don'ts that would determine my safe arrival home or not. The life lessons parents hope to burn into their children's subconscious like a scar from a branding iron. A permanent reminder they couldn't lose if they wanted to.

On this day, her preparations would be put to the test. Despite my experiences of bus drivers running late, never had I faced a bus breaking down from a mechanical failure. Additionally, never had I had to wait for a new bus at a stop I was unfamiliar with. My anxiety, beset by my upcoming ghetto pop quiz, must have been evident.

"Hey, don't worry, little man. Just wait right here with everyone else until another G bus comes. When it does, just hop back on, and it'll take you to the same stop you always get off on," the bus driver reassured me. "Just don't fall asleep again. The next bus driver might not wake you up like I do when you nod off. Okay?"

"Uhhh. Okay?" I responded timidly.

"You'll be okay," he assured me.

"Uh-huh, yeah. Got it."

The truth was, I wasn't sure if I had it. Not even close. The moment I stepped onto the curb, the bus driver closed the door behind me. The last thing I remembered of the bus was its hazard lights turning on before black smoke shot out its exhaust, choking the group of us jockeying for position on the curb for the next bus. When the smoke cleared, I watched the bus limp its way around the corner before parking itself to wait for repairs or a tow. The jockeying for position intensified. Even I knew the farther you fell back in the fray, the less likely you'd get a seat on the next bus, especially this deep into the route.

The busy intersection was overwhelming. Hundreds of people crossed in four different directions, knocking into friends and strangers alike. Other SEPTA buses, large delivery trucks, and cars leaned on their horns, urging pedestrians along so they wouldn't be caught by the pending light change.

"Move to the back, li'l nigga!" someone shouted from behind me. "This nigga think he slick. Trying to jump the line—I said move!" The shout became louder, more aggressive, but this time, I felt a yank on my book bag that almost toppled me over backwards.

"Get the fuck off me!" I shot back, not even aware of who my aggressor was. I leaned forward to counteract the force. I threw my left arm and small fist back wildly. My skinny, undeveloped arms didn't break the grasp of the teenager towering over me.

"Ohhh shit! Young bohl swung on you, Roc," another voice, Roc's friend, exaggerated. The truth was, I couldn't have sincerely swung on him if I tried. I was too short and my arms not long enough to even reach his face without jumping. Later in life, my growth spurt would kick in and my frame would top out at six feet three inches, but that wasn't helping me in the here and now. That day, I was underage and undersized.

My mother had convinced school administrators to accept my enrollment a year early, since my birthday was only three months after the start of the school year. She'd made an agreement with them that if I fell behind like they'd feared, they could always just have me repeat the year. The administrators accepted the agreement because repeating a grade equaled an extra year's tuition for the diocese of the parochial school. It was a win-win for the school and at worst, an educational day care for my mother, who would have to spend money regardless for someone to watch me while she was at work.

But that gamble meant that I would be less developed mentally and physiologically compared to my peers. Today, standing toe to toe with someone significantly older and meaner placed me at an even greater disadvantage.

"You trying to give me a fair one, li'l nigga!" Roc demanded between gritted teeth.

"I ain't scared of you, motherfucker!" I shot back, using the biggest curse word I could remember, projecting confidence to disguise and convince my trembling legs.

"This geeky muh-fuckah said motherfucker all proper and shit! That's how y'all cuss in Catholic school, you li'l bitch?"

"Suck my dick, bitch!" I shot back. Genuine anger revealed itself, seeing he was trying to punk me. I was only eight years old, but my pack had taught me better.

Never let anyone punk you.

Even in your own neighborhood, surrounded by familiarity, you were tested, sometimes by the same people you found protection with, your own friends. Ironically, and as twisted as it sounds, that's how some of us eventually became friends. You show up as the new kid in the neighborhood and they test you. You run or tell your mommy or daddy and you'll be running forever. A castaway and a neighborhood reject. Running guarantees your confinement to home obscurity your entire childhood.

But once you stand tall, face your fears, fight your aggressor, shed some blood, earn a scar or two, those same guys who tested you will eventually accept you as their friend. And you find yourself perpetuating that same violent cycle when it's your turn to haze the new kid on *your* block. I'll admit instigating a fight was never my jam. The one time I did start a fight, I lost, badly.

Before facing Roc on the corner of Fifty-Seventh and Walnut, I'd already fought enough times between my neighborhood and school that a dust-up wasn't anything to fear. My battle scar, on my right temple, from what fight? Only God knows. On my right thumb is another scar after cutting it on glass while breaking into a car. On the top of my right hand, two small scars from my fist greeting a foe's two front teeth with my fist. All of them, still visible to this day.

"Suck ya dick, huh?" Roc said, pushing me violently with all his might. I went falling back into another set of teenagers.

"Yo! Get the fuck up off me!" one of the teenagers yelled before grabbing a hold of my coat, tossing me back toward Roc and his crew. I regained my balance and footing during the shoving match and charged at Roc, jumping to launch myself into the air. With a little luck and the element of surprise on my side, I landed my undersized fist with Roc's left cheek. A modest smack sounded off when my knuckles met his larger face, barely moving him.

"Ooooh shit! Young bohl snuck you, Roc!" someone from Roc's crew with a thick scar across his face instigated as I stumbled back to the ground again. Roc grabbed one of the straps of my book bag with his left hand and reared back with a clenched right fist. I guarded the sides of my face between my two skinny arms, bracing myself for Roc's ill-intentioned blow.

"Don't hit that fucking kid!" a voice shouted out from behind Roc, grabbing his right arm before he could lean into delivering his blow. The large maintenance man from the bus grabbed Roc by his collar with one hand and grabbed me with the other, separating the two of us with his body.

"Let 'em fight, old head! Let 'em get that fair one!" the scar-faced instigator continued.

"He's a fucking kid! You bess leave him alone unless you wanna kick me a fair one," the maintenance man warned.

"Look at 'em, now. Nuffin' to say," another older man said, walking over to help the maintenance man squashing the fight. The new stranger stood between Roc and his friends while the maintenance man walked me away around the corner.

"You might want to wait for the bus after the one coming, young'n. We won't be able to keep these nut-ass kids off you after we get off the bus." The maintenance man released his grip from my book bag.

"I'll stand at the corner till the G bus comes to make sure they don't fuck with you while I'm here, but you better figure out whether you gonna wait for another bus or fight them once we get off. I can't miss work fuckin' round with you li'l niggas," the maintenance man said.

"I'll wait for the next one," I said.

"Okay, go that way and loop back around the block. We all should be on the bus and gone by then. A'ight?"

"Okay. Thank you," I said, knowing he'd saved me from getting jumped. He just shook his head and snickered.

"You welcome, young'n. You might wanna grow some more before you punch somebody bigger than you. You got lucky today," he said before returning to the corner of the bus stop, pointing, and shooing the teenagers back around the corner as they strained to see where I'd retreated to. I surveyed the rest of the intersection, not confident enough to walk around the long, dank corners I was a stranger to, but I had to. Staying put would only entice Roc and his crew to miss the bus on purpose just so they could jump me once the maintenance man and the other good Samaritans were gone.

I started walking down the street away from the bus stop. I didn't run. I didn't want to entice a chase from the crew of delinquents. My stride was just brisk enough to put a hurried distance between myself and Roc's crew. Plus, I was still adjusting to my West Philly surroundings. It might as well have been a whole new world compared to my Southwest Philly home. Everyone was a stranger, every corner and vagrant potentially dangerous. Once at the end of the block, I made a sharp right turn and continued my power walk past unfamiliar row houses, seeing groups of kids who may have been friends or foes. Adults shot me peculiar stares, not recognizing me as one of the familiar faces in the neighborhood, and my anxiety probably presented me as someone who was lost.

At the middle of the block, I saw an unusual break in the length of the street. The break revealed a side street and a one-story, long, rectangular building that suddenly sparked a memory.

I've been here before.

My pace increased and my eyes scrutinized the building. I crossed the street, jaywalking, dodging oncoming traffic in both directions, making my way to the corner where the building resided slightly up a hill. I reached two heavy, steel doors with matching metal caging covering the windows. Above the doors was a large sign with the name of the elementary school I'd just stumbled upon.

My memory jolted again, and a smile spread across my face. I pulled the handle of the metal door and it opened. More memories flashed in my mind.

Make a left, down the hall, I mouthed silently, traversing the empty, dimly lit hallway.

Now, right and look for the sign that says GUIDANCE COUNSELOR OFFICE.

Mrs. Fay.

Just like I saw in my head, the door was the first office after making the right at the end of the hall, but no lights were on inside and the door was shut. I perched myself up on the tips of my toes and peered through the glass window of the office door. Sunlight shone through the window, revealing the same office with a sofa and two chairs facing a metal desk with another cushioned chair behind the desk.

Mrs. Fay isn't here.

I pulled the door open to the cold, silent room, flipped the switch along the wall, and the buzzing sound of the office lights igniting could be heard before they illuminated the entire space.

I slung my book bag off my shoulders and hopped onto the middle cushion of the dated sofa. I let out a comfortable sigh as my feet dangled off the edge a foot above the linoleum floor. I glanced at the clock on the wall.

The little hand is at seven and the big hand at five, six, seven, eight: 7:08 a.m.

I did more math in my head.

That's another twenty-two minutes before my mom's friend gets here.

Like clockwork, at seven thirty, Mrs. Fay, one of my mother's best friends, pulled open her office door. She met eyes with me, comfortably seated with my hands folded like the nuns at my schooled trained us to do when not doing anything productive with our hands.

"Tarik? W-What are you doing here?" she asked in startled disbelief. "Where's your mother? Is everything okay? Why aren't you in school?"

"My bus broke down. I remembered my mom bringing me here a while back. Can you call her? She should be at work by now," I said calmly, almost nonchalant now that I was in the presence of someone familiar. Someone I trusted. She dashed over to her office phone, pulled her phone book out of her purse, and dialed my mother's number at work. While we waited for my mother to arrive, I filled her in on the remaining details of my eventful bus ride. An hour later, my mother burst through the door and hugged me hard. Her hair was out of place, and she was both flustered and happy at the same time.

"Oh my God, how did you remember me bringing you here? That was over a year ago."

"I don't know," I muttered, not realizing at the time how lucky I'd been to have my bus break down in one of the very few places I'd traveled with my mother outside my neighborhood. When I was older, and my mother and I recalled the day, she confessed how the event had shaken her. Unbeknownst to me, during that same timeframe, there were a few child abductions happening in Philadelphia. And that's how sometimes unforeseen circumstances could alter an adult's or child's life. Especially in a time that predated the internet and mobile phones.

Many circumstances lined up for me to make it home safely. But what if my bus driver hadn't cared enough to give me instructions to stick with the other passengers? What if that maintenance man had not stopped Roc's crew from jumping me? What if he'd told me to circle a different block to avoid their wrath? What if he or any other people in that four-block square had been predators and I'd been abducted? What if I'd found the closest pay phone and dialed 9-1-1 and the police decided my mother had made an error in judgment and placed me in custody of Child Protective Services? What if my mother didn't have me with her that day she visited Mrs. Fay and I wandered past the school? Sometimes life tests you; that day it tested me. And I passed.

chapter 20

Many may disagree with me here, but the discussion needs to be had. African-American collective culture, although not monolithic, must take a hard yet fair evaluation of our use of intimidation and violence as a tool for disciplining our children. We must ultimately decide if it truly renders the results we desire. It is my humble opinion that our leveraging of spanking, switches, extension cords, paddles, etc., to discipline our children is antiquated and unnecessarily brutal.

As a point of clarity, I am *not* grouping everyone who's used the spanking method into the category of child abusers. I also equally dispute that everyone who has been spanked has been abused. But that subset of "spankers" who employ methods like beatings with extension cords and then ordering their child to take a bath immediately after so the welts can burn and further torture the kid may need to seek therapy, because that shit right there is sadistic. You might as well tie them down and rub salt over their wounds.

For the record, I'd never been spanked with anything other than a belt, well, except that one time when a belt wasn't accessible, and my mother pulled her leather sandal from her foot and used that instead. What I am saying is, there are an overwhelming number of parents in households, both nuclear and single, who have successfully raised well-behaved, respectful, law-abiding contributors to society and humanity overall without the threat of violence and intimidation.

It is my belief that members of our community, specifically, have unknowingly adopted, normalized, and assimilated the violence we experienced during slavery in this country as a civilized method of discipline, when, in fact, it is not. It is my contention that the same way slave masters leveraged whippings, brutality, and torture to scare and intimidate our ancestors into obedience is comparable to how Christianity leverages the fear of hell to scare and intimidate Christians into obeying God's laws. And that is comparable to parents who leverage spankings and whippings to scare and intimidate their children into obedience.

Have I lost you? Hopefully not. Keep reading.

The use of violence in this country is ingrained in our culture. We're the only country to have dropped a nuclear bomb on another…twice! Our local law enforcement officers are trained to shoot to kill instead of the focus being de-escalation and using firearms as the absolute last resort. The Second Amendment makes it too easy for too many of our citizens—who are not responsible enough or mentally stable enough—to own weapons designed for battlefields. We have an epidemic of gun-related shootings and killings that have wandered from our streets and into our schools. Shrouded in all this violence, it's no wonder we have parents who think the most effective way to discipline children is to literally hit them.

Then we're surprised and want to raise holy hell when our child is hit by another child when they begin to attend school. We're even more surprised when those same children grow into adults who choose the most violent method available to them—murder—as a conflict resolution tool. What do we expect as a society? We've taught our children from the moment they had common sense that when their parents need to resolve a conflict with their own children, the solution is violence. So why would our children have a conscience about using violence to resolve conflict with strangers?

We African *Americans* have become so Americanized that we don't even question how we've adopted American violence into our own culture. In some cases, we instinctively rebel against the notion there is an alternative method of discipline. We are literally brainwashed when we are so set in our ways we can't even fathom considering an alternative to any process or methodology.

In my own personal experiences as a parent, I've spanked my son on his behind with my hand once and from that single experience, I saw genuine fear in his eyes—the level of fear I'd only witnessed from award-winning actors on television and movie screens. For two days after that, my son shied away from me, ultimately resulting in him crying at the sight of me because he associated me with violence and fear. It was at that point I decided that spanking my son to discipline him or to encourage obedience would no longer be an option. I began a search for alternate methods of discipline that didn't involve intimidation or violence.

Now, I realize in my community, the idea of placing a child in the corner or in time-out is often ridiculed. To put it frankly, we associate those forms of discipline, at least in the circles I've traveled in, as ineffective Caucasian methods of discipline. And if I'm being completely transparent, we African Americans stereotype Caucasian methods of discipline as the root for White children throwing embarrassing tantrums where they call their mothers bitches in public. We also quietly attribute Caucasian methods of discipline as factors in why mass shootings are perpetrated by predominately White males after their first real taste of the world not catering to their every whim and desire.

However, my personal experiences have led me to challenge these notions. Perpetuating the stereotype of time-outs being so-called "White disciplinary methods," can been seen in the same light as African Americans speaking "proper" English and enunciating being classified as "speaking White."

Once I began adopting a method of nonviolence to discipline my child, we never had another instance where I would witness fear from him when he was in my presence. His behavior also changed once the fear disappeared, further incentivizing my desire to continue using alternate methods to discipline him.

Twenty-three years later, as I write these words, my son is a college graduate, respectful, and has never had any encounters with law enforcement. He's never spoken disrespectfully to me, his mother, or any parents, teachers, or elders he's crossed paths with. He's the poster child for a well-behaved and disciplined young man—all achieved with him never having felt the lash of a belt.

I, on the contrary, have experienced being beaten with mostly belts, once with a flat leather sandal, and oh yeah, I forgot about my last whipping with a wire dry-cleaning hanger. The wire hanger beating was the moment my mother realized that beatings didn't work on me anymore because I'd built up a pain tolerance to the belt. I was in my sophomore or junior year of high school. Puberty had kicked in and one irritable morning, the baritone rumble of my voice betrayed me as I said something smart under my breath.

"Oh, you think you're grown!" she declared when she overheard what I thought was covert back talk. I knew a beating was soon to follow. After hearing her rifle through her closet for her weapon of choice, she charged toward me. I calmly put my book bag down on the floor next to me, placed my hands in my pockets, and stood defiantly face-to-face with her punishment. Armed with a dry-cleaning wire hanger, she beat me on the top of both my shoulders, alternating when she didn't receive the flinches and recoils from the blows she'd anticipated.

The silent whistle of steel cutting through the air competed with the soft chirps of the birds singing outside. I refused to display any fear or pain as the now-bent steel heated my welting skin, rivaling the warm comfort of the polo shirt I'd just pulled from the ironing board.

At the conclusion of eight or nine futile lashes, she relented, defeated.

"Now, go to school!" she yelled, and I complied. Not because of the beating but out of respect for her being my mother, providing for and loving me. I sighed, picked up my book bag from the hardwood floor of our home, threw it over one of my beaten shoulders, and calmly walked out the door like it was any other day.

For cinematic representation of my defiance, think of the Denzel Washington whipping scene in the movie *Glory*, minus the single tear he shed.

Like Denzel's character, I refused to surrender any satisfaction to the person flogging me, staring her in the eyes as Denzel did the sergeant who carried out his punishment for running off to look for a pair of shoes. Like Denzel, I wanted to silently stare her in the eye and let her know her punishment and her tool of choice were not justifiable for such a minor transgression.

When it was over, without a single word, I put my mother on notice that her choice to use a lazy and uninspired method of punishment didn't affect me any longer. That she would have to try harder to reach me in another way, like conversing and using her words, to communicate how what I did made her feel instead of being short tempered. I wanted her to know she didn't deserve a single tear or wince. But I couldn't express that same sentiment years earlier while on the receiving end of the worst beating I'd received from my mother.

"Tarik! Did you wash those dishes?" my mother yelled from her bedroom when I was about twelve or thirteen years old. I don't remember exactly when it was, to be honest; I just remember I wasn't in high school yet.

"Wha— Huh?" I responded, jolted out of my dream, still half asleep.

"I said, did you wash the dishes before you went to bed like I told you to do?" she repeated, now barreling down the hall toward my room before my eyes could adjust to the darkness. The door flung open. Light flooded my dilated pupils.

"If you can't remember doing them, that means you didn't do them. Now go downstairs and wash those dishes. I'm not going to tell you again!"

"Okay, I am," I responded in a sincere and remorseful tone, prompting her to walk her way back to her bedroom and back to bed. I slowly woke myself up, slid my feet into my slippers, and rose from the mattress that lay on top of the box spring, with only a wooden floor to serve as my bed frame. I lazily slid my feet across the wood floors, careful to grab the banister leading me down the stairs to the living room next to the kitchen, where that night's dinner dishes were waiting for me. I'd convinced my mother before she went to bed that I would let them soak for a while, so it'd be easier to hand wash them before I went to bed. My negotiation was successful, but my follow-through left much to be desired.

In hindsight, I probably figured I could wash them in the morning before school and she'd be content with my executive decision. Instead, all I accomplished that night was a display of overriding her better judgment. Once downstairs, I turned the switch for the lamp on one of the end tables to break the darkness of the living room. Still not fully awake, I stopped short of the kitchen and collapsed on the couch nearest the lamp. I prompted my head forward into the palms of both my hands, rubbing my eyes and yawning, trying to ignite the will to drag myself into the kitchen only a few steps away to finish a fifteen-to-twenty-minute task. Then it happened. I momentarily leaned back into the welcoming caress of the soft suede cushions, yawned once more before releasing an arm stretch, and that was the last thing I remembered before...

"*Tarik!*"

I shot awake from the sound of my mother's war cry to find myself still engulfed in the couch.

Oh shit! I fell asleep. Get up and wash the dishes before—

It was already too late. She hadn't called me from her bedroom. She was already perched at the top of the steps snarling at what looked like, from her perspective, my purposely being defiant of her orders. We made eye contact and before I could explain, she disappeared from the top of the steps. I could trace her steps through the hallway towards her room. I knew what was coming next.

"You want to go back to sleep, huh? I got something for you!" she threatened.

"I didn't mean to fall asleep. I'm doing the dishes right now," I confessed as I approached the foot of the stairs, but my pleading fell upon deaf ears. I could hear the metal buckles of the belts she hung in her closet clanking against each other, but she didn't come down immediately after the ruckus. Seconds later, I heard her testing three or four different belts—honestly, I lost count—against her mattress, trying to decipher which carried the most punishment. Finally satisfied with her choice, she stormed through the hall, down the steps, and made a beeline directly toward me.

"I didn't fall asleep on purpose," I pleaded again but it didn't matter. She had made her decision how this night would go.

"*Yes, ya did!*" were her last words before the sound of the thick, leather belt of her choosing repeatedly floated through the light cotton fabric of my pajamas. I screamed out in pain, instinctively trying to protect my thin body from the fury of her feeling disrespected and disobeyed. Now, I'm no stranger to this form of discipline. My family is Southern. Like go-pick-your-own-switch-from-the-bush outside Southern.

Now, in comparison to beatings some of my friends confessed, with extension cords, wooden spoons, and other sadistic methods I would define as child abuse, my beatings with a traditional belt were a blessing, despite it still hurting.

But this night, this beating was more ferocious, and the time lapse had an uncustomary duration. In short, mother had lost her temper, she was angry, and that anger translated through each lash of that belt. I remember worrying between the flashes of pain.

When is this shit going to end?

"*Move your hand!*" she continued, lash after lash, as she kept reeling back, enraged. My legs, my arms, my back, my butt, and my hands were trying to temporarily relieve my screaming body of the searing pain.

Stop already!

Then suddenly, my dog, Ranger, a Siberian husky-German shepherd mix, came darting down the stairs barking and startling my mother long enough for him to purposely place himself between me and her belt. And he didn't move. He stood there. He didn't growl at my mother. He didn't try biting her. Once in place, he never barked again. He just stood there protecting me.

"*Move, Ranger!*" my mother commanded while pulling at his collar. "Ranger! Basement!" she ordered, using the command we'd trained him to obey whenever we had visitors over. For the first time, he ignored the command. I slid to the floor with my welted back pressed against the wall and Ranger pressed against my chest, my arms wrapped around his torso. She pulled at his collar again. "Ranger! I said basement!" He stood his ground. I could hear his long nails dig into the wood floor, resisting the woman who paid for his food and provided his shelter.

Thank you, Ranger! Thank you! Thank you!

Then, Ranger's uncharacteristic display of defiance snapped my mother out of her rage. When I think back to that night, I can only surmise from what I now know about canines and their heightened senses. Ranger sensed the same thing I was painfully experiencing in real time. My mother had lost her temper and something bad was going to happen if he didn't intervene. Ranger would continue to live a full life and passed away not long after I left home for college. He was a great dog and the most loyal of companions.

Despite my familiarity with a belt, ninety-five percent of the time, I was a good kid who developed into a good adult. Much like my son, I probably could have gone through life without ever being spanked. The beatings I received were for mistakes or missteps I did make but my lesson on how to correct those mistakes could have easily been communicated through conversation or some she could have chosen some other method to communicate the lesson I needed to learn .

Instead of a weekend spent playing with my friends and running the streets, tasking me with cleaning the entire house on my own would have driven the point home. Taking my Nintendo or Sega video games away for an extended period would have worked. Not being allowed to participate in the next season's sport and watching my friends win another championship while I sat in the bleachers would have taught me the same valuable lesson.

As a community, we must practice removing the emotion from determining our method of disciplining our children when they're disobedient. I believe an overwhelming majority of children don't purposely defy their parents. We are simply developing vessels figuring out how to navigate life. And like any explorer, we're going to make wrong turns and bad decisions. It's the teachable moments spawned from these wrong turns and bad decisions that mold both child and adult into better human beings.

If any parent reading this has the courage to do so, sit your child down and literally ask them to describe what they're experiencing or feeling when you beat them. I promise you if you give them the safe space to sincerely do so, you'll be moved by their response. My mother and I never had this conversation. It just wasn't how we did things. However, if we did have it today, if she asked me to communicate to her my feelings or opinion on the beatings, I would say the following:

My overexposure to violence in the environment in which I grew up, in addition to the occasional beating I received, only resulted in making me more comfortable with experiencing and participating in violence. It's equally honest and disturbing for me to admit I'm okay with violence. It doesn't faze me. I'm not repulsed by it. If I see it, experience it, or participate in it, I shrug it off. It is what it is.

I've grown accustomed to it. I don't run from it. I'm not fearful of it. It's been normalized to me. Essentially, I've become Americanized, akin to a soldier charging the enemy on a battlefield after graduating basic training. I've been groomed to accept it as part of life, like a soldier has been trained to accept war. And I think we can all agree that's not a healthy existence for anyone or society.

The violence of being beaten or spanked only hardened me

emotionally. I don't cry; I only shed a tear under the most extreme of circumstances. I don't experience a certain range of emotions as I should. I know I carry the effects of being subjected to discipline that didn't match my "crime." That isn't a criticism of my mother—she is and always will be amazing. However, as human beings, we all must accept that part of the price we pay for this experience called life is our willingness to grow and evolve.

My mother's growth in this area just didn't mature evenly with her generation's progression in society. I didn't need beatings to turn out to be a good person. My community has assigned a false equivalency to children who turn out well in life to, "Oh, their parents must have beaten them. That's why they listen so well." No, these *good* kids are just *inherently good* and obedient. They've developed a respect for their parents before ever seeing the belt. If anything, you're reversing the instinctual respect they already have for you when you beat them.

My mother was just repeating the traditions practiced on her, like her mother before her, etc., etc. I get that—that lesson isn't lost on me. My sole motivation in sharing these two specific instances of excessive punishment is to challenge the traditions we've adopted and carried over from our darkest of days in this country. We must objectively consider relegating these barbaric and sadistic methods of discipline we've unknowingly assimilated into our culture during our oppression. They're antiquated and unnecessary.

And this is for the fathers who may be potentially spanking their daughters: I hope to God you aren't. You must seriously consider the message you're sending to the young ladies you're helping develop. We all have heard or know the age-old adage, a father is their daughter's first love. Their relationship with their father is their first exposure to how a man should treat them. That's why we see campaigns encouraging fathers to take their daughters on dates, opening doors for them, etc. Fathers have the responsibility of demonstrating to their daughters how men should treat them. Right?

Well, here's something to ponder. For all these great fathers who take their daughters on dates, open doors for them, in addition to all the other chivalrous acts of love, consider what these little girls, these young women, all these daddy's girls psychologically experience or are learning when their first love spanks them or uses intimidation or perceived violence to discipline them. Have you considered that you're unintentionally teaching your daughters that a man can simultaneously love them and beat them? Have you thought about how you're prepping and grooming your daughters to accept domestic violence in their future relationships?

Think about it. If these young women arrive at a psychological state of mind and reasoning where they can accept that their own father, their daddy, their first love, can love, protect, *and* hit them, then they will eventually subconsciously rationalize that being slapped, smacked, hit with objects by the man they choose as a boyfriend or husband is also okay. We've seen enough movies and Lifetime shows where the woman being abused retorts robotically, "I know he hits me, but he loves me." Some of our daughters are learning that conditioned response from their fathers first.

Human beings are programmed to evolve. We find and invent better ways of accomplishing tasks. Just look at the quantum leaps we've taken in technology and how it has affected the behavior and culture of an entire generation through social media apps. We must apply the same creative genius and innovation to not only technology but also our way of thinking and how we resolve disciplinary issues and conflict overall. We're at a point in human evolution where leveraging fear of the lash as a primary method of developing our children into responsible contributors to society. The steps I've taken to break that cycle of violent discipline and their results are evident in the good person my son is. The shit works.

chapter 21

My senior year in high school, I would encounter my second round of blatant, in-your-face racism by students and school administrators alike. But unlike my previous experiences, where I employed the Christian brainwashing of turning the other cheek and retreating, I'd engage my oppressor head on. My first of these two encounters would be with what I'd thought was a friend. I don't use that term loosely, either. I'd always been purposeful about whom I let in my orbit, and Travis (not his real name), despite being White, had earned his way into not just mine but other Black students' circles.

The school where I chose to finish my high school education, Sicklerville Technical High School, was the opposite of Camden Catholic, except for their both being predominately White. However, where Camden Catholic had developed a long reputation of academic excellence and white-collar affluence, Sicklerville Technical High School's White student body weren't the beneficiaries of privilege and wealth. They were the offspring of blue-collar parents who either specialized in the trades of construction, plumbing, and electrical work or were the socioeconomic equivalent of my city's poverty stricken. In short, many of the Caucasian students at my school were considered "poor White trash" by their ethnic counterparts from Cherry Hill.

Travis was no exception. In fact, he was one of the few who were obviously poor—and worse, he was so poor not even the poor White kids were his friends. My sophomore year in high school, before the home room bell and during lunch, students would congregate in the front of the school where the basketball courts were to play three-on-three games of pickup. Sean was tall, about my height at six-feet-two, but not athletic at all. A group of my friends from Camden noticed him standing beneath the basketball courts one morning by himself, not talking to anyone. You know, that look of a lonely kid, devoid of social skills. One where if you didn't approach him first, he'd sit there quietly in the background? That was Travis. We did notice his height and he had some weight on him, so that morning, when we were missing one of our usual teammates, we picked Sean to even out our numbers. We figured he could at least play defense and rebound if he couldn't dribble or shoot.

Sean had us all fooled. He couldn't jump, so he was outrebounded by everyone. He had heavy legs and zero lateral movement, so he was also a defensive liability. Then on those rare moments where he was left open to shoot, forget him even coming close to making a shot. He would shoot the ball so hard we joked about checking the metal backboards for dents. For those not paying attention, with their backs to the game, they were startled by the booming collision, wondering if the backboard was about to come crashing down on top of them. This is not an attempt at humor or my being facetious; he really was that bad. Sean was a good sport about the playful ridicule that's customary in our culture.

"What's your name again, man?" one of my friends asked Travis after we'd lost the game. Once the opposing team realized he couldn't shoot, they left him unguarded the rest of the game. That meant they could double-team whichever remaining two of us got the ball.

"Travis," he said, not volunteering any information except what was asked of him. My friends and I instantly began sizing him up, gauging if his short responses were a result of him being intimidated by Black people or if he was just shy or soft-spoken.

"Man, you shoot like you've never played before. What were you, nervous?" my other friend asked.

"No. You're right though, I don't play that much," he responded, his face slowly flushing red in embarrassment.

"Damn, all that height and never considered picking up a basketball. You had us fooled. We won't be picking your ass again," another joked just as the homeroom bell sounded. We headed to the sidelines, picked up our book bags, and moved toward the door like we always did. Only this time, Travis followed slowly from a distance. Not exactly with us but keeping in proximity, almost hoping someone would continue the conversation, even if it meant him taking a few more insults on the chin. At least someone was talking to him.

Over the next couple of weeks, Travis would post himself beneath the basketball court where we'd play, and he occasionally got picked by other teams who made the same mistake as us and figured his height would be an asset. He couldn't dribble so he relegated himself to the outside and shot his set jump shot that would make his big belly pop out from under the shirt that was obviously a size too small for him. After a couple of weeks, I realized he wore the same pants and would rotate through a carousel of four or five shirts that were always clean but not all that memorable. Travis was no-name-brand-white-sneakers type of poor. Complete with a kitchen-haircut-done-by-one-of-his-parents type of poor.

By the end of the first marking period, he was hanging with us. He was cool, never said anything off-color, was a genuinely a nice kid, and after a few months playing with us every morning, he developed a respectable jump shot and would occasionally grab a rebound or two, so he wasn't a liability when we played anymore. At one point, he even tried out for the basketball team with me but got cut and never tried out again. Based on how much he developed in that short period of time, I guess he was content with being good enough to be picked up for three-on-three with the Black kids in the morning or during gym class.

Travis would stay in our circle of friends as one of the rare White guys who hung out with us and joked around with us in class, until his senior year. By then, his confidence had grown and he became more sociable. His friend group expanded, and he'd even developed some new friends who were White and from the same city he lived in. The kids he was hanging around with weren't the type who mixed with Black kids, though.

This new group wore Metallica and Harley Davidson T-shirts and we city kids knew they weren't too fond of us. Truth is, we weren't fond of them, either. We knew their type. They were mullet and tight jeans-wearing kids who chain smoked Marlboros. They knew better than to call someone a nigger to their face, but we knew they said it amongst themselves when they were in their own safe spaces.

Travis and I coincidentally shared the same major in high school. For three periods at the end of the day, after taking our typical courses of math, science, English, and an elective, we spent three periods learning the intricacies of computerized electrical technology, or CET. There was a morning three-period class and an afternoon three-period class. I was the top-ranked student in my afternoon class while some other kid was top ranked in the morning class.

My teacher, Mr. Johnson, much to my surprise, wasn't shy about encouraging me in front of my coaches and mother to be an electrical engineer once I graduated. It was in his classes those three years where I got my first lesson about the intricacies of White friendships. Specifically, when some Caucasians assume a level of perceived comfort where they believe it impossible for them to be racist or bigoted simply because they have one or two legitimate Black friends.

"Hey, Tarik, want to hear a joke?" Travis asked me one day while I was busy completing a class assignment, not paying him full attention. Had I been more aware, I would have noticed he'd asked me after congregating with his newly acquired group of mullet and Metallica T-shirt-wearing White friends who were off in the corner of the classroom laughing obnoxiously.

"Sure, go ahead," I responded, putting the finishing touches on an electrical wiring diagram I needed to finish before class ended.

"What's long and black?" he asked.

"I don't know, what?" I said dismissively.

"The welfare and unemployment line," he concluded as he and his group of friends exploded with laughter. My brow furrowed, I dropped my pencil, and my fist clenched as I turned to find Travis. I saw red and power-walked at him.

"Fuck you say?" I could feel a throbbing heat in the cartilage of my ears as I closed in on him. The smile fell from his face, but the group behind him, whom I surmised had coaxed him into spewing the insult, laughed even harder with sinister eyes.

"Why do White boys get black eyes?" I shot back at Travis, now only twenty, nineteen, seventeen, thirteen feet away. "For saying dumb shit like that."

Eight, five, zero feet.

I reared my right hand back, and just before I could let it fly forward, Damien, my basketball teammate, grabbed it from behind. Travis lurched back in shock, seeing Damien had stopped me from making him the literal punchline of my improvised joke. Mr. Johnson wasn't in that day, so instead, our substitute teacher shot out of Mr. Johnson's office.

"Stop it! Stop it now," she yelled, but was hesitant to fully confront me, seeing me enraged. "You! Go to the dean's office! Now!"

"Why am I going? He's the one telling racist jokes! Tell him to go to the dean's office," I shot back while my teammate, who had by now wrapped his arms around me, was pulling me in the opposite direction of Travis.

"It was just a joke, Tarik," Travis announced sincerely. He was honestly in disbelief that I'd tried to hit him. "You know I didn't mean anything by it. It's just a joke."

"Fuck you! I'ma beat yo azz when Damien lets me go!" I threatened.

"That's it! Go to the dean's office or I'm calling security!" the substitute teacher yelled.

"Come on, Tarik! They'll call the cops on you," Damien said, trying to protect me. The substitute and I locked eyes. I saw fear in her. The type of fear I'd only seen on television when White women suddenly grow uncomfortable in the presence of Black men despite there being nothing to fear.

Don't do it, Tarik! They won't let you graduate!

For a moment, I thought the words that were my better judgment guiding me were Damien talking in my ear, but when I snapped my head around, he was silently yelling a warning at Travis.

"Don't come over here, Travis!"

Go to the dean's office. Be smart. Let him hear your version first.

The substitute turned quickly and headed back into her office and grabbed for the phone.

"All right! Get off me, Damien. I'm leaving!" I shouted.

"Don't play!" He shot back with a tilted head, nonverbally warning me not to bolt at Travis the moment he let me go.

"I said all right. Now, let me go, got damn it!" I assured him through pursed lips and still-clenched fists.

"Ms. Substitute or whatever your name is, he's going to the dean's office now. No need to call anyone. I'll walk him down." The substitute, still holding the receiver of the phone in her hand, pointed it toward the door. There was a noticeable trembling. I turned and looked one last time at Travis and silently mouthed the enunciated sentence, "I'ma fuck…you…up!" before I stormed out with Damien close behind.

Moments later, I told the dean what happened, and Damien and the substitute teacher corroborated my version. Travis would be suspended for a week, excommunicated from my group of friends and all the other Black students he'd developed associations with once word got around about what happened. For the rest of our senior year, he was reassigned to the morning CET classes while I remained in the afternoon session to keep us separated.

Now traveling in different circles, Travis and I didn't cross paths again until graduation. On the day of our graduation, classmates took our last personal photos with each other before we would all go our separate ways. Some to college, others to the military, and some directly into trade work and hopefully a union. Right before I headed over to meet my family, Travis called out to me.

"Tarik!" I recognized his voice, and the joy of finally being finished must have been pulling at my heartstrings to make me turn around and acknowledge him.

"What!" I shot back.

"I'm really sorry, man, for what I said," he said sincerely. Even to this day, I admit I could see he was truly remorseful. My heart softened slightly, despite my common sense advising me otherwise.

"What's done is done. We're graduating now," I replied.

"I didn't think you would take it that way. You know that, right? Or else I wouldn't have said it."

"But you did. And the fucked-up part is you didn't even have friends until you met us. Where were those muh-fuckas you were telling racist jokes with when you were standing by yourself alone sophomore year? Junior year!"

"You're right," he admitted. "But I got suspended. Doesn't that make us even?" He extended his hand for a handshake.

"Nah, we're never going to be even. Ever!" I said, turning my back to him and heading toward my family. I locked eyes with my kin. Some had already picked up on the tension between us.

"Come on, Tarik. I made a mistake," he pleaded, running up behind me, lightly grabbing my shoulder and refusing to concede our friendship had died the moment he delivered the punchline of his joke. One of my cousins' eyebrows raised and he began walking toward me with a heightened sense of aggression. I knocked Travis' hand off my shoulder and looked him up and down, sizing him up, posturing so he'd know he was now in danger.

I turned my head to look back at my kin who were en route, my mother grabbing at one of them in futility. Her fingers closed, grabbing nothing but air.

"Cousin, you a'ight?" he shouted, his gait quickened, his fists balled to the size of mine if I were holding a softball in each hand. I nodded my head and waved him off.

"Yea! I'm straight!" I announced, tempering him momentarily. He slowed and came to a rest after a few more steps, scowling past me, shooting laser stares that burned through Travis. They held their ground as I asked but didn't retreat one step. I turned back to Travis.

"Yeah, you fucked up," I acknowledged. "My conscience is clear. You're the one who has to live with what he did. Now get the fuck outta here before you wake up in a hospital." I turned my back on Travis for the last time. He heeded my warning and didn't follow, not a single step.

"Tarik! I'm sorry, man. I really am," he said once more as I threw my arms around my two oversize cousins and led them away from Travis, back toward our family. I never acknowledged Travis' final plea and I never saw or heard from him again. And I was perfectly okay with that.

chapter 22

Now that I'm an adult, I have a firm grasp on certain intricacies of life. I can understand and even empathize with the compulsions, biases, and tendencies of human nature. I can come to some educated conclusions about why we human beings treat each other so badly. What I mean by this is, looking back on my time at Camden Catholic, communing with children who come from extraordinarily privileged backgrounds, I can surmise, even if I don't agree with, how they've come to behave and think the way they do. In the same capacity, I can comprehend how the people I most identify with in my community have come to practice some of our cultural, nature-versus-nurture behaviors.

I can logically surmise why my White peers, despite not truly knowing me outside of the name I was given and my zip code, can so easily fix their mouths to call me a racial slur. I can surmise that anyone who does such a thing, or even worse, attempts to justify why, has had limited exposure and experiences with people who do not look like them or share the same culture as them. In addition, there is a high probability that someone influential in their lives planted the seeds of bigotry, discrimination, and non-inclusion to carefully mold an ignorant perception of people who don't look like them.

I can also surmise the twisted and misguided logic my former high school friend Travis exhibited when he figured I would harmlessly receive his racist joke as jest. That somehow, after three years of demonstrating through his friendship that he was not a bigot, his words were not a fair and clear representation of his true feelings and moral fabric. That his truth was he housed no ill will toward me, my friends, and my community, the community that embraced him during high school before his own did.

It wasn't until Travis' own community saw him develop friendships with those they saw only as their enemy did they decide to wrap their arms around him in lukewarm friendship. The idea of one of their own assimilating or befriending a culture outside of theirs unnerved them. That perception of one of their own realizing we are not the threat they believed us to be was the catalyst for their desperate effort to reinforce the negative stereotypes they'd been taught and to bring Travis back into their fold of White superiority. Even if that meant embracing Travis under false pretense and disingenuous friendship on their part.

At my very core, I believe Travis was a good person despite making an egregious mistake. For that mistake, I punished him with excommunication and deservingly so. One thing I do regret is not knowing whether he learned from my turning my back on him or if he fell further into the cesspool of hate his newfound friends were cultivating for him. I sincerely hope his fate is the former and not the latter. I hope he evolved into a man who would ensure his family and children would not grow to be replicas of the boys who encouraged him to ruin our friendship.

Some I've shared this story with believed that I should have forgiven Travis, turned the other cheek, and continued to cultivate our friendship. I see their point of view, but I respectfully disagree. My reasoning? Frankly, bigotry and racism are problems of the bigot and racist. It will never be the responsibility of the oppressed to change the hearts of the wicked. The wicked must choose to evolve with humanity or be left behind, whether that be by humanity making a conscious effort to excommunicate them, as I did Travis, or their wicked ways ultimately being the catalyst to their eventual extinction.

As a society, we must confront the many ways we're cultivating another generation of willfully ignorant and sinister supremacists. Supremacists who will take on professions such as high school guidance counselors, like mine, who "advised" me to be a teacher rather than an engineer, despite the promise I showed in technology. Had I not chosen to ignore my guidance counselor and revere the advice of my instructor, Mr. Johnson, I may not have decided to major in Electrical Engineering and ultimately Information Science & Systems when I matriculated into undergraduate study.

It's easy to surmise how my high school guidance counselor was nothing more than my mother's generation of the bigoted kids, like those who wrapped their arms around Travis in faux friendship because they had more sinister motivations of undermining goodness. Comparatively, I can surmise my instructor, Mr. Johnson, who was a tattooed Harley Davidson biker raised in the same environment as Travis, chose a different path of acceptance and inclusion. Hopefully, the consequences of losing a friend led Travis down the same road as Mr. Johnson. Ultimately, I just hope he didn't become the contemporary version of my senior year physics teacher, because if he has degenerated into a Gen X version of, we'll call him, Mr. Asshole, then I was right to shun Travis and he will forever be my enemy.

Now, about Mr. Asshole. He was my physics teacher my senior year, and unfortunately, he and I were destined to butt heads over his racist comments.

"Okay class, you have fifteen minutes to complete your velocity experiments before the bell rings. When you're done, just place your exercise sheets on my desk before you leave," my physics teacher said, finishing his lesson on the board. Math, science, and any class with the word "computer" in it always kept my attention. Critical thinking and, specifically, problem solving always intrigued me. My friends knew this, so whenever they needed help, I rarely said no, and this day would be no exception. My friend Desso and I made sure we sat at the same lab table in our physics class. In total, the large table with sinks could accommodate six students, three on each side. He and I were two of the three African-American students in the class, with our senior class valedictorian being the third.

"Hey, did you follow all that?" Desso asked.

"Yeah, what's up?" I asked, already knowing the answer but not wanting to hurt his pride by being presumptuous.

"I got most of it but that last part lost me," he said.

"I didn't understand any of it," another student from the neighboring table whispered to both of us before raising his hand to get the teacher's attention.

"Mr. Asshole, I didn't understand any of that. Can you explain it one more time?"

"Yeah! Me either. Can you go over the example one more time?" another student requested from the table where our valedictorian sat.

"Okay, but if you don't finish the exercise, you'll have to take it home, in addition to the homework I already assigned," Mr. Asshole said before turning toward the blackboard to repeat his lesson. I moved my chair closer to Desso so he could show me what part lost him.

"Hey! Tarik! Desso! You two better pay attention. I'm only going over this one more time," he directed. We both knew the drill. Just look up and look engaged for the first twenty to thirty seconds until he falls in love with his voice, then Desso would have my full attention again.

Desso's chair was in front of me, so when the time elapsed, I tapped him on the back.

"All right, show me where it stopped making sense for you," I whispered to Desso. He turned toward the table and pointed to his worksheet and where his calculations ended. I looked over his numbers and compared them to the formulas in my notes and nodded my head in acknowledgment.

"I see what happened. You skipped a part. First, you gotta calculate average velocity. Then, find the values that represent displacement and then divide that by the change in time."

Desso tilted his head.

"Basically, how much time has passed. For example, how many minutes will pass between now and the end of class?"

"Oh, okay! Why he ain't just say that!" Desso said a little too loudly. Mr. Asshole whipped his head around and peered at Desso.

"Oh! You think just because you're Black you don't have to pay attention?" Mr. Asshole scolded loud enough for the entire class to hear. Embarrassed, Desso bowed his head to avoid eye contact with our classmates. A mixture of snickers, gasps, and laughter followed. I peered angrily at my classmates, not finding any of it funny.

This wasn't the first time he'd uttered those exact words to Desso under similar circumstances. Desso didn't say anything back then, either. I wanted to curse Mr. Asshole out, throw a chair at him, anything that would deliver the message.

I don't give a fuck if you're a teacher. I'll beat the shit outta you!

I had warned Desso when it first happened that if he didn't say something to defend himself, it was sending a message to Mr. Asshole that it was okay for him to say it again. Silence equals compliance. Desso hadn't wanted to draw any more attention to himself, so I didn't respond, either, out of respect for him. Now, just over a month later, just like I predicted, Desso's silence only emboldened Mr. Asshole to spout his bigoted views at my friend again. I looked at Desso and silently mouthed, "I told you."

"You hear me talking to you? You think you don't have to listen to me and my lessons just because you're Black?" he repeated, and I snapped.

"Who da fuck you think you talkin' to!" I shouted at him, standing from the metal stool, broadening my shoulders and staring Mr. Asshole directly in the eye, letting him know I wasn't intimidated by his title and I was bigger and stronger than him.

"Don't you—"

"Shut the fuck up!" I shouted, cutting off any chance of him regaining control. This was my class now and I had a lesson to deliver. "You think I won't kick your ass just because you're a teacher? Disrespect me and my friend again and I will fuck…you…up!" I threatened. My classmates' eyes lit up while some jaws dropped.

"Us being Black has nothing to do with your lame-ass lesson. If you were a better teacher, I wouldn't have to reexplain to Desso what you just taught to the class." The class erupted in laughter. I was always the quiet, laid-back, and studious kid, so hearing me lash out in this tirade shocked them all. I'd had enough of Mr. Asshole, Travis' joke earlier that year, the LAPD who'd just been exposed for beating Rodney King, my guidance counselor's attempt at steering me away from engineering, the dean from Camden Catholic, the asshole who called me a nigger two weeks into Camden Catholic, the chubby "it" kid from South Philly, all of it.

"Get out of my class! Now!" Mr. Asshole demanded, face bright red from both embarrassment and rage.

"Come make me get out, *bitch*!" I defiantly dared. The rage in me poked at his manhood, hoping to instigate him to engage. I'd never liked him. It was no secret that he had a reputation for being an asshole to minority students; even my history teachers had warned me about him. "Whatchu waiting for? Kick me out, you *pussy*!" I challenged again.

"Ooooooh!" a growing section of the class jeered and instigated. Mr. Asshole looked around, unsure of what to do, seeing he'd lost control of his classroom.

"Yeah, that's what I thought," I said, grabbing my book bag and throwing my books inside. I looked over at Desso. He was in as much shock as the rest of the class.

"You a'ight?" I asked. He quickly nodded his head twice with raised eyebrows and a slight smirk. I zipped up my book bag and threw it over my shoulder before locking eyes with Mr. Asshole punching numbers on the wall-mounted phone in front of the class next to the blackboard.

"Tell the dean I'm on my way," I said, slowly heading for the door past the rest of the students, this time locking eyes with our Black valedictorian. I had no words for her, but I wasn't surprised. She mostly hung with White students rather than those who looked like her. I shook my head at her silence. She broke eye contact and put her head down.

"Hello! Dean—"

"Tell the dean I said Mr. Asshole can suck my dick for being a bigot!" I said, ceremoniously exiting the door to the roar of my classmates.

"*Oooooohhhhh!*"

I spent the next period in the dean's office explaining what happened and what sparked my outburst. This would be my third trip to his office that year. The last time was due to the incident that stemmed from Travis' racist joke. The one before that was after a school administrator claimed I tried to "incite a riot" after he tried illegally searching my friend's book bag, claiming he had drugs on him. I told everyone in earshot that this administrator was not the police or any form of law enforcement and had no right to search his personal property. Honestly, at the time, I didn't know if what I said was right or not, but I said it with such confidence it sounded like I knew what I was talking about.

And now my third visit, all in my senior year, would be in retaliation for another racist incident. I'd learned my lesson about being passive in the face of racism and bigotry at Camden Catholic, and I wasn't going to let it happen again at this school. The lessons I'd absorbed reading more literature authored by revolutionaries like Huey Newton and Fred Hampton had armed me with not only knowledge but also the strategies of fighting back intelligently while also shielding myself from the potential fallout.

I intentionally wore outward signs of my inner grace via revolutionary Black power and Malcolm X T-shirts. My basketball strength and conditioning coach, Coach Mitchell, invited me to join an extracurricular group at the school called the Self Awareness Group. Its mission was to teach young Black men at the school about our true history before the American education system whitewashed it to make us believe we had no history outside of being freed slaves.

Our educational system and country acts as if we should be

grateful—we're free now—instead of being strategically resentful or even vengeful for the centuries we'd been held in captivity like zoo animals. Appreciative that no one is punishing us with lashes across our backs much like orca whales who are starved into performing the tricks patrons pay to see for their entertainment. Rewarded with the basic necessities of life, like food, once they or we finally comply to subservience.

The Self Awareness Group taught us of our shared collective history of scholastic, cultural, and military achievement dating back to our roots in Africa. They sponsored a field trip to see Spike Lee's new movie *Malcolm X*, starring Denzel Washington, that was released the same year.

The lessons I learned from Coach Mitchell's Self Awareness Group, in addition to the books I read to educate myself about my celebrated African lineage, were instrumental in my successful navigation of bigotry and racism I experienced post-Camden Catholic.

All three instances where I confronted bigotry and racism head-on resulted in my perpetrators being disciplined. I never received a single disciplinary consequence. Instead, in each instance, the dean instructed both my perpetrators to apologize to me—in private, of course—and remember, Travis was suspended from school for a week. I'd be lying if I said I didn't revel in those moments of triumph. I was slowly learning the rules of the game. A game my oppressors created, and I was now beating them with it. It was my first taste of speaking truth to power, and I savored every morsel of those meals.

chapter 23

The Transatlantic Middle Passage was the launching pad that condemned a people who would later identify themselves as African Americans to four centuries of forced, unpaid manual labor, otherwise known as slavery. At the conclusion of slavery, American culture seamlessly rolled into another century of law-enforced and sustained oppression via segregation, Southern Jim Crow laws, and deliberate, targeted incarceration. At the conclusion of Jim Crow and the passing of the Civil Rights Act, my people thrived for the following twenty years. We thrived because there were finally no *legal* barriers to outright deny African-American progress. In response to our upward trend, American culture contrived another calculated plot to stunt our progress and return my community to bondage.

Historically, every generation of my people has had their battles to fight and overcome. My family's story began with my paternal and maternal lineage being kidnapped from Nigeria and the Bioko Island, west of the Equatorial Guinea coast, respectively. Their offspring were forced into a brutish and deliberate system of slavery, predominantly in the Carolinas. Their offspring would endure Jim Crow laws and the Ku Klux Klan before eventually fleeing the South and settling in Philadelphia and New Jersey.

My generation, Generation X, has at times been critiqued by its predecessors as surfing through life haphazardly. We've been charged with reaping the benefits and sacrifices of the Baby Boomers who endured the Civil Rights struggle. They attribute our thriving to the pavement they laid. They are correct; my generation has experienced an existence of minimal resistance, in comparison to the Boomers, because of their sacrifices.

Another stark criticism for what Baby Boomers describe as a lackadaisical approach to life is that my generation never had our own war to fight that equally paralleled our predecessors'. Coincidentally, my generation similarly criticizes Generation Z and the Millennials. We've equally labeled them as lazy, self-entitled, and hypersensitive. I'm admittedly guilty of such criticism and I've struggled to reconcile that I have been unjustifiably judgmental of the generations following mine.

It is now my contention that each generation will have its criticisms of those who come after them because our experiences seem mutually exclusive. Wars, much like culture, adapt to their adversaries. For instance, those who stand firm in the belief my generation is lackadaisical or underachieving because we had no war to fight are mistaken. As in any war, where the unrighteous instigators of a conflict find themselves losing momentum and coming face-to-face with a pending, unceremonious end, they must change their tactics to turn the tide of that war.

When the tide of power begins to shift against the unrighteous, they must change tactics and leverage new methods of waging war. Once their laws of reducing African Americans to two-thirds of a White man, denying us the right to vote, access to safe and affordable housing, and a fair wage were all rendered useless, they chose to exterminate us. As such, the new tactic my generation would have to face and overcome would be Nixon and Reagan's shared war on drugs and the American-funded crack epidemic.

―――――

My mother, finally able to buy her own home, moved us from

Philadelphia to Camden, New Jersey, in the Fall of 1985. Coincidentally, that would be the first time the name "crack" first appeared in the *New York Times*. For those of you not familiar with the history of how the American government, specifically the CIA, worked with Colombian drug cartels to purposely flood American ghettos with crack cocaine so they could use the profits of this drug to fund the Iran-Contra Affair, just Google it. For those who don't wish to read and prefer a more cinematic representation of the course of events from beginning to end, watch the television series *Snowfall*, created by John Singleton.

The same course of events that plagued the Black and Brown communities of Los Angeles would also befall my community of Camden, New Jersey. The crack epidemic unleashed the most sadistic and cruel acts in a person once the drug reduced them to addicts. Routinely, my peers and I encountered the worst of unscrupulous people who didn't care about others' lives and even worse, their own lives. In the January 20, 1992, issue of *TIME* magazine, the featured article was titled, "The Other America," followed by the words, "Who Could Live Here? Only people with no other choice—and in Camden that usually means children."

I remember it like it was yesterday. The unflattering article that highlighted the crime, the drugs, the dilapidated, abandoned homes, and an above-average poverty rate infuriated my city. To make things worse, during that time, Camden topped criminal statistical charts as one of America's most dangerous cities. For a run that spanned several years, we were either ranked number one on that list or were a constant in its top-ten rankings.

To give you some perspective, Camden had a population that has never exceeded eighty-five thousand people. In comparison, our per capita crime statistics would rival cities like Detroit, Michigan's, whose population was seven times ours at *six hundred thousand* people. In Camden, we had Mischief Night, whereas Detroit had Devil Night. These two unceremonious nights were designated by local delinquents from each city, who would purposely set fire to abandoned homes and vandalize businesses and cars the night before Halloween. For two consecutive years, approximately one hundred fires were set in Camden. One urban legend claimed someone ran a trail of kerosene methodically down the middle of the street that spanned the entire length of a city block. Then they lit the kerosene on fire, lighting the entire street, leaving cars unable to traverse the street until the fire was ultimately extinguished by adult residents.

During the worst Mischief Night of those two years, the quantity of fires exceeded the capabilities of the city's fire department. The mayor and fire chief had to enlist fire departments in neighboring cities to assist their overwhelmed Camden Fire Department. In 1992, my junior year in high school, the union that represented my school's bus drivers demanded my school's early dismissal under the threat of strike. The drivers who had bus routes in Camden were afraid of being caught in the city during that year's Mischief Night. Especially after bus drivers had rocks and bricks thrown at their buses the previous year. The union won and my high school complied, and we were home by noon and our bus drivers with routes in Camden were out of the city before 1 p.m.

I won't deny Camden was a rough city and there were some experiences I wish I didn't have to live through or witness. In dueling fairness, I can also attest that the entire city and its people weren't the Godforsaken cesspool *TIME* made it out to be. The city block I lived on consisted predominantly of homeowners. We had annual summer block cleanups with a block party to follow. It was a harmonious celebration of our collective love for our homes and city.

However, if you walked around the corner, two blocks from my home, the environment instantly changed. A stone's throw away, my neighborhood degenerated into a "hood," where the concept of neighbors was nonexistent. The hood is where people not native to these surroundings should not traverse haphazardly. And for some, even if you were from the surrounding hoods and knew who the local hustlers, stickup boys, crackheads, and dope fiends were, you'd be unwise to take those commonalities for granted.

Even if one was fortunate to live on a pristine block like mine and relegated themselves to their own street to avoid certain pitfalls, the criminality two blocks away would easily spill over our borders. I washed away a stranger's blood from my mother's white Toyota Tercel twice as a teenager while it sat parked in front of my home. Once from a broken nose sustained during an everyday street fight that morphed into a jumping. The second instance was more severe and stereotypical of inner-city living. It made my mother's pristine white car resemble that of an artist's canvas painted only in the brightest of reds.

"Tariiik! Phone," my mother yelled from downstairs, waking me from an afternoon nap. That summer, I'd come home from college instead of staying in Baltimore because I had acquired my first internship that paid more than the minimum wage jobs of pizza delivery and cashier at the local Wawa off Moravia Road. I rolled over on my mattress, eyes still closed, to grab the cordless phone from my nightstand.

"Hey, you," I answered, already knowing who it was. I had worked overnight at my second job the night before, so I told my college girlfriend from Philly I needed to sneak in a few hours of sleep before picking her up for our late-afternoon dinner and movie date. I'd always been a heavy sleeper, so her call was an established routine to make sure I didn't sleep through my alarm. She didn't like being late, and luckily, neither did I.

"I'm up," I said, lying in bed with my eyes still closed.

"No, you're not. You're still lying down. I can hear it in your voice," she said as I rolled out of bed onto my feet.

"For real, I'm up."

"Yeah, *now* you're up," she said with a slight sense of jest. I walked down the hall and into the bathroom and quickly turned the water on.

"See, I'm already in the bathroom and about to brush my teeth and head over to you in a few."

"Yuck! No shower?" she questioned.

"You know we don't have a shower head. I took a bath and ironed my clothes before my nap. That's called thinking ahead," I teased while simultaneously starting to brush my teeth, knowing she would have a clever retort and I could use that time to finish brushing.

"Keep it up, smart-ass, and there won't be any kisses waiting for you when you get here, fresh breath or not. Did you make reservations or are we trying our luck this time?"

"Huh?" I replied, stalling my response so I could finish brushing.

"Huh, hell. You heard me."

"It's Olive Garden—do they even take reservations?" I asked in between shoveling water I cupped in my hands from the bathroom faucet into my mouth.

"I'm not even sure, to be honest. If they don't, we'll be at the bar getting drinks then."

"Fine with me," I said, finishing my rinse and wiping my mouth of the excess toothpaste and water dripping down my chin before leaving the bathroom. I made a quick right out the door headed toward my mother's room at the front of the house, where I'd carefully laid out my clothes on the ironing board in the corner of her room.

"Hold on for a second while I get dressed. Matter fact, it's only going to take me a few minutes to get dressed and head out the door. So, I'll just see you in a little bit. No need to sit on the phone—"

Pop! Pop! Pop! Pop! The sound of what I initially equated to balloons popping floated through the open window in my mother's room. I immediately crouched down toward the floor, cordless phone pressed against my right thigh.

"Mom! You okay?" I shouted downstairs.

"What was that?" my girlfriend's muffled yell demanded.

"Hold on!" I yelled down at the receiver, listening intently to see if a volley of return fire would follow.

"Mom!" I shouted again.

"Yes! I'm fine. Are you?" my mother shouted from downstairs. From the sound of her voice, she was in the kitchen at the back of the house, farthest from the gunshots.

"Yeah, I'm good!"

I bear-crawled to the open window to peer down toward the street where my block's kids played. Where my neighbors sat on their porches or stoops on nice sunny days like today. Where my mother's car was parked, freshly vacuumed and washed in preparation for my date.

"Tarik! You there? What was that?" my girlfriend asked frantically.

"Tarik!" my girlfriend yelled again.

"Hey! Yeah, I'm fine," I responded, taking another look. This time, I parted the shades from the side of the window, looking left, then right. Off in the distance, I could see a teenager only a few years younger than I riding his bicycle off in a hurry. My gaze traced the origins of his escape route and then, finally, just below me, I saw him. Another teenager of similar age on the sidewalk in front of my house. His back leaned against the passenger side door of my mother's car. He frantically pulled at his shirt, lifting it up. His eyes initially lit up with shock, followed by fear after seeing blood flowing from the small hole in his torso.

"Heeeelp!" he cried out desperately. "Mutha-fuckah shot me!"

I released the window shades from where I spied the boy.

"Somebody just got shot in front of my house. I'll hit you back," I said, before hitting the button on my phone to end the call. I tossed the phone on my mother's bed, then hurried to retrieve my clothes and sneakers. I threw them on in haste and ran down the stairs. My mother was now at the front window peering out at the same victim I'd seen from upstairs. I ran past her through the house vestibule, and in one swift motion, unlocked the screen door and pushed it open, stopping at the top of my porch steps. Twenty feet in front of me, a collection of my neighbors and passersby were huddling around the shot teenager. Some were afraid, others in awe, but only one not familiar to me was enraged.

"They shot my nigga!" a teenager yelled, crouching down next to his friend.

"Anyone call 9-1-1?" Aunt Rose called, clutching at her chest.

"*They shot my nigga!*" the teenager repeated before redirecting his attention away from his fallen comrade. He scooped up the bike his friend had been shot off of, pushed it through the crowd, and pedaled off in the opposite direction from where the shooter had made his escape. Within seconds, he disappeared after making a sharp right around the corner. I retreated into my house past my mother, who was still looking out of the window, concerned and silent. I grabbed the keys to her car and my wallet and headed back to the door, where blue and red lights were now heading down the street toward the scene.

I exited the house and saw my neighbors creating a perimeter around the now-unconscious victim, who was no longer propped against my mother's car and instead was lying on the red bricks that made up the sidewalk in front of my porch. The crowd of onlookers had now grown larger and engulfed the front of my porch. I shoved my wallet in my left pocket and secured my mother's car keys in my right hand. Rather than pushing my way through the crowd, I threw my long legs over the three-foot metal railings on the side of my porch and jumped down onto the pavement.

Pop-pop! Pop! Pop-pop-pop! Pop! Pop! Everyone outside crouched down in unison at the sound of more gunfire sounding off from around the corner where the victim's friend had sped off in a vengeful fury. *Bang! Bang! Pop-pop-pop!* Everyone scattered in the opposite direction of the sound of the war that had just commenced. They ducked behind cars, trees, and protruding brick porches, anything that would provide cover from a stray bullet. I dashed toward the space between the front of my mother's car and the back of my neighbor's car. I periodically peeked through the back window of my neighbor's car, trying to spy potential danger.

The police took off running in the direction where we all heard the volley of gunfire, talking inaudibly every few steps into their shoulder radios. I took this as my opportunity to make my escape as well. I emerged from between the two cars and dashed to the driver's side of my mother's car, unlocked it, and reclined my seat as far as possible while turning the ignition.

"Tarik! Where are you going?" my mother yelled, pushing the screen door of our home open and poking her head out from the safety of our brick house. Concern filled her eyes. I responded quickly and simply through the glass passenger window that was smeared with blood.

"Away! Far away from here!"

She didn't respond verbally. The eyes of a person can speak volumes, allowing the mouth a necessary break. When my mother heard my response, her eyes shifted from concern to pride. With a quick and simple glance exchanged between the two of us, I let her know that eventually I'd have to leave the city that raised me. The city where she had provided a stable home for me. The city that taught me its version of how to be a man. I'd let her know a time would soon come when I'd be leaving my pack's den. And her mute response let me know she was okay with that.

chapter 24

During my life, I've developed an appreciation for history. In fact, my favorite movie genre has always been rooted in films where the storyline is based on real-life events. My favorite movie adaptation to this day is *Glory*, the 1989 war drama that highlighted the heroic accomplishments of the first all-African-American regiment, the "Fighting" 54th Massachusetts Volunteer Infantry, which earned Denzel Washington his first Academy Award, for best supporting actor.

For me, being both entertained and educated about humanity's collective past and the gift of wisdom history bestows us is so satisfying. So satisfying I find difficulty properly formulating it into words. What I can confess is I believe our forebears have inscribed invisible cautionary tales with their blood on the sheets of time. And our fate will be determined solely by our own choice to evolve from these lessons or to perish if our choice is to willfully ignore the consequences of our indifference to the routine cruelty we inflict upon one another.

I remember the first time I learned, as an adolescent, about the bloody Hatfield-McCoy feud, a conflict involving two rural American families of West Virginia and Kentucky. I was weirdly intrigued by the documentary's historical depiction of the two families' blood feud while channel surfing one Saturday afternoon. The narrator's description of the warring clans mystified me because, up until that point, I'd reserved the concept of war for rival countries, not families. Looking back, I realize my perception of life was naive. Now that I am fully aware of the human capacity for cruelty, I wonder if this was the universe showing me a precursor to my own experience. Perhaps some cruel preview to prep me for the blood feud that would befall my own clan, my pack.

My grandmother, rooted in Southern gender roles and traditions, cooked for her family every day. No days off were even had on weekends, and for holidays, she put on an even more elaborate feast. She never fed us fast food. Despite us living on concrete rather than soil, after her migration to northern cities, she cultivated a garden in a fenced-off area of the manicured front lawn of her life partner, Mr. Jesse. That garden is where she grew her own herbs and spices and staple vegetables, like tomatoes and carrots, that eventually found their way onto her dinner table.

Our family, much like the Hatfields and McCoys, maintained a healthy distribution of offspring, but mostly male. My generation of boys, despite our inner-city geography, were Southerners in culture and stature. Being the descendants of men who'd worked the land, we all had broad shoulders, thick necks, wide hands, and thick fingers. When huddled together, the collective stature of the men in our pack is intimidating.

The unwritten rules and social norms of our city were a breeding ground for conflict. Out of survival, we drew nigh to each other, always knowing protection was afforded to us through our numbers. If our opposition wanted to fight, the men in my family obliged them with boxing, and we won. Our family's women were no exception, either. The concept of hair grabbing and face scratching are foreign to our pack. Our women also knew how to ball a fist and throw a right cross that left many opposing women with blackened eyes and broken noses streaming with blood.

For me, the bulk of my fisticuffs were during my elementary school years in Philly. Since all my family lived across the Delaware River in Jersey, there was no one to protect me and my mother.

Street fights for me were a regular occurrence until I recorded my first and only knockout at the expense of a neighborhood kid I once thought to be a friend.

Because I was new to the neighborhood and typically alone, this kid thought I'd be an easy win because his older brother was there when he decided to pick on me. By today's politically correct standards, I was being bullied. But this bully was a poser, and with a single right hook, he found himself stumbling to the ground, crashing into the Huffy bikes surrounding us like a makeshift ring. Now, admittedly, I'm not an exceptional fighter. My opponent simply made the mistake of not striking first. I, on the other hand, did strike, and I struck true. I'd made my mark, gained the respect of my block, and that would be the last fight I'd have to have in my own neighborhood.

That same year, my mother surprisingly moved us from Southwest Philly to Camden. She wanted to own her own home instead of renting, and my grandmother had moved into a new home with her common-law husband, Mr. Jesse. They lived in a section of Camden called Parkside, where the affluent White people of the city once lived before White flight happened, after the shipping industry collapse. The Polish people who thrived as longshoremen once occupied their own area of the city, dubbed "Polack Town." They disappeared when the dock jobs left, relegating the neighborhood to a place where only African-American and Hispanic people now live.

The oral agreement my mother and grandmother made was simple. She could take over the home with the understanding the house needed extensive repairs. In exchange for my mother taking on the responsibility of rehabbing the dilapidated house, my grandmother would sell the house to her for $1 and transfer the deed to my mother's name. The house my grandmother purchased for $4,900 is now mine to place tenants in and is worth six figures.

That modest, three-bedroom, one-bathroom house has served my family well. Whether it was a home that housed a family or a momentary stopgap to help someone get back on their feet after losing a job, separation from a spouse, or to give them a roof over their head after being released from prison, that home on Trenton Avenue just two blocks from Cooper Hospital had history and a reputation only our lineage could account for.

On the ride to our new home, I pressed my back firmly against the seat of the U-Haul truck, sandwiched between my mother and my older cousin, Cyrus, who was driving. I looked to my right past my mother out the van's half-open window as we passed through Center City, Philadelphia. Looking past my mother and at the mirror on the door, I could see my mother's green Datsun bouncing from lane-to-lane at my older cousin Speedy's will, jockeying for a closer position behind the U-Haul. My cousin was my mom's age and looked and acted more like an uncle than a cousin to me. Soon, the Benjamin Franklin Bridge, with its freshly painted blue suspension cables and steel beams, came into view.

Although I had lived in Philly my entire life, this was the first time I'd really seen the Philadelphia skyline—the tall centerpieces of Liberty Place and Mellon Bank Center. The picturesque urban design was quickly ruined as the litter and debris tumbled in the streets, substantiating the unflattering nickname of Filthadelphia.

As we sat at a traffic light, a few panhandlers made a beeline for our and the other cars being held hostage at the intersection. Most drivers ignored them, but not my mom. She instinctively reached into her purse, retrieving two dollars and sticking them out the window for the sign-carrying pedestrian to pocket. Seeing her wallet made me wonder.

"Mom, don't you have a license?"

"Yes, I do," she responded, smiling and waving at the grateful homeless man.

"Then why is Cousin Cyrus driving?"

"I don't like driving on highways or over bridges—they scare me."

"Why? It's the same as driving on a regular street, except you get to go faster and higher," I persisted, nudging my cousin with my left elbow. "Right, Cyrus?"

Cyrus flashed a sly smile in return.

"Like I said," my mom repeated, "I don't like driving over bridges," just before popping me on the lips. "And if I have to repeat myself again, you'll be walking to the new house."

I covered my mouth with my hands to protect my throbbing lip and slumped down in my seat. Cyrus chuckled.

So that's why we always took the train to Jersey.

I slyly saw Cyrus chuckle at my being disciplined. When he noticed, he broke eye contact to glance at his driver's side mirror to check where Speedy was driving my mother's car.

Finally, our truck pulled around the curve that traced the perimeter of Philadelphia's police department headquarters. I watched as my mother closed her eyes and dug her nails into her thighs.

"Mom, you going to be okay? If Cyrus's driving is making you nervous, I can drive us the rest of the way," I said sarcastically, obviously too young and small to reach the pedals, let alone drive.

She didn't open her eyes, but still managed another pop on the mouth with the precision to make a sniper jealous. "I warned you about your mouth…didn't I?"

A minute later, we were on the downswing of the bridge. The Camden skyline was no Philadelphia by any comparison. Cyrus pointed to the only tall building in the downtown business district.

"That's where I work, City Hall. I know the mayor and most of the city officials."

I wasn't impressed by the building. The only noticeable difference between Philadelphia and Camden was that this new city was much smaller, and the only White people I saw in their business district were unkempt drug addicts and prostitutes.

We passed the transportation center where my mother and I would catch the train whenever we visited Jersey. Now that we had successfully traversed the bridge, my mother opened her eyes and her posture relaxed. Our new home would only be ten minutes away, right off Haddon Avenue. When we made the turn onto Trenton Avenue, plenty of children my age were already clustering the sidewalk and street, busying themselves in fun. Some of them waved. I smiled and waved back.

The protection I lacked in Philly would soon be abundant and cover me as a cloak before I even passed the threshold of our new home. Once we parked the truck and my mother's car in front of our new home, one of our neighbors came to sincerely welcome us. She was accompanied by her son and daughter, who would eventually attend the same Catholic elementary school as I. We began exchanging pleasantries the best kids could manage while our mothers did the same a few feet away. Less than a minute into our parents' conversation, it ended abruptly and my potential new friends were pulled away hastily while my mother walked toward me donning an unfamiliar sneer.

"Tarik, don't be surprised if those two are hesitant to be your friends," she warned.

"What do you mean?" I asked, more confused than disappointed by the unexpected news.

"Their mother, Ms. Priss over there, had the nerve to ask me, 'How could you live next door to those people and their children?'"

Awww, shit!

"I told that uppity, chicken-head, river rat those *people* are my family!" my mother declared, invoking the country culture I warned you about earlier. To give you some perspective, my entire family in South Carolina lives along the full, two-mile stretch of road and we're all kin by blood, not marriage. When my grandmother migrated north, those of her generation who also followed her had adopted the same tradition of living in proximity. Living in the same city wasn't enough; they all bought houses in the same neighborhoods and on the same block, if possible.

My mother's new mortal enemy had just insulted one of her closest sisters, my Aunt Ronnie and her children, her nieces and nephews, my cousins. Their confrontation would not be the catalyst of me instantly developing new friendships, but alternatively, it was good knowing my street-fighting days had almost instantly concluded. My guilt by association bestowed upon me the respect the house's previous occupants had earned.

Even in those rare moments when neighborhood kids, ignorant of my association, tested the new kid, there was always someone among them who knew better. Initially, I was also ignorant of it but would later notice the discreet whispers, followed by a finger point, and my opponent's aggression would magically dissipate.

My mother was the beneficiary as well. One evening, after my football practice, she'd gone to the bodega around the corner for an item she needed to make dinner. I busied myself with homework while she walked the half block to the neighborhood store. While she was leaving the store, an amateur hooligan attempted to snatch her purse as she emerged from the door. Luckily for my mother, he wasn't a seasoned criminal and failed to snatch her purse cleanly. She retained her grip and instinctively resisted by punching the teenager in his eye. She told me how a look of shock washed over him once he realized she'd managed to strike him first. Then, as the rest of the story goes, her would-be mugger threw a punch back that somehow failed to land its mark. Then my mother followed up with her own knockout punch—metaphorically, that is.

"You know who my nephew is?" she threatened while a tug-of-war with her purse ensued. "Kevin! And he's going to fuck you up when I tell him." Her name-drop turned her attacker into a coward. His eyes lit up, his jaw dropped, and his grip loosened on her purse.

"Ohh, shit! You better hope she lyin', young'n!" a loiterer near the bodega instigated from the sidelines, almost entertained by the whole scene. The attack concluded and the would-be mugger ran away in a full sprint without looking back once.

Months later, after we settled in, one Sunday would be my first Pop Warner football game for the Centerville Simbas. I was in the living room, in full uniform, watching television and anxiously counting down the minutes before my game, when there was a knock at the door. When I opened it, I lit up with excitement seeing my older cousin Kevin on the opposite side of the screen door. I unlocked it and pushed it open.

"What's up, little cousin?" he said, accompanied by his ever-present smile.

"What's up? I got my first game today. You coming?" I asked, heart racing.

"Hell, yeah. I wasn't going to miss your first game," he said, extending his hand and engulfing mine. His facial expression changed.

"That's not a handshake. Grab mine like you mean it and look me in the eyes. Always look a person in the eyes when you talk and especially when you shake their hand. Nah mean?"

I corrected my shake and posture as instructed.

"There you go!" His smile returned. "Where's Aunt Sheila?"

"She's upstairs getting ready."

He didn't even make it into the house after inspecting my uniform. He stuck his head just past the threshold and yelled, "Aunt Sheila, I'ma take Tarik to the store real quick before the game—we'll be right back, a'ight!" He informed more than asked for permission as we headed out the door.

"Okay," she responded, uncharacteristically nonchalant, just before the door slammed shut behind us.

"You ready?" he asked.

"Yup!" I responded enthusiastically.

"How many touchdowns you gonna score?"

"I don't know. They only have two plays for me, and I don't even know if Coach is going to call them."

"Well, if your coach calls your play, you make sure you score. Don't let anyone tackle you," he loosely ordered.

"A'ight, I won't," I assured him as we turned the corner and headed to the same bodega where he used to work as a teenager, the same one I frequented with neighborhood kids, and the same where my mom had her altercation. I was happy someone else was going to the game beside my mother. She didn't even like, let alone understand, football at that point. My thoughts initially distracted me from noticing many of the older kids in the neighborhood deliberately acknowledging Kevin's presence with a nod of the head from a distance or giving him dap, even if it meant inconveniencing themselves to walk up to him.

When we got to the bodega, he bought me a bag of chips, a soda, and a new pair of tube socks with black and gold stripes at the top that matched the color of my uniform.

"Go 'head and put your new socks on while I talk to my peoples real quick," he said, pointing at an empty stoop where another kid was leaning up against the brick wall. I ran over to the stoop, put down my chips and soda, unlaced my cleats, and pulled off the socks I had on before he got there. They were a dingy, off-white-color and the elastic had worn from me hand-washing them repeatedly, so much that every few steps, I had to reach down and pull them back up my leg.

"What's up?" the kid leaning against the wall said to me, periodically scanning the intersection as if looking for someone.

"What's up?" I responded with a nod before ripping at the plastic wrapping with my teeth to retrieve my new, bright white socks. I yanked them out, making sure they didn't touch the ground, and pulled them up my skinny calves and shins.

"How you know Kevin?"

"He's my cousin," I responded, paying more attention to my new socks and tying my cleats back up, excited to see how my uniform was going to look, thanks to Kevin.

"Oh, a'ight. I'm Dawuan."

"Tarik," I responded, shaking his hand with the same ferocity Kevin had just taught me. I gathered the empty plastic bag and discarded it on the ground next to the stoop of an abandoned house. I looked over to where Kevin was talking to a collection of three loiterers near the store, out of earshot.

"Pick that off the ground. It's a trash can in the store," Kevin said, administering my second lesson of the day. Dewaun playfully laughed at me as I followed his orders and ran over toward the store.

"Hold up," Kevin said, grabbing me by my shoulder pads. "This my li'l cousin. He the starting tight end for Centerville's eighty-five-pounders. Tell these niggas how many touchdowns you gonna score today."

"I only have two plays but if my coach call them, I'm scoring both times," I said, emboldened by Kevin's confidence.

"That's right, and his uniform is looking right!" he said, letting my shoulder pads go and motioning me into the store.

As my years in Camden passed, my perception of the world matured, and I saw it for what it really was. I eventually realized Kevin's impromptu visit and tour of my new neighborhood, his old stomping grounds, was more deliberate than a spontaneous gift of a snack and socks for my first game. I would finally realize that my city was small and the circle of its players even smaller. After my mother's declaration of who her nephew was, the streets started talking.

Word had gotten back to him. His cameo appearance wasn't a social call. It was a bulletin, putting everyone on notice that the family home he'd been raised in was now occupied again...by family. That day, he would accompany me and my mother to my football game. My old coach was once his coach, so when he volunteered to work the sidelines by holding the first-down marker while I played, his request was granted.

My coach would eventually call one play for me at the end of the game, and as Kevin instructed, I scored a sixty-yard, game-winning touchdown. It would be the first of the eight touchdowns I would score that season. After the game, he walked with me to the concession stand, bought me a hot dog and soda to celebrate my touchdown, and bragged on his little cousin so everyone in Parkside would also know who I was related to. From that day forward, despite living in a city where crime swirled like a tornado in a trailer park, my mother and I never had a problem.

She was never mugged again, I never had another street fight, our house was never broken into, my bike was never stolen, the hustlers never tried to recruit me as a lookout or corner boy. Unlike many of my counterparts, my only concern was getting good grades and doing well in sports.

"Tarik! Get in the basement! Now!" my mother yelled from my grandmother's kitchen into the living room. I was occupying my usual spot in front of the television before our traditional Sunday family dinner. Everyone in our pack knew that if you needed a meal, Edith Jackson's house was the place to be on Sunday evening. And you didn't need an invitation. Unfortunately, for that night, word of our Sunday tradition wasn't contained to just family.

"Get up!" my mother ordered, dashing toward me and securing a death grip on my left arm before I could even react to her first command. My feet barely touched the green carpet as she dragged me with every running step I took to keep pace with her frantic state.

"What's wrong?" I asked desperately, but she didn't respond. Out of the living room, past the dining room, around the corner into and through the kitchen, past the brown refrigerator, and down the stairs that led into the basement. When we finally came to a stop, I saw the rest of my cousins my age hunkered down on couches in the finished basement.

"Stay here and don't move! I'm going to get your coat," she ordered before running back upstairs. I watched her disappear upstairs and slam the door behind her, locking it. I looked back at my cousins and locked eyes with Tiffany, who was the closest to me in age.

"Why we down here? It's not even a TV here," I questioned. Tiffany shrugged and walked to her Easy-Bake Oven.

"I'll make us dinner tonight," she said, busying herself with the plastic pots, pans, and utensils. I turned my attention back to the dark stairwell. Amid the collage of muffled voices of older family members who'd remained upstairs, the sound of the house telephone ringing could be heard.

"Don't answer it!" someone yelled as the phone continued to ring before dying out. The once-muffled voices escalated to a heated debate now. Again, the ringer of the house phone sounded off. Only one ring this time. Everything went quiet but only for a moment. One of my older cousins broke the eerie silence.

"Yo! Who the fuck is this? I swear to God—"

"*Shut your mouth, damnit!*" my grandmother commanded. Everything went silent again. It was one of those rare moments when, not only did she raise her voice, but the churchgoing lover of Christ also doubled down with profanity. Everything went silent again until I heard my grandmother's anger morph into painful sorrow.

"*Oh, my lord Jesus! God noooo!*" she cried out. Shouting from other voices followed my grandmother's painful pleas.

"Yo! We out of here!" one of my older cousins declared as the door unlocked and swung open furiously. That older cousin stomped down the basement stairs in a hurry, past me, and grabbed her son. His legs wrapped around her torso and his arms around her neck, she ran back up the stairs. She and my mother brushed by one another. My mother, as promised, stormed down the steps toward me, coat in hand.

"Put this on. We're leaving!" she said, fighting back tears and panic. I did as I was told as her bottom lip and hands trembled. Soon as I had my coat on, she rushed me up the stairs past other parents heading downstairs to retrieve their children after seeing my cousin's evacuation, then back through the kitchen, past the dining room where we ate, and to the front door before she came to a screeching halt. Placing me directly behind her, she looked through the decorative windows of the front door. Quickly but carefully peering side to side before turning the doorknob, she grabbed me and made a mad dash toward her green Datsun hatchback.

She held me closer now that we were outside, and her head swiveled back and forth, her piercing eyes inspecting every parked and passing car. It was winter and her car was old, so according to the routine, we would sit in the car approximately five minutes while it warmed up before pulling off. But not tonight. As soon as the car turned on, she threw the manual shift into first gear and peeled out of her parking spot. The old car sputtered along in a different direction from the one we usually took to go home. That wouldn't be the only deviation we took.

Our typical, ten-minute drive stretched to fifteen, due to the many uncustomary detours. With every turn, she feverishly peered into the rearview mirror.

Something's wrong.

I couldn't hold my tongue anymore.

"Mom? You okay?" I asked my visibly shaken mother, but she didn't answer. My question did instigate an outburst.

"I told those boys! I told them! *I told them!*" she shouted, making another sharp turn down yet another unfamiliar street and repeating her inspection of the dark streets behind us via the rearview mirror. I turned to look through the back window, seeing nothing but dimly lit empty streets the entire way. Once we arrived home and parked the car, she rushed us into the house as quickly as we had left my grandmother's. She slammed the door behind us, locked it, and turned off all the lights. I sat in the dark in the kitchen, coat still on, for an amount of time I couldn't keep track of.

My mother repeatedly peeked through the blinds of our two front windows, pacing back and forth between both. After a while, she finally took a seat next to me in the kitchen, rocking back and forth in her chair, arms crossed, hugging herself periodically, sniffing and wiping away tears. Then she finally spoke.

"Tarik, your Aunt Janice is dead," she spoke through a cracking voice.

"What? What happened?" I asked, disappointment washing over me rather than sadness. Members of my pack dying prematurely wasn't new to me, not anymore. In the short time between us living in Philadelphia and Camden, I'd already lived through two of my family members dying. The first was mom's father when I was five or six years old. I honestly don't remember my exact age. In my opinion, I was too young to have gone to a funeral. I just couldn't comprehend what was happening, let alone what death really was. I remember sitting in the church with my family, everyone crying… except me.

I felt bad, wondering if something was wrong with me for not feeling sad, not crying, and wailing like everyone else. You see, I'd never met my mom's father. I didn't know his name. I didn't know where he lived. I didn't even know, at that point, how he even died. He was a stranger to me.

Despite that, I knew deep down I should have felt some sense of loss, but my brain couldn't rationalize it. I couldn't manifest sadness for someone I'd seen for the first time lying motionless with grayish skin in a casket. My second funeral was not long after that when my cousin Larry, Kevin's brother, was murdered. Being so young, exposed to death, and with no one to talk to me about how to process it, I gradually developed a mechanism of desensitization. I wouldn't cry at a funeral until the age of twenty, when my grandmother died of cancer while I was in college.

"We don't know how yet," my mother said in response to my question about how my aunt, who was barely a few years older than my mother, had died. I noticed she broke eye contact with me when she responded.

She's lying.

A week later, my cousin Tiffany, who lived with my grandmother, would confess to me what she found out about that night. Much like the Hatfields and McCoys, my family had become part of a blood feud. The other family had unsuccessfully been trying to settle a beef with someone in my pack. In lieu of not being able to track him down, they figured out the Sunday tradition my family had. They staked out my grandmother's house, hoping my family member they were looking for would show up there.

Knowing the heat was on him, he stayed away from the family and his enemies grew impatient. So, instead, they set their sights on his mother, my Aunt Janice, and followed her from my grandmother's home to an elevated train station. They followed her into the station and onto the platform, assaulted her, and threw her onto the tracks in front of an oncoming train.

As is the custom of the cities I've been raised in, no one talks to the police. No leads were developed in the investigation of her death. The lack of cooperation meant the investigators ruled her murder as a suicide and closed the case. But the streets and my family knew it wasn't suicide. Those mysterious phone calls to my grandmother's house weren't the only calls she'd receive. More calls would be made by the same people who'd stalked and murdered my aunt. They would eventually call and anonymously claim responsibility with a few simple words.

"You tell Chub we watchin' y'all crib." Then they would abruptly hang up.

My family's version of the Hatfields and McCoys had begun. We were at war with another family, and my aunt had become a casualty. A vicious and unsanctioned casualty. Despite the outward appearance of the streets being unruly and lawless, there are understood *unwritten* rules of hood life:

No snitching.

No civilians.

No children.

No women.

Absolutely *no mothers*!

The murder of my aunt caused a rift in my family. A rift we struggle to recover from to this day. That awful night forever altered how and where we lived. Sunday family dinners at my grandmother's became scarce. Our family dynamic and methods of fellowship would never be the same. Already, we rarely entertained at our homes. Going forward, the locations of where we laid our heads would only be disclosed on a need-to-know basis. For years, it was weird not knowing exactly where some of your closest family members called home. Some even moved their loved ones out of the city to undisclosed locations while the men remained and "went to the mattresses."

One of my cousins was shot a ridiculous number of times during one attack and survived it, decades before the rapper 50 Cent made it his calling card. Another cousin carries a bullet in his body that can't be removed by operation, so he must live with absorbing its lead, hoping it doesn't cause him long-term health issues. I have another cousin who was shot point blank in the face, survived it, and had to have reconstructive surgery on his jaw—also like the rapper 50 Cent. I have a cousin who's been stabbed. I have a cousin who's done the stabbing. I have a cousin who is currently doing time for three murders and two attempted murders. The two who survived were his own cell mate and a correctional officer who disrespected him after he was arrested for his third murder.

That's why I laugh at wannabe gangsters who play tough because they think it's cool. I'm talking about the guys who have college degrees like me, who come from loving, two-parent households. They watch too much television and gangster films and pop off at the mouth because they feel safe when their fake wannabe gangster friends are around. They know they can't fight so they participate in jumping people. The same guys who, if pulled up on while they're alone, are suddenly humble and apologetic. The ones who turn into track stars the moment it's time to kick a fair one or confronted with, "Can I get a drop?" My pack simply looks at your perfectly manicured nails and the smooth unblemished skin around your knuckles and surmises you're a poser, a bluff, a bitch! And we'll tell your momma you're a bitch!

Wannabe tough guys who think just because they lift some weight in a gym, they can throw hands. Those who fill out an application and took a conceal carry class thinking it's cool flashing their weapons for clout. Where I'm from, if you pull, if you flash, you better shoot. Flashing will only expedite your reservation at the cemetery. There's a difference between hearing gunshots from afar and being up close enough to see that muzzle flash, feeling and hearing the whistle of a bullet violate your personal space.

In my family, my pack, we've carefully crafted the nuances of how we live and how we maintain and manage our personal, family, and home security. Eventually, our urban version of the Hatfield-McCoy blood feud concluded. A conclusion that, unlike its country predecessors, did not end with an arrest and trial. The police never solved the case of who murdered my aunt. Detectives ruled it suicide. But one thing is for sure: my pack never lost another one of our kin to "suicide"…ever again.

epilogue

So, now what? What was the point? What has been gained by this exercise of transparent vulnerability? These are the questions I ask myself now that my collection of formidable traumas have been purged upon paper. My response to my self-imposed question is simple.

I've been willfully ignorant of my moral underachievement. In denial far too long about my approach and methods of navigating life. An uneven balance of my life decisions have been misguided. Some were innocent. Mere repercussions of the growing pains of this experience we call life. Others were made out of pure ignorance. Leaving the most sinister rooted in selfish survival yet still repugnant.

The good news is I've finally learned from them, resulting in a more peaceful existence guided by a refurbished moral compass that now guides my behavior and decisions. The truth is, I had to change. That's my own self-realizing conclusion, not my therapist's, although she does agree. In return, I've thanked my therapist profusely for everything she's done to help me heal and become a better human being.

"You've come a long way, Tarik. I'm proud of you. But the work never ends. There's no magic pill. No easy fix in undoing a lifetime of bad habits. Never forget our first session together?" my therapist cautioned.

"I was worried about you," she reminded me.

"Yeah, I dumped a lot on you that first session didn't I?" Recalling it now makes me laugh in pure comedy. The same type of innocent comedy spawned by my recalling losing my virginity. I'd compiled so much repressed emotion that I talked, nonstop, the entire hour of our inaugural session. Her allowing space and time for my purge revealed my very first lesson on the validity of therapy—sometimes you just need someone to talk to. Someone who's just going to listen—not judge, not propose fixes—just genuinely and actively listen and allow you to be heard. To her credit, she did just that while I vented as much poison I could fit in that inaugural hour.

Turns out I'm an emotional person after all. A little too honest for these days and times of political correctness I can admit. My words and emotions flowed like Niagara Falls, giving my therapist a glimpse into my emotional state of mind. When my rants had concluded, she suspected I may be a sociopath. Don't worry though, I'm not. We both laugh and joke about it now whenever we recall her inviting another therapist to our second session together. She wanted an objective second opinion so for the first thirty minutes of session two I was tag teamed with the help of her colleague to give an even more thorough evaluation of my mental state and I passed. Hahaha!

Now, after years of denying I was in therapy to friends and family, I'm comfortable admitting that I do go periodically, much like the routine preventative maintenance with my primary care physician who ensures my physical health is intact. The shit works too because I've never been happier.

I've noticed a change in my behavior, others see it as well. I'm confident in my ability to avoid making life decisions devoid of compassion and righteousness. I'm free of leaving a wake of people I encounter. Especially those who don't deserve it.

The purposeful, wolflike decisions and behaviors—those I knew to be wrong from their inception, potentially wrong after calculated egomaniacal consideration, or the ones I convinced myself were justified—now embarrass me. Those terrible decisions were the ones I needed most to confront before they destroyed me. Not "destroy" in the sense of a superhero annihilating an archenemy by literally killing them, reducing them to ash, where they disintegrate into nothingness; I'm speaking of destroying the inherent good that remains in me.

That good, I'm now clear enough in mind and spirit to carefully cultivate and grow abundantly before I degenerated into the character of someone bereft of any moral compass and honor. Someone my family, friends, and loved ones would no longer recognize. Or even worse, someone *I* wouldn't be able to recognize.

If that were to have happened, I would have become a person or a sum of characteristics I mentally persecuted others for. How ironic would that be? Judging and condemning individuals who act the same way you do. It would be the ultimate form of self-hate. I don't want that for myself, but most importantly, I don't want that for those in my orbit. Writing this book was bigger than me. Ultimately, I want my life's story to be bigger than I am. I want to be able to say sincerely that I've given more to this world than I took from it. That I added to the lives of the people in my orbit instead of taking away.

Unfortunately, I have too many memories of leaving people worse than I found them. For some reading this book, I'm sure there were moments when you've hated the day I walked into your life. Especially my failed romantic relationships that have spanned the last three decades: my college girlfriend, Yas, and Dee—you didn't deserve to experience the worst version of me. And I apologize, this time in writing, so that my act of contrition is documented. Maybe one day you'll believe I'm a good person at my true core, despite the layers of flaws you had to penetrate to get momentary glimpses of what good was in me.

For those I've named and the others I've purposely omitted for their privacy, I know I don't fully comprehend how you withstood my dysfunction. I'm thankful for your friendships, even at the safe distance you've maintained from me. Trust me, I get it, and

I understand your skepticism; your lack of trust in my sincerity is warranted.

Now, I understand not all my encounters have ended badly, of course, but there are one too many that have for my conscience to be at peace. I've been terrible, mean, and coldhearted to many—I acknowledge that in the same way many drug addicts must admit they are addicts first to be able to continue with rehabilitation and recovery. This is my taking accountability, especially now that I know the origins of those behaviors, how they developed into patterns, why they merged with my character as behaviors that gave me an unceremonious reputation.

Hopefully, my reliving, acknowledging, and taking accountability for my questionable behavior will play its part in removing these flawed characteristics with the precision a surgeon uses to remove a cancer from a vital organ before it consumes and kills its host. The same way pancreatic cancer consumed and killed my mother while I was writing this book.